D0852826

Peter Leslie

The
Liberation
of the *Riviera*

The Resistance to the Nazis in the South of France and the Story of Its Heroic Leader, Ange-Marie Miniconi

Wyndham Books / New York

Copyright © 1980 by Peter Leslie
All rights reserved
including the right of reproduction
in whole or in part in any form
Published by Wyndham Books
A Simon & Schuster Division of Gulf & Western Corporation
Simon & Schuster Building
Rockefeller Center
1230 Avenue of the Americas
New York, New York 10020

WYNDHAM and colophon are trademarks of Simon & Schuster

Designed by Irving Perkins
Manufactured in the United States of America
1 2 3 4 5 6 7 8 9 10

Library of Congress Cataloging in Publication Data

Leslie, Peter.
   The liberation of the Riviera.

   Includes bibliographical references.
   1.   World War, 1939–1945—Underground movements—France—Riviera—
Biography.   2.   Miniconi, Ange-Marie, 1911–   3.   Riviera—
Biography.   4.   Guerrillas—France—Riviera—Biography.
I.   Title.
D802.F82R584   940.53′44   80-10389

ISBN 0-671-61048-1

Acknowledgments

Among the many sources providing background material to this story, the interviews in Armand Panigel's mammoth television documentary *Ce Jour-là, J'en Témoigne* were particularly rewarding. Each of the following books yielded invaluable information in one way or another:

The Larousse encyclopedia of *La Deuxième Guerre Mondiale;* Jacques Robichon's *Le Débarquement de Provence,* in the Robert Laffont *Ce Jour-là* series; *Code-name Marianne,* by Edita Katona (Collins & Harvill, London); *Missions Secrètes en France,* by Peter Churchill (Presses de la Cité, Paris); Philip Erlanger's *La France sans Etoile* (Editions Plon, Paris); Eda Lord's *Extenuating Circumstances* (Hodder & Stoughton, London); *Adventure in Diplomacy,* by Kenneth Pendar (Cassell, London); Henri Michel's *Histoire de la Résistance en France* (Presses Universitaires de France, Paris); and the monumental four-volume study of the same title written by Henri Noguères and Marcel Dugliame-Fouché (Robert Laffont, Paris).

My thanks are due to Monsieur Francis Vagliano, Monsieur Sam Kadyss and others for the loan of precious photographs and docu-

5

ments, and to Madame Veuve Jean Tonner for her courtesy in receiving me.

Most of all, of course, I am grateful to the principal character, Ange-Marie Miniconi himself, without whose prodigious feats of memory and unfailing patience during many, many hours of questioning there would have been no story at all. I thank him especially for the loan of many documents which are irreplaceable and for continuous access to his remarkable contemporary archives.

Three privately printed chronicles I was privileged to see were *Historique de la Libération d'Antibes* by Commandant A. Vérine, *Vingt-cinq Ans d'Administration Préfectorale,* by Auguste Pierangeli of Grasse, and *Hôtes de la Gestapo,* which is unattributed but was in fact written by the mother of Hélène Vagliano. Finally, acknowledgment must be made to the current part-work, *Les Années 40* (Tallandier/Hachette, Paris), and to the files of *Nice-Matin, Le Provençale,* and *Le Patriote.* It was in 1964 that the last-named prefaced a series of articles recalling Resistance exploits in Cannes with the words:

> We have done the best we can to make the past live. Perhaps one of the people we contacted has mistaken a date or confused a name. Maybe somebody has failed to mention such-and-such an action. But there were so many, and twenty years is so long a time, that such lapses are easy to forgive. The important thing, surely, is that the story should be told?

A similar apologia for the spirit rather than the letter of the tale is more relevant than ever today, when yet another fifteen years have passed.

—P.L.
Tourrettes-sur-Loup, 1979

This book is dedicated, with respect and admiration, to the memory of Hélène Vagliano, Francis Tonner, Louis Périssol, Captain Maurice Derché, Henri Bergia, and all the others who fought and fell.

Prologue

Must we continue to jail, execute, exile our ecstatic visionaries . . . and then enshrine them as tomorrow's heroes?
—THE HARVARD REVIEW

SOON AFTER the second World War, it became a joke among travelers that, however many people you met in Germany, none of them had ever had any connection—no, not the remotest connection—with the Nazi party. France displayed the opposite side of the coin: however many people you met, it was impossible to find any who had *not* been "in the Resistance." Latterly, it has become fashionably cynical to swing to the other extreme and say that virtually nobody resisted; that the great mass of the population acquiesced in their defeat and actively collaborated with their conquerors. This statement is probably less true than either of the others. But any definition of truth must be empiric rather than categoric—and if the maneuvering of the Free French, the wheeling and dealing between Churchill, Roosevelt, de Gaulle and Giraud seems complicated to the political historian, the rivalries and animosities between resistants within metropolitan France were more complex still.

There was, for one thing, no single organization entitled to call itself *the* Resistance. Defiance of the occupier manifested itself in many ways, from the single chalking of a victory sign on a wall to the sabotage of a munitions train; from the illegal reception of a BBC broadcast to the assassination of German soldiers. Between these extremes came the gathering and dispatch of information useful to the Allies, the production and dissemination of false documents and clandestine newspapers, the acquisition of arms and explosives, the hiding of fugitives, the active support of outlaws, the operation of secret radios, and the smuggling to neutral countries of refugees and shot-down aviators. Some of these activities were carried out individually or in small independent groups, others by larger, organized formations.

The latter were more numerous than is generally realized. Most readers will be familiar with the terms Maquis or FFI, but who, outside of France, has heard of the FTPF or the MUR, the ORA, the NAP, or the Group FER? Yet not all these organizations could properly be called part of the French Forces of the Interior, and few of their members were *maquisards*. They were all, nevertheless, important.

Organized resistance fell broadly into three categories: political, paramilitary, and intelligence. These were "aimed," respectively, at the Vichy French, the Nazi occupiers, and the Allies. Toward the end of the war, attempts were made, not always successfully, to assign specific categories to specific groups. But immediately after the capitulation those prepared to continue the fight underground —and at first they were few—were content to let *any* form of defiance express itself, however small and unimportant it might seem. Political, religious, and personal differences were forgotten in the battle against the common enemy.

It was after the Axis armies invaded the unoccupied southern half of France at the end of 1942 that relations between the paramilitary formations became at times strained. Rivalries and jealousies proliferated as the chiefs of the various networks competed for the limited amount of money and material available from the Allies. The problem was exacerbated at the beginning of 1943 when many thousands of men who would not otherwise have been resistants took, literally, to the hills in order to escape being drafted to Germany as slave laborers. These were the true *maquisards,* later to become the backbone of the FFI. By 1944 there were 22,000 of them living rough in small groups, and a further 8,000 enduring an outlaw existence as loners. Drilled by dedicated leaders into disciplined guerrilla units, these men were reinforced after the D-Day landings by members of the "demilitarized" French army and by patriotic civilians from towns and villages in the battle zone. In the Brittany peninsula alone, 80,000 FFI pinned down several German divisions and liberated most of the major towns at a crucial point in the adjoining Normandy campaign; in the Alps, General Henri Zeller raised a clandestine army of 10,000 men to help vanquish the Nazis in Marseille.

It is impossible to evaluate the aid given to the Allies in this way by the FFI and by those other groups outwardly living normal lives but secretly plotting against the Reich. General Eisenhower put it at the equivalent of 15 divisions. Kaltenbrunner, the German security chief, estimated the number of active resistants *before* the Normandy invasion as 80,000.

The problems of supplying these undercover forces were immense. To put them on anything like equal terms with the enemy, they would have needed 60 tons of arms and equipment parachuted to them *each day*. The best the Allies ever achieved was 20 tons—for the whole month of March, 1944. Theoretically, this could easily have been bettered. But the American and British Chiefs of Staff were wary of arming the *maquis* too well, for this could have encouraged an uprising which would have drawn German reinforcements into the country and thus made the eventual establishment of beachheads more hazardous still. They preferred to distribute the arms after their forces had gained a foothold on the continent.

In fact, between 1943 and 1945, Allied airplanes flew 8,455 supply missions over France, of which 5,634 were rated successful. These included the parachuting of 868 secret agents and 8,455 tons of war material. Lysander light reconnaissance planes, which could land and take off from a large field, deposited and recuperated the agents, along with politicians and Resistance chiefs, only eighteen times in 1943. The number of such missions flown the following year rose from 137 in January to 1,262 in June, when the planes arrived, according to one Resistance leader, "with the regularity and reliability of flights on a scheduled airline."

Limited though it was, this aerial assistance permitted units of the Resistance to accomplish useful work. In one week in 1944, the FER network, which restricted itself to sabotage of the railroads, put more locomotives out of action than the whole of the Allied air forces had done in the previous four and a half months—without the casualties and damage to civilian property caused by aerial bombardment. In the month of July, the FFI in the *département* of Côtes-du-Nord, Brittany, organized 40 derailments, cut the railroad tracks 200 times and the telephone lines 300, destroyed a huge gasoline dump, ambushed 50 German patrols, and mounted 30 attacks on enemy observation posts. In April of 1944, information networks sent 2,622 telegrams to London via Spain and Switzerland. The following month, clandestine radios parachuted into France transmitted 3,700 messages giving almost daily reports on Nazi defenses and troop movements all over the country.

The cost was high. Twenty thousand French resistants were executed or died under torture. A further 60,000 were deported to concentration camps, and of these less than 50 percent survived the war. Of 393 men and women infiltrated into France by the British and French secret services, 110 were arrested, shot, or deported to Germany. Only 15 of the deportees returned alive. The *maquis*— regarded by the German High Command as a serious threat to morale—were treated with a savagery that beggars description. Once a unit had been located, whole divisions, complete with armor, heavy artillery, airborne troops, and dive-bombers, were called up to subjugate it. Survivors were executed on the spot, frequently after being tortured. The villages which had sheltered them or supplied food were annihilated, their inhabitants butchered. At Ascq, in the north of France, after a troop train had been delayed by sabotage of the track, the SS assembled the men of the village and started murdering them one by one with pistol shots to the head. Eighty-six had perished before word came that the break in the line had been repaired and the train could continue. At Oradour-sur-Glane, near Limoges, 200 men of the infamous *Das Reich* SS division machine-gunned, asphyxiated, or burned alive 634 men, women, and children. The whole of the village was then set on fire and later razed to the ground. One teenage girl only escaped alive. The reason for the massacre? A *maquis* roadblock ten miles away in which four SS men had been slightly injured.

Fear of such random reprisals inhibited a great number of people who might otherwise have cooperated with the Resistance. Often, it made the undercover fighters unpopular with their fellow countrymen. It led also to innumerable betrayals. The Nazis did succeed in introducing double agents into some networks, but by far the majority of arrests were the result of denunciations. Those who subsequently escaped, or were released, were in an invidious position, shunned by the ordinary people as troublemakers, and by their former comrades lest they should have broken under torture and agreed to work for the enemy. There was the additional risk, too, that they had been set free so that they could unwittingly lead the Gestapo, German military intelligence, or one of the specialized Vichy police squads to the remainder of their network. For these reasons, many Resistance groups imposed an inflexible rule never to renew contact with a member who had been arrested and then released, no matter how important or trustworthy he had been considered before.

It was against such a background of deceit, suspicion, mistrust, and frequently poverty that the resistant lived his daily life. Even if he was one of the luckier ones hiding his clandestine activities under a "legitimate" cloak of house and job and family, he must learn to keep his mouth shut, to avoid old friends, to watch his every movement, perhaps to brave public opinion. And the more he was honest, the greater was his danger. The Resistance became like a whirlpool, engulfing more and more surely those who ventured within its orbit. It might start with a promise to look after some compromising papers, hide a gun, pass on a message. The next step would be to hide a refugee. Perhaps, then, a minor part in some mission—and the responsibility, if companions were arrested, to carry on where they left off. Finally—the moment of danger, when it was necessary to risk arrest or cut all ties with the past.

Renouncing his life, his family, his career, the resistant then would find himself in that shady half-world of forged documents and dyed hair, schooled to show no fear when his fake papers were examined, leaving cheap hotels at dawn before the daily arrival of the police, never entering a house by the front door before checking if there was one at the back. For him, life would now be a matter of meetings in stations and public squares, a life in which the least noise at daybreak, an unfamiliar voice on a stairway, a glance that lingered a little too long, could all signify the dread word—Gestapo.

With this daily fear would go the knowledge that, apart from the enemy, there were powerful forces of his own countrymen hunting him down—the anti-Jewish police, the anti-Communist squad, and the Special Section of each *préfecture*.* There would be the knowledge that he must always have the odds stacked against him, that one day, through tiredness, through ignorance or simply inattention, he must make the fatal slip, the tiny mistake that would give him away.† And then, more surely still, would be the certainty that

* Between 1941 and 1944 one French squad in Paris alone arrested 2,071 suspects, of whom 495 were handed over to the Germans on various charges. One hundred and twenty-five of these were condemned to death and shot.

† A woman agent parachuted into France was caught by an alert Gestapo officer in Paris after he had noticed her involuntarily looking to the right before crossing a busy street—

the road could lead only to the torture chamber, the firing squad or the long, slow death in a concentration camp.

Happily there were enough men and women with faith, enough human beings with the courage and the will to win through, enough people who believed in a better future, to face those intolerable risks and surmount them. This book tells the story of just one of them— a village schoolmaster who managed, although he was already under suspicion, to raise a guerrilla army of more than 600 men under the eyes of the Germans—and then used it to liberate Cannes, on the French Riviera.

---

instead of to the left like everyone else. The officer recalled that traffic in Britain kept to the left of the road, and deduced that anybody automatically checking on vehicles coming from that direction must be English.

Act I

In Defense

To live with defeat is to die a little each day.
— Napoleon Bonaparte

Scene One

THE RAILROAD was only a few hundred yards from the coastal highway and the sea. In between, parasol pines cast, in the dying light of the sun, long shadows across the hillocks of an abandoned golf course. Beyond the road, gray waves broke among anti-invasion obstacles studding the foreshore.

For the five saboteurs hiding in the bushes that masked the sunken section of track chosen for the derailment, the afternoon had seemed endless. As the lower rim of the sun touched the crest of a tree-covered ridge to the west, they covered their anxiety in rude banter.

There were hazards for anyone wishing to make the cut unseen. The tracks ran across a flat valley floor separating Mandelieu in the west from the Cannes suburb of La Bocca, where there was an infantry detachment detailed to mount permanent guard over the freight yards. Half a mile away in the other direction, sentries were posted at the bridge where the railroad curved south toward La Napoule and the wooded Esterel massif. In addition, German patrols constantly policed the shore road and the workshops of *Les Aciéries du Nord,* where the work force constructed boxcars and repaired rolling stock for the French SNCF system. To make it more dangerous still, there was the risk that the Nazi armored train, with its deadly flatcar-mounted 88mm. gun, might make one of its unscheduled runs at any time.

The tall man knelt upright and peered over the tops of the bushes toward Mandelieu. The sun had disappeared, leaving a deepening blush in the sky above the Esterel; already the chill of the evening was raising layers of white mist from the banks of the River Siagne where it looped down the valley on its way to the sea. It was November 2, 1943. In cemeteries all along the Côte d'Azur, chrysanthemums set in 24 hours previously for All Souls' Day glowed bronze and yellow and red in the gathering dusk.

"Alert north," someone said urgently.

The five men flattened themselves beneath the bushes.

A rustling of leaves on the landward side of the tracks. A low whistle: two notes, repeated. An answering signal from another of the saboteurs: the same notes in reverse order.

Two young men appeared on the bank at the far side of the track. They were short, dark, tanned, typical Mediterranean types. Francis and Fernand Tonner, sons of a farmer who grew flowers, fruit, and vegetables farther up the valley. Making the rendezvous wouldn't have been too difficult for them: it was just a question of crossing a few fields.

"Any sign of Brochet and Goujon?" the man in blue asked.

Francis Tonner nodded. "They're on the trail beyond the fields. They should be here at any minute. They've gotten hold of a couple of uniform caps, and Brochet's pushing one of those galvanized handcarts from the Department of Roads and Bridges!"

"That's a smart way to hide the tools we need," the man in blue said—and then he swung around to face the sea as one of the other men called to him: "Sanglier! I can see Ablette and Le Héron!"

The whole squad turned toward the highway. Beyond the overgrown fairway and the weed-filled bunkers of the golf course, two men on bicycles were approaching from the direction of La Napoule. When they were opposite the cut, one of them appeared to have a puncture. He dismounted and wheeled his machine to the grass verge. His companion rode on a few yards and then swung around in a U-turn and pedaled back to see what was the matter. Together they upended the stricken cycle and balanced it on its

handlebars and saddle. The rider spun the back wheel and unclipped the pump from the frame. While the other man glanced up
and down the road, he made a show of screwing the hose into the
nozzle of the pump.

What should have happened then—once it was established that
the coast was clear—was a quick plunge into the bushes bordering
the golf course, a moment spent concealing the machines, and then
a second dash, dodging from bunker to bunker until contact was
made with the group hiding by the tracks. Unfortunately the coast
was not clear.

There was a sputtering roar from the direction of La Bocca, and
two German motorcycle combinations sped along the highway,
heading west. The riders were wearing steel helmets and the soldiers in the sidecars were armed with Schmeisser machine pistols.
"Shit!" Sanglier said under his breath. "The bastards have changed
the time of the shore patrol! Let's hope those boys can spin a convincing tale—and that their papers are in order."

The patrol bikes changed down and angled into the verge, brak-
ing to a halt one on either side of the French cyclists. An NCO
climbed out of the leading sidecar and approached with his Schmeisser at the ready. The hidden saboteurs held their breath. In the still,
late afternoon air, Nazis' voices were clearly audible over the splashing of the waves. The Frenchmen were expostulating, making ex-
planatory gestures. Papers were produced. The German from the
second sidecar joined the NCO and one of the riders dismounted,
his right hand resting on the pistol at his hip.

"Keep down!" Fernand Tonner hissed. "There's something on
the line." Faintly, the watchers could hear the rhythmic clicking
transmitted by the rails which signified that a train was approaching.

Sanglier looked at his watch. "It's the *michelline*,"* he said. "Stay
as far back from the tracks as you can . . . and don't look up as she
passes by."

On elbows and knees, he shuffled crabwise into the shelter of a
low-growing *pistache,* peering through laced fingers as the two linked
couples of red and cream cars came into sight around a distant
curve on the outskirts of La Napoule.

The shuttle rocketed past, the rails sinking slightly and then rising

---

* *Michelline:* a diesel railcar running a local shuttle service.

again as each pair of wheels passed over the joints. They heard the brakes applied as it neared the station at La Bocca; a signal wire jerked beyond the cinders on the far side of the track, and the semaphore swung into the *Stop* position. In three minutes' time, the Nice-Marseille *rapide* was due to pass in the opposite direction. After that, nothing was scheduled but the munitions train they hoped to derail.

But darkness would have fallen before it was due. Time was very short, and there was no margin at all for error. Sanglier rose to his knees and looked anxiously toward the road.

The passage of the railcar seemed to have distracted the attention of the patrol enough to kill their curiosity. The two Frenchmen were handed back their papers and the Germans rode away. Sanglier was already running across the golf course, bent double as he zigzagged from cover to cover. He made the highway as the two men were about to haul their bicycles into the bushes. "Forget it!" he panted. "Get the hell out of here and ride into town as fast as you can. Go to the Taverne Royale, Toni's place, anywhere, just so long as there are folks there and they can see you. Go to the Taverne: there'll be krauts drinking there and that's better still."

When Sanglier got back to the cut he found that the two men with the handcart had arrived. So had another couple who had been making their way to the rendezvous on foot from La Bocca, sheltering behind boxcars in the sidings, swarming over backyard walls, making detours around the bridges, and walking the ties on the few stretches of track that were not visible from above.

They waited for the eight-coach *rapide* to steam past on its way to La Napoule and all stations to Marseille, and then hurried to collect the tools from the handcart, which had been left by a gate in the country lane beyond the embankment. "We're two short and we've got to move," Sanglier said. "Let's hump this gear and get started in while we can still see." The furnace glow was fading from the sky above the hills and the light was visibly thickening beneath the pines. In the east, a single star glittered already over the high ground behind Cannes. Black smoke from the locomotive hung beside the twin tracks in the cut.

Quickly and efficiently, they carried crowbars, jimmies, pipe wrenches and hammers down the bank to the track. Two of the men were plate-layers working out of the maintenance sheds at La Bocca;

Sanglier himself was a freight clerk. Under their direction, the squad began its task with furious but controlled energy. For what seemed a long time, there was no sound but the scrape of boots on the ballast, the clink of metal on metal, and occasional sharp taps with a sledgehammer as chucks were driven out from the steel cradles holding the rails in place. Bolts were unscrewed and fishplates loosened and then removed. Half a dozen men wielding crowbars levered in unison, prying the track out of position.

Dusk clouded the air as a sediment dulls wine. The scarves of white mist wrapped themselves more closely around the banks of the river. It grew very cold. Each man in the sabotage squad worked with the knowledge that discovery would mean torture and death, perhaps for his whole family and not just for himself. Each was comforted by the knowledge that if he broke under torture he could betray no more than two, or at the most three companions—and even this would be of little use to the inquisitors, because the names he knew would be code names only: rigid security and a tight cell system in this branch of the Resistance demanded that no member could ever be referred to by anything but his personal number or a *nom-de-guerre.*

By the time the short southern twilight was over, two lengths of rail had been freed at one end and then splayed outward, and a third had been removed from the track altogether. The effect would depend upon the speed of the munition train when it hit the length of doctored track. If it was going fast, there was a chance that the locomotive would follow the curve of the splayed section, and then topple over on its side when it ran out of rail, perhaps dragging the first two or three cars with it. If not, the wheels would simply leave the track and grind to a halt in the ballast. In either case it would be necessary to bring out a breakdown gang to repair the damaged track, and then to call up a mobile crane from Nice to lift the locomotive and any derailed cars back into place.

"Two hours' delay at least," Sanglier said. "Maybe three if we're lucky and she hits it at speed." He paused, his dark head tilted to one side. Very faintly, over the sighing of the sea, they could hear the mournful wail of a distant train whistle.

Francis Tonner had his ear to the rail. He looked up and shook his head. "Not in this section yet."

"She'll be coming out of the cut after Anthéor, on the downgrade to Théoule," Sanglier said. "Now get the hell out of here. You'll be hearing from me later."

The Tonner brothers and two other men collected the tools and took them back to the handcart. Once they had arrived at the farm, the tools would be hidden beneath the shingles of the roof. The cart would be wheeled to some neutral place and abandoned the following day. The man who had complained about not being able to smoke hurried across the golf course toward the coast road: he had a bicycle concealed in a culvert which ran beneath the highway. The others melted away into the darkness, singly or in pairs, on the landward side of the railroad. Finally only Sanglier was left. He waited for a moment, listening—the puffing of a steam locomotive was now clearly audible—and then turned his back and began hastening along the permanent way toward La Bocca. It was his duty to stay close enough to report on the effectiveness of the sabotage, but the armed guards riding shotgun on the train would be triggerhappy, expecting an ambush the moment it was halted; he had to watch from a position where his escape line would be clear.

Three hundred yards up the line, the high wall of a timber yard followed a curve in the tracks. Halfway along, a signal gantry was attached to the brickwork, and from the shelter of its girders, he could survey the whole section back to the cut. It was quite dark now. As he clambered up to sit astride the wall, he saw the headlight of the train sweep around the bend to the east of La Napoule.

Sanglier swore. He could tell from the sound that the booster engine which had helped the big 4-6-2 haul the heavy train up the steep grades of the Esterel was still coupled to the front of the locomotive. Which meant, unless they were traveling at a pretty fair clip, that there was a chance the booster alone would run off the track, leaving the train itself still on the rails. He watched the light approach, heard the hiss of steam and the shrill squeal of brakes when the engineer saw the gap in the line, and then listened to the receding clatter of bumpers as the long line of boxcars abruptly decelerated. The headlamp beam swung wildly from left to right, careened toward the center of the permanent way, but finally remained upright as the train shuddered to a halt. At the same time there was a confusion of noise—the screech of steel on cinders, the sudden frantic huffing of a locomotive freed from load, a splintering of wood and metal, and then the angry voices.

From his vantage point, Sanglier could see in the reflected light what had happened. The booster had jumped the gap in the rails, plowed into the ballast, and torn up a length of the opposite track. But there hadn't been sufficient impetus for the engine to topple over, and only the leading bogey of the second loco had been derailed. The rear of the tender was stove in and the leading car damaged.

It could have been more dramatic, with the engines overbalanced and telescoped wagons spilled all over the line. But it could have proved less effective, if the engineer had been able to stop the train before it reached the break in the line. Then it would simply have been a matter of replacing the rails before they could continue. As it was, heavy-duty cranes would have to be brought up and the booster lifted out of the way before repairs could begin. Five or six hours, working with floods, Sanglier thought contentedly. Perhaps even until daylight; it depended on the breakdown gear the Germans had available.

A searchlight was sweeping the banks of the cut now and armed guards were deployed among the bushes. Officers shouted queries at the train crew. Two men were sent hurrying along the track toward the signal cabin outside La Bocca. Sanglier figured it was time he was on his way. He jumped down into the yard and ran between stacks of lumber to a pass door beside the entrance gates.

Half an hour later, he pushed aside the blackout curtain and walked into a small bar behind the port in Cannes. The place was crowded with fishermen, local shopkeepers, a few brassy-haired prostitutes, and a couple of German soldiers. Sanglier wedged himself between the wall and the counter at the end nearest the door. He ordered a *bock*, took a folded newspaper from his pocket, opened it, and then lit a cigarette. After a cursory glance at the front page, he put the paper down on the bar. He took three deliberate puffs at his cigarette and then stubbed it out in an ashtray. At the far end of the bar, a short, red-faced man with a heavy black mustache drained his cup of *ersatz* coffee and plucked at his right earlobe. He laid a coin on the bar, pushed past a girl who was propositioning one of the Germans, and went out into the night. Sanglier breathed a sigh of relief. The message had been received, understood, and would be passed on. It was safer not to make direct contact: there were plain-clothes Gestapo everywhere, and you never knew, in a public place, who might not be an *indic,* an informer. He finished his beer and went home.

The red-faced man walked along the quayside toward the customs house. A hundred yards short of the building, he stepped onto a gangplank and made his way to a fishing boat in the second line of small craft moored by the harbor wall. As the boat rocked to his weight, he dropped down into the cockpit and took an electric flashlight from a locker beneath the stern thwart. Crouching on the duckboards, he scrutinized the port from one side to the other. There was a Wehrmacht sentry patroling the mole, and French *Défense Passive* wardens talking to the guards by the customs house. In between, the yard and the street beyond it were dark and deserted. Beyond the casino, on his right, the shuttered villas and grand hotels of the Croisette stretched away along the shore. To his left, bulked against the stars, he could see the ancient roofs of Le Suquet, the neighborhood built on the rocky promontory overlooking the harbor.

Straining his eyes to pierce the grains of the dark, he located the silhouette of the square, twelfth-century Mont Chevalier tower, lowered his gaze to take in the ruined abbey and the church of Our Lady of Hope, and then paused at a rectangular outline marking the remains of Roman fortifications. North of these and some way below, tall, narrow houses spilled downhill toward the bus station and the market. He counted the chimney stacks against the skyline: one, two, three, four, five, six. Beneath the seventh, in the row of ancient buildings on the lower terrace, was the roof of the Mont Chevalier school. And in a first-floor classroom Sanglier's chief would anxiously be awaiting his message.

The red-faced man held his breath and listened. Water slapped and gurgled between the moored boats. Somewhere along the Croisette a dog barked. He could hear dance music from a distant radio, and over by the town hall the boisterous echo of a Nazi drinking song was punctuated by bursts of male laughter. But no jackboots rang on the cobbled surface of the hard; no sentry strode along the quay toward the boat. Carefully, he supported the electric lamp on the gunwale and slanted it up in the direction of the invisible school. He pressed the button three times, waited a full second, and then flashed the torch three times again.

Immediately, astonishingly, light blazed from a window among the jumble of houses climbing the promontory. For an instant, the bright oblong was printed against the night—and then, as some civil defense warden shouted angrily from the street, it was as quickly extinguished. Message received and understood.

The red-faced man crawled to a bunk in the tiny cabin, pulled the door shut behind him, and made himself comfortable for the night. It was not yet curfew time, and he was fairly sure that nobody had seen him signaling. But if there had been a derailment it was better to keep off the streets: in vengeful mood, the Germans were liable to pick anybody up as a hostage or shoot them as a reprisal.

Behind the window through which the illumination had briefly been permitted to escape, Commandant Jean-Marie, head of the local partisans, fixed the blackout in position and switched on the light again. The bare schoolroom with its rows of scarred desks smelled of dust and chalk. He went to the teacher's rostrum and sat down by the blackboard in front of a pile of uncorrected essays—a short, wiry man with a prominent nose, dark hair slicked back, and restless, piercing eyes. During the past year, although himself under police surveillance, he had recruited a clandestine army of more than two hundred men. They had established regular radio contact with the Free French in London, hidden refugees, arranged the escape of Allied agents, and disseminated forged papers and anti-Nazi propaganda, but tonight's attack on the railroad beyond La Bocca was the first positive offensive action they had been able to take.

The Resistance leader's anxiety to know that it had been carried out successfully was emphasized for a variety of other reasons. The group he had formed in Cannes had lost men through denunciations; since the Germans had chased the Italians from the occupied coastal zone two months before, friends and colleagues had been arrested, tortured, shot, or deported to concentration camps. He was now in the process of forming a second company in La Bocca. Its members would be drawn chiefly from the railroad workers based there and from the personnel at *Les Aciéries du Nord*—where opportunities of hindering the German war effort occurred most frequently—and its main task would be sabotage. Tonight's action was therefore in the nature of a pilot operation, not least because several of the men involved were "borrowed" from another Resistance network. Its importance for him lay not only in its organization and security, not only in the smoothness of liaison with other patriots, not just in the delay and disruption of German schedules, but also in the occupiers' reaction and any reprisals they might make against the civil population. Much of his future planning depended on the extent of this.

But he would have to be patient. None of the questions posed by these factors could be answered until morning. And like the man who had signaled him from the port, he thought it more prudent to stay off the streets now that he knew the derailment had been a success. He would spend the night in the schoolroom, where his presence early in the morning would occasion no comment: Salignon, the principal of the Mont Chevalier school, was a member of his company, was indeed one of the few people alive who knew that the near-legendary Commandant Jean-Marie, chief of the guerrilla group bearing his name, and Ange-Marie Miniconi, schoolteacher and eldest son of a Corsican mailman, were one and the same person.

Banishing all thoughts of his Resistance work from his mind, Miniconi willed himself back into the rôle of a teacher—history and literature to the fourth grade, math to the third. He pulled the pile of French compositions toward him and began to read.

But the clandestine activities which now swallowed so much of his time and placed him always in peril could not so easily be forgotten. As he deciphered the pages of childish scrawl, pausing now and then to mark a neat marginal comment in red ink, his thoughts ranged back over the past four years, like the buoy swinging with the tide at the entrance to the harbor, casting a beam of light now this way, now that.

Flashback I

Spring – Summer, 1940

I

IT HAD begun soon after the New Year in 1940—when Miniconi found himself playing as it were the rôle of resistant even before France was defeated. The war was four months old. Finns fought Russians in the snow. Warsaw had fallen. In Alsace and in Lorraine, along the frontiers with Belgium and Luxembourg, French soldiers in the concrete emplacements of the Maginot Line faced Nazi Germany across the Rhine, the Moselle, the Saar, and the Meuse. But no shots were fired, no bombers flew, the expected gas attacks never came. Despite the official Declarations, northern Europe seemed to be paralyzed by that military stalemate the British called "the Phoney War."

In France's Alpes-Maritimes *département,* the idea of actual combat seemed increasingly remote. Along the Riviera coast, the holiday villas were shuttered and the pleasure boats hauled ashore under tarpaulin wraps. But the sky was blue, food had not yet become scarce, the olive crop was better than usual, and they said it would be a good year for the vines. Only the fact that an abnormal number of conscripts and reservists were away from home distinguished the month from any other January.

In Peille, an eagle's-nest village perched on a mountainside a dozen miles from Nice, Ange-Marie Miniconi stood on the steps outside his school and shaded his eyes against the sun. Peille was 2,000 feet above sea level: the wide valley that opened out to the southwest below its confusion of shingled roofs framed a panoramic view of Nice, St. Laurent, Cagnes-sur-Mer, and the crocodile head of the Cap d'Antibes. Even at this distance, the light reflected from the surface of the Mediterranean was dazzling. Through the open schoolhouse windows, the voice of a radio newscaster announced that the National Assembly in Paris had voted a law suspending elected deputies who were members of the Communist party.

"Morning, Miniconi." A prim, gray-haired man of about sixty raised a hand in greeting as he passed the iron railings outside the school.

"Good morning, Monsieur Giammet."

"Still no news from the front!" Giammet was a retired army officer, an honorary commandant of the old school who acted as secretary to the mayor. In his spare time, he tended hives of bees among the thyme and lavender on the barren limestone slopes above his house.

Miniconi shook his head. "It's unbelievable," he said. "What a way to run a war!"

Giammet grunted and walked on toward the Mairie. The schoolmaster turned and went indoors. It was time to ring the bell and call the children in from the yard for the first lesson of the day.

The following day, the two men went through an almost identical routine. Commandant Giammet lifted his hand in a half-salute and said, "Good day, Miniconi. Nothing happening up there!" Miniconi sighed. "It's a phoney war, all right!" he said.

It was perhaps a week later that a bugle call shrilled over the village as he was dunking bread in his bowl of breakfast coffee. There was nothing unusual in that: a battalion of *Chasseurs-Alpins*, reservists in training who had yet to be called to the front, were encamped on the slopes behind the church. Miniconi recognized the common calls—reveille, taps, chow, and the orders to muster, advance, or retreat. But although it was vaguely familiar, this particular succession of notes stirred no precise recollection from his own short service as a conscript in the early '30s. He rose from the table and walked over to the window.

Outside, the sun was shining again in a cloudless sky. Behind the village, cultivated terraces climbed toward the forest of oak and pine covering a shoulder of the mountain that hid the 4,000-foot bulk of the Pic de Baudon. To the south, rocky bluffs buttressed the peak of Mont Agel, which lay between Peille and the peacetime playgrounds of Cap d'Ail, Monte Carlo, and Menton. Miniconi could see no unusual activity in the small square separating the schoolhouse from the entrance to the village. Most of the inhabitants were busy among the olive groves brimming the valley far below, rattling canes among the branches to bring down the fruit before birds ruined the crop. "I wonder what that was all about?" he said thoughtfully, returning to the table.

"The bugle call?" Claire Miniconi was dark and petite, even shorter than her husband, with a trim figure and blue-gray eyes. "It's just the *Chasseurs* on maneuvers, I expect," she said placidly.

"It's odd, just the same. A quarter of eight's a funny time for them to be blowing. Usually it's much earlier—or later on in the morning."

"Finish your coffee," Claire Miniconi said. "The children will be here at any minute."

Her husband was at that time twenty-nine years old. A brilliant student, he had graduated early and turned into an equally impressive teacher, stern but just, with a reputation for getting results. When the couple had arrived at Peille in 1934, no pupil from the village school had gained a *Certificat d'Études* * in twelve years. By the following year, Miniconi was able to present three candidates for the examination. Two passed, and the third only lost out by half a point. The success, however, had not been without its dramas. From Christmas until Easter, the school's two classrooms were crammed to overflowing. But from then on the numbers dwindled until sometimes in the senior class he found himself talking to no more than two or three children. Things were almost as bad in the junior class taught by his wife. The people of Peille, he discovered, liked to have

* A leaving certificate or graduation diploma.

their children help with the family business. And since four-fifths of the population produced flowers, fruit, and vegetables for sale in the markets of Monte Carlo and Beausoleil, this meant that they were out in the fields during the whole of the spring and summer seasons. Miniconi invoked a law of 1883 requiring all parents to send their offspring to be educated, summoned the gendarmerie from the nearest town, and sent them ranging over the terraces above and below the village to see that it was enforced. In 1936 three pupils sat the leaving examination and all passed. The figures were the same for 1937. One passed and one failed in 1938. And in the year war was declared the school scored four out of five.

It was going to be difficult in 1940. There were seven candidates, the papers seemed to get tougher every year, and the kids were naturally unsettled by the uncertainties of the war, even if there was no actual fighting yet. Miniconi forgot about the mysterious bugle call and started collecting the homework he had marked the previous night.

It was at 9:30, in the middle of the math period, that a heavy knocking shook the front door.

Since the school was built on a steep hillside just below the road, this door was on the upper floor. Miniconi hurried up the stairs, calling, "All right, all right. Who is it?"

"Police! Open up."

He swung open the door and stood staring in astonishment.

Three men stood on the step, two of them in uniform, the third, a lean fellow with a hard-bitten face, wearing a belted trench coat busy with shoulder straps and buckles. Beyond them, the whole small *place* seemed to be swarming with soldiers—and suddenly Miniconi remembered the bugle call that had puzzled him. It was the General Alert.

"Messieurs?" he began. "What can I—?"

"Miniconi, Ange-Marie?" The civilian stepped forward with a piece of paper in his hand.

Miniconi nodded.

"Born, Ocana, Corsica, on June fifth, Nineteen-eleven?"

"Yes, but I don't understand. What—?"

"Deuxième Bureau," the man in the trench coat said. "Office of Counterintelligence. We have a warrant to search the premises." He held out the paper. With stupefaction, Miniconi saw that it was signed by General Montagne of the 2nd *Chasseurs,* the officer commanding the Armée des Alpes, and that it bore the stamps of the *Préfecture* and the schools inspection board.

He shook his head. "There must be some mistake . . ."

"No mistake. What's the layout of this place?"

The teacher shrugged helplessly. "It's simple enough. The schoolrooms are downstairs—senior on the left, junior on the right. Beneath them are the cellars. This is the part we live in, up here . . . sitting room, bedrooms, bathroom, kitchen. There are attics under the roof."

"We'll start with the sitting room. Lead the way."

Miniconi stared past the three men again. The road that climbed up to Peille from the valley entered the square just past the schoolyard and then turned immediately through 180 degrees to continue upward and circle the village to the north. At the apex of this hairpin there was a fountain. The colonnade surrounding an old chapel stood on the opposite side of the square and between the two were walls of heavy masonry, stretching up to the higher reaches of the road on one side, and down to Miniconi's garden on the other. Troops now lined the walls and sealed off the entrance and exit roads. There were soldiers among the orange trees and geraniums in the yard outside the schoolrooms on either side of the house, and more still strung out among the scrub on the steep slope below. An army truck parked by the chapel blocked the narrow entry leading to the stone stairways and cobbled alleys of the medieval village center. The school had been surrounded in a textbook military operation.

Miniconi glanced at the two gendarmes as he led the way to his sitting room. These were not men he knew from the barracks at l'Escarène in the valley below; they were members of the field gendarmerie attached to the army. "Just what is this all about?" he asked as he opened the door and stood aside. "What's the operation in aid of? What are you expecting to find?"

"Subversive literature, perhaps," the taller of the two gendarmes said. He fingered the handcuffs clearly visible through the stuff of his pocket in a meaningful way. "It wouldn't be the first time in a school, believe me."

Miniconi compressed his lips and went to fetch his wife.

The search was exhaustive. It took over two hours and left the place in chaos. Drawers were emptied, bookshelves examined, desks rifled and cupboards explored. Before it began, the children were sent home—but not before each one had been searched and the contents of his or her satchel investigated by a sergeant and two soldiers stationed at the foot of the stairs. Whatever the man from the Deuxième Bureau and his two uniformed companions were looking for, they appeared to draw a blank. Nothing was put aside, nothing requisitioned; no notes were taken. Finally one of the gendarmes said, "Where did you print the posters then?"

"Posters? What posters?"

"You know what posters," the policeman said sourly. "Who helped you put them up?"

Miniconi suddenly remembered. A few days before, a rash of small notices had appeared on the walls of the village. Some amateur bill-poster had been at work, damning the authorities in Paris for their dilatoriness, criticizing the conduct of the war, impatiently demanding to know how much longer the men called to the colors would be kept away from home. He hadn't paid much attention; he shared the anonymous demonstrator's impatience. "I don't know anything about them," he said. "I can't even remember what they said."

"We shall see," said the gendarme.

But there was nothing to see, and finally they went away. The soldiers were recalled to the square, paraded, and marched back to their camp in columns of four. The two gendarmes and the civilian climbed into an official Citroën and drove away. The few villagers who had been looking down on the scene from the upper road dispersed.

Behind the school railings, twin flights of stairs curved gracefully down to the yard from the front door. Miniconi stood on the top step and watched the Citroën, beetle-black in the bright sun, spiral between the olive groves toward the Nice-Escarène highway below. There were thirteen hairpin bends and half a dozen sharp curves to negotiate in the three and a half miles before the road from Peille joined Departmental Route 21 by the Vicat cement works at La Grave de Peille. Staring absently at the dwindling shape of the automobile, he turned over in his mind the possibilities that might lie behind the inexplicable and alarming visit he had just received. Indoors, his two young children, Guy and Félix-Henri, were crying.

Mme. Miniconi was trying to restore some semblance of order to their violated home before she prepared the midday meal.

It was after all perhaps not surprising, Miniconi thought, that he should have been suspected as the author of the "seditious" posters. He belonged to no political party but his views were what today would be considered leftist or liberal. All his life he had fought against the stuffiness of officialdom, the persecution of the weak, the inefficiency and hypocrisy of those in high places. And he had not been afraid to speak his mind. He had brought the children of Peille out on strike against the policies of Pierre Laval when the unpopular minister had vetoed government plans to impose sanctions on Italy during Mussolini's rape of Abyssinia. Nor had he disguised his approval of Léon Blum's Popular Front when that left-wing coalition had voted laws limiting the hours of work and guaranteeing paid holidays for all Frenchmen for the first time in history. On Armistice Day, 1938, still smarting from the shame of Munich, he had delivered a piece of typical French oratory after the ceremonial placing of a wreath on the monument to those who had fallen in the Great War. Reminding his listeners that it was only twenty years since the end of that holocaust, Miniconi recalled that it was supposed to have been a war to end wars—and then turned to the storm clouds which were once more gathering over Europe. "Instead of calling a halt to Fascist expansion with a categoric ultimatum," he cried, "the democracies fall back before the risks of a war that exists only in their imagination! Backtracking on all their commitments, they do not hesitate to sacrifice a Czechoslovakia in flames on the altar of the Nazi god! From ancient Asia to martyred Spain the Fascist assassin sows death and destruction, his murderous weapons sparing neither women nor children." He gestured toward the war memorial and added, "May this shameful abdication of responsibility not lead to evils with effects too fearsome to contemplate. May those whose names are engraved on this stone remain uncontaminated by that which the living have been so eager to accept."

The Peille war memorial stands on a rocky boss, a precipitous spur rising up from the age-old walls and commanding the Faquin ravine. By the time he had completed this piece of rhetoric, Miniconi and the stone soldier on his plinth were alone among the wreaths and the tricolor ribbons.

Given his reputation as an anti-Fascist, it seemed strange to Miniconi now that he should be pursued by the authorities on the suspicion of indulging in what one of the gendarmes had confided to him was "activity prejudicial to the successful conduct of the war." After all, even if he had been the author of the offending posters, he would only have been agitating for more efficiency, more action, whereas the charge was customarily leveled at those thought to be negative and defeatist. On the other hand, he had come to the notice of the authorities on more than one occasion through personal, rather than political, views.

He had been a brilliant student, admitted to the *Ecole Normale* at the unprecedentedly early age of sixteen, and was graduated as a full-fledged teacher before he was twenty.* First employed as an exchange teacher in Nice and then at St. André, he soon gained the reputation of a disciplinarian who could "handle" unruly classes. He restored order at a mutinous village school at Plan du Var, in the back country, where southern Italian immigrant children had driven three previous teachers to the border of nervous breakdowns, and then made himself popular with the elderly staff at the Montfleury school, Cannes, by volunteering to supervise extra classes in music and physical education. When he was drafted, however, for his compulsory eighteen months' military service, a certain inflexibility of purpose—his superiors called it pigheadedness—manifested itself.

To begin with, he volunteered once more—to enlist ahead of his class because this gave him the right to choose which formation he was to join. He chose the artillery rather than the infantry quartered in Nice. Then there was the question of the officers' training school. All *Ecole Normale* graduates, being considered potential officer material, were required to sit the entrance examination for this course. But Miniconi had no wish to be an officer: at the time, before the Nazi menace had revealed itself, he was an ardent pacifist, believing wars and the preparation for them to be useless occupations followed only by fools. He detested the rigidities of the martial mind. And so, quite deliberately, he wrote a paper that brought him zero marks. The result was too much at variance with his brilliant record as a student to go unnoticed. The damning comment *"Unenthusiastic"* was written into his dossier.

* An *Ecole Normale*, at that time, was a specialized institution where *lycée* (high school) students with the highest grades were taught, after an extremely stiff entrance examination, to be teachers. The three-year course included practical work with actual school classes, so that the graduate took up his first post with a certain amount of experience.

He had made his point, but at the expense of a reputation that now tagged him "a bit of a bolshie," a potential troublemaker.

He spent three miserable winter months helping to man an unheated gun emplacement high on the cliffs near the Italian border. Then, with the help of a staff major who was a friend of his, he obtained a discharge on health grounds.

Back in civilian life, he was appointed to teaching jobs at Spéracèdes, near Grasse, at Toulon, and then at St. Sauveur-sur-Tinée, a tiny village in the valley leading seaward from one of the highest massifs in the Alps. This was a two-teacher post, designed for a husband-and-wife team, and it was while he was here that Miniconi met and married Claire, a pretty brunette schoolmistress from Sistéron in the Basses-Alpes *département*. Their elder child, Félix-Henri, was born at St. Sauveur in 1934, just before they were transferred to Peille, where Guy was born a year later.

And it was partly due to the two boys, Miniconi thought wryly, that the search of his house had produced nothing to satisfy the man from the Deuxième Bureau. During a pre-bedtime romp the previous evening, a row of books had tumbled to the floor. Claire had picked up most of them, but two or three had fallen down behind the shelves—and these included works by Marx and Engels as well as Hitler's *Mein Kampf.* Fortunately the gendarmes had not discovered them, for although none was proscribed, their appearance in a context of suspected antiwar activities could have been embarrassing.

The searchers had missed two other things. Miniconi possessed an old 6.35mm. automatic, a small target pistol given to him by his father years before. For some reason it was kept in the linen closet, but although sheets, pillowcases, and blankets had been pulled out, the gun had remained hidden under a pile of hand towels. The last item could have proved the most "unfortunate" of all. It had been given to him by Pierre Simondi, a short, nut-faced professional soldier on furlough from some Maginot Line fortress near Strasbourg. "Hell of a thing," Simondi had said. "Here we are, ripping off all our identification flashes, our divisional signs, even our badges of rank, a hundred miles before we get there—and we don't even know where 'there' is until we arrive. And then, before we've even had time to stow our kit, there's this boche loudspeaker on the other side of the river blaring out, 'Welcome to the Seventh Division of General Condé's Third Army, and the men of the One-hundred-twenty-second *Chasseurs Alpins* from Nice!' You can imagine how we felt, after all that security bullshit!" He shook his head and added, "A few days later, a hun plane dropped a load of these." He handed Miniconi a cutout pamphlet shaped like a leaf from a plane tree.

On the green paper, black lettering announced: THE LEAVES WILL FALL IN THE AUTUMN—AND SO, TOO, WILL YOU FRENCH SOLDIERS FALL UNLESS YOU LAY DOWN YOUR ARMS AND MAKE PEACE WITH US.

"You'd better leave that with me, Pierre," Miniconi said. "It wouldn't look too good if some snooping MP caught you with it. You'd be on a charge for sowing despondency—if not for treason!" And he had put the leaflet on the chimneypiece in his sitting room, intending to keep it as a curiosity, and thought no more about it—until the knock on his door that morning.

By this time it was too late to do anything about it—and if the leaflet could have made trouble for a soldier on leave, how much more could it make for a man suspected, however unjustly, of hindering the war effort! Miniconi contrived to fold the leaflet in two while the searchers' backs were turned, and then covered it with the square base of a candlestick. It was not discovered.

The report that would eventually be handed in at the préfecture would therefore be negative. There would be no follow-up to the search warrant and the military encirclement of the school. Apart from the indignity and the inconvenience of that slightly ludicrous operation, the only repercussion would be an awareness for the next few days that neighbors were whispering and staring curiously. But somewhere along the dusty corridors of police headquarters in Nice, there would be a door behind which a dossier had been started. And once a name is on file, the papers inside the buff and orange and blue folders have a habit of multiplying.

Miniconi didn't even mind this. He had a shrewd idea that despite his work record the civil authorities, like the military, already had him labeled as a potential rebel. What was more alarming was a single fact that lay behind the official search.

The warrant had been signed by General Montagne. The regional GOC would have done this only at the request of the Deuxième Bureau, and the Bureau must have been alerted by the préfecture in Nice, acting in concert with Spinelly, the Inspector of Schools in the Peille district. But neither Spinelly nor the anonymous bureaucrats at the préfecture would have acted on their own. They had better things to do than check out the authorship of mimeographed posters in a mountain village. They must, Miniconi knew, have been investigating "information received." In other words, someone must have lodged a formal complaint, naming him personally.

The black Citroën had almost reached the highway. It vanished among trees below the long gray scar where the cement works had stripped the vegetation from the marl and pudding stone that floored the valley.

If someone had made a complaint, the schoolteacher reflected as he turned and went back indoors, particularly if it concerned the mysterious posters, that complaint could only have originated in Peille. Therefore—and it was this that bothered him the most—he must have an enemy in the village.

II

SOON AFTER the war started, the French authorities set up Commissions of Enquiry to re-examine the cases of those who, for medical or other reasons, had been excused from military service, discharged, or otherwise released from the duty of defending their country. When Miniconi's class was called before the commission sitting in Nice in December of 1939, he took the bus from Peille to the city, determined to get back into uniform.

Since the commission's brief was obviously to net as many extra bodies for the army as possible, most of the men called before it were exaggerating their health problems to counteract a suspected lack of impartiality in the examiners. The anteroom to the conference hall in which the tribunal was installed was loud with consumptive coughing, crammed with what appeared to be terminal cases. Many of the twisted or limping occupants were taking a final look —often through thick-lensed spectacles—at sheaves of papers signed and stamped by doctors, mayors, lawyers, employers, all of them swearing that it was absolutely essential that the bearer should not on any account be displaced from his present activity. Miniconi marched briskly in when his name was called and stood at attention before the long table at which the commission members sat. "You were only in for three months when you were called up for military service," said the colonel who was presiding. "Where are the papers justifying the continuation of your discharge?"

"I don't have any, sir," Miniconi replied.

"You don't *have* any?" The colonel sounded scandalized.

"No, sir. I'd be perfectly content to be drafted."

"But. . . ?" The officer looked down at the typed sheets littering the table. "Show me your pay book, your army ID papers, the original discharge documents."

"I'm . . . afraid I forgot to bring them, sir. But I'm perfectly fit. There's no reason at all why I shouldn't re-enlist."

The colonel stared at him. "You'll be hearing from us," he said gruffly. "Next case."

A week later, Miniconi was astounded to receive notification that he was *définitivement réformé*—permanently discharged.

On his way into Nice to query this inexplicable decision, he chanced to meet the staff major who had helped release him from his military purgatory six years previously. "You owe me a drink, *mon vieux!*" the major chuckled. "Did I do you a favor the other day!"

"What do you mean? What favor?"

"The commission was all set to have you drafted," the officer said. "Luckily for you, I happened along at the right time. I was able to swing the lead and get you reclassified instead."

"But . . . but I *wanted* to enlist!" Miniconi protested.

"You're crazy! You've got a nice soft job in a nice quiet village. A useful job, too, instructing the young. Why on earth should you want to trade that for a life of square-bashing and tours of duty in the Line? I thought you were the great pacifist anyway, the man who couldn't stand army life."

"I was, I was. But Munich changed all that. Seeing all those crowds cheering and applauding on the newsreels, I felt like echoing Daladier: 'The idiots don't know what they've let themselves in for.' Well, they know now. Anyway, it's all written down in black and white if you read *Mein Kampf*. Hitler's done what he said he would—up to this point. Why should anyone kid himself that he won't do the rest? Unless we say, Stop! That's enough! And Munich, I felt, was when we should have started to say, Stop! It's still not too late, but I can't stand this stupid inactivity. That's why I want to join up; that's why I feel we should be—"

"All right, all right," the major laughed. "So you want to join the army now! I suppose you want me to put in another word . . . this time to reverse the decision and get you *up*graded?"

"It would help," Miniconi said. "I'm on my way to see the commission now."

It was thus that the army was finally persuaded to accept him as a volunteer—provided that he absolved them of any and all responsibility and accepted the fact that he joined at his own risk. Ostensibly on account of his previous discharge because of ill health, this shabby maneuver in fact required him to sign a quit form depriving himself of a disability pension in case of "injury or ill health suffered in the course of duty," a not unlikely hazard in wartime. Miniconi didn't care. He was going to get back into uniform.

November 22, 1939, was the date he signed on. His call-up papers did not arrive until April 16, 1940. In between came the drama of the posters and the search warrant. The day after this disturbing incident, Miniconi was standing as usual on the stoop outside the front door before school started. Commandant Giammet passed as usual on his way to the Mairie. He was a few yards beyond the fountain when the schoolteacher realized that he had neither saluted nor wished him good day. Seized by a sudden suspicion, he ran out into the road and called after the ex-officer, "Monsieur Giammet! Excuse me—but you wouldn't by any chance have been behind the—er—little difficulty I had yesterday, would you?"

In Miniconi's own words, many years later: "He swung around and he stalked up to me. His face was contorted, the face of a man I didn't know. He spoke like a snake striking. 'Yes,' he hissed. 'It was me! And I pride myself on the fact. Men like you should be eliminated. They should be removed from society. They are noxious, noxious, noxious!' "

This was Miniconi's first encounter with the kind of mentality that would later shape the typical collaborator: a reactionary and bigoted brand of patriotism that valued order above freedom, blind obedience above initiative, and was to see in Hitler no menace but a preserver of the status quo. Aghast at the thought that he had been denounced as a dangerous extremist simply because he held liberal opinions and had flippantly criticized the running of the war, Miniconi reached out and grabbed the old man by the lapels. Despite his spare frame, he was strong; he lifted Giammet momentarily off the ground. Then their feet slipped on the wet cobbles by the fountain and Giammet fell to his knees. Miniconi mastered an overwhelming urge to smash his fist into the informer's face, muttered "What's the use?" and went back into the school.

The two men carefully avoided one another in the remaining weeks before Miniconi's call-up, but he left for the 152nd Infantry Depôt in Nice with the uneasy knowledge that there were influences at work in France of which he as yet knew nothing, that the war was not quite the black-and-white, good-against-bad crusade that he had imagined.

Miniconi was once more required to sit the exam for the officers' training course. This time, with an aim and a purpose, he passed with high marks and was posted to an officers' training school at Hyères, a peacetime holiday resort near Toulon. But if he had imagined the course to be a shortcut to action against the Fascists, he was doomed to be disappointed. Life at the Vasogne barracks, where the school was situated, involved even more parades and drill and bullshit than it had when he was a rookie conscript six years previously. Instead of learning how to set up an observation post or enfilade an enemy position, the trainee officers spent up to five hours a day, in full kit with packs weighing 65 or 70 pounds, marching up and down the interminable series of salt pans fringing the lagoons on the outskirts of Hyères, shouted at by NCO's and pestered by untold millions of mosquitos in the damp heat. "It was," Miniconi said later, "absolutely crazy. Before long, even the toughest among us was literally on his knees."

He himself, after more than a month of this curious preparation for war, had to be transferred to a military hospital at Fréjus for remedial treatment. While he was there, the war suddenly broke wide open. On May 10, instead of attempting to storm the Maginot Line, Hitler's Wehrmacht outflanked the impregnable fortifications by marching through the low countries and attacking France from the north. Rotterdam was dive-bombed into oblivion. Massed attacks by parachutists were used for the first time. Holland and then Belgium fell. More than a quarter of a million British and French soldiers were evacuated from Dunkirk in small boats after the Allied line around Lille crumbled. The war suddenly seemed very near to the people of Provence when Marseille was bombed on June 2. There was an air raid on Paris the following day.

Once the blitzkrieg panzer divisions of Guderian and von Rund-stedt had made their successful surprise attack through the Ardennes, the German forces swept through France like a scythe in a cornfield. In three successive days during that sweltering summer they took Dieppe, Rouen, Compiègne, Fécamp, Beauvais, Reims, Pontoise, Senlis, and Château-Thierry. The Nazis marched into Paris—which had been declared an open city—on June 14, and then stormed on south to Nantes, Vichy, Dijon, Lyon, and eventually Bordeaux and the Spanish frontier. In the meantime, Mussolini had declared war on Britain and France and his troops had warily occupied Menton, on the Italian border, and a few frontier villages.

By the time Prime Minister Paul Reynaud had resigned and his successor, the aging Marshal Pétain, had asked for an armistice, Miniconi was on his way back to the 152nd depot in Nice. Once the terms of the armistice were known, he was sent to a demobilization center at Cogolin, among the vineyards in the hills behind St. Tropez. He returned to Peille on July 26, 1940. The discussions which led to the formation of the original Groupe Jean-Marie began the following day.

Scene Two

IF THE attempted derailment of the munitions train at La Bocca was a pilot operation for the Groupe Jean-Marie as a whole, the next action organized by Miniconi was a baptism of fire, so to speak, for the new company he had recruited from among the men staffing the freight yards and the workshops of *Les Aciéries du Nord*.

Like the first operation, it was directed against the railroad itself; like the first, it was planned for the day after a public holiday, when the concentration of police and occupiers might be expected to be marginally less alert. Unlike the pilot action, it was designed to disrupt rail traffic as a whole and not to hold up any particular train.

It took place in the early hours of the morning following New Year's Day, 1944. And this time the small sabotage squad was provided with explosives.

Shortly after Christmas, Miniconi had received a message telling him to rendezvous with a courier outside a shelter at the bus terminal near the port. Miniconi was to arrive on a bicycle. The courier would be carrying a matchbox. Miniconi was to approach him and ask, "Have you by any chance a pump?" And the courier would then reply, "It would be easier to find one nearer the gasworks."

When this exchange had been duly effected, the messenger—whom Miniconi had never seen before and was never to see again—told him to be at a certain small hotel at six o'clock that evening, when he would receive a small, precious delivery of *plastique*.

The hotel was next door to a large hardware store in one of the narrow streets twisting down from the railroad bridge to the covered market behind the harbor. The contact was a tall, thin man with a lined face. He had just arrived from Nice by train and had booked a room for the night. Miniconi met him as if by chance in the small bar at the back of the building. As they struck up a conversation about the food shortage and the difficulty of finding accommodation, the thin man slid the strap of a rucksack from his shoulder and leaned it against the brass rail by his feet. "There's about four and a half pounds there," he said. "You're to use it as and when you think best, just so long as the traffic stops. What are you going to have to drink?"

When Miniconi left ten minutes later, the rucksack was slung over his shoulder. The plastic explosive was wrapped in a striped cotton shirt underneath a sweater and a blue pajama suit. There were detonators among the toothbrushes and tubes of dentifrice in a zippered, oiled silk toilet pouch, and primacord was stuffed into the toes of a pair of brown oxfords.

"God knows when we'll get any more," he told Léon Raybaud, the man in charge of the destruction company. "So every ounce of this must be made to count. I leave it to you to find the place where it can do the most damage."

"Better be somewhere away from a built-up area," Raybaud said, "as it's the first time we're making a real bang. Don't want to be caught on the street with any of that stuff in your pocket!"

"Right," Miniconi said. "In practice, I guess that means someplace west of La Napoule, maybe along the Esterel corniche?"

The company commander nodded. "I'll scout around tomorrow," he said.

Forty-eight hours later he contacted Miniconi again. "Found just the place," he reported enthusiastically. "A little way this side of Anthéor."

"Good God!" Miniconi sounded shocked. "You don't mean . . . ? Not the viaduct?"

Raybaud laughed. "Not this time! You'd need mortars, marines, and a squadron of Stukas to get anywhere near that! Apart from the antiaircraft battery, they've got a blockhouse at either end and heavy machine guns covering the tracks all the way across. No, there's a cut half a mile this side of the bridge. It's steep and it's deep; with luck, quite a small charge could tear up the track and produce a rockfall as well."

"Very well. You can gather enough men living not too far away? It looks suspicious if people get caught up in a routine check when they're off their normal beat."

"Sure. There's a couple at Théoule, and two more at Miramar and Le Trayas—plus a quarryman who can come over the hill from Les Adrets."

"Good. Just keep me a bit of *plastique* for later, that's all."

"There'll be enough for your Independence Day fireworks!" Raybaud said.

The tree-covered sugarloaf hills of the Esterel rise from the sea to the west of Cannes, with Théoule and La Napoule at their eastern extremity and St. Raphael to the west. Between the two, France's Highway No. 7 skirts the inland flank of the massif and No. 98 follows the contours of the coast—a twisty, swooping, soaring route that divides its time between beachcombing and cliff-hanging. At Anthéor, 15 miles from Cannes by road, it curves between a sandy beach and the great arched railroad viaduct spanning a cleft in the rocky mass, and then climbs to a clifftop perch from which in summer the Mediterranean can be glimpsed postcard-blue between the pines.

On the night of January 1–2, 1944, the sea was an infinity of darkness below branches dripping with moisture in the windless air. The moon was obscured by low cloud and, although it wasn't actually raining, white mist smoked from every hollow and depression among the scrub on the clifftop. It was very cold.

Raybaud had chosen a place where the rock walls of the cut were almost vertical. In this sector, the railroad and the highway were constantly passing one over or under the other, and there was a bridge at the far end of the cut where a byroad slanted away up the mountainside. The rendezvous was at this bridge, two hours after midnight. The six men chosen for the operation arrived within five minutes of each other. Between Mont Vinaigre and the Pic de l'Ours, the Esterel is webbed with forest tracks and lumberjack trails, firefighters' roads cut between the cork oaks and pines, and coast-guard paths where the slopes face the sea. All the saboteurs had traveled by one or the other of these routes, two of them with bicycles and the rest on foot. There was too much risk of running into a German patrol on the coast highway, especially after dark, and for the same reason this time the men were armed: there would be no question of a simple demand for ID papers if they were to be discovered in this place at such an hour—even if they managed to get rid of the explosive before they were caught. The weapons they carried were long-barreled Mauser pistols stolen or looted from the Germans.

Javel, the section head, had brought the *plastique* up from La Bocca in a briefcase strapped to the carrier of his bicycle. He had spent the afternoon with friends at Mandelieu so that he could be on the fringe of the forest as night fell and could lose himself without attracting too much attention. He knew the two resistants from Théoule, but the quarryman and the two who had climbed up from the coast were strangers to him. As soon as the proper identifications had been exchanged, he took a torch from the briefcase and leaned over the parapet of the bridge. A thin ray of light sliced into the darkness from the hooded lens.

"A flashlight that works!" one of the men from the coast whispered. "How in hell did you get the battery? I haven't seen one in a year!"

"Italian officers' mess a couple of months ago," Javel replied. "One of the boys worked as a steward there, and it was easy enough to liberate one or two at a time." He shifted the light beam so that it played over the damp rock wall of the cut. "*Merde!* I figured we could get down to the track by the side of the bridge here, but the bastard's too slippery and too steep. Apart from the noise we'd make, I can't risk a fall with this lot."

"What are we going to do?" asked one of the men from Théoule.

"Walk along the lip until we find a place where we can get down quietly."

"There's a tunnel a hundred yards farther on, this way," the quarryman said, nodding his head toward the east. "We'll have to go nearer the viaduct."

Javel swore softly again. They were not encumbered with T-shaped keys and crowbars this time, but six men walking across rough ground, along the edge of a defile, in the dark, were scarcely going to manage it noiselessly. "We'll take the higher side, away from the road," he said quietly. "That way, if we're rumbled, we can scatter up the mountainside. If we were caught between the cut and the highway, we'd be fucked. I'll go first and use the light whenever I dare. The rest of you follow on at ten-yard intervals . . . and for God's sake try not to slip or dislodge any stones!"

Geologically, the rhyolites and red sandstones of the Esterel form one of the most ancient land masses of Europe. The igneous and sedimentary rocks of the Cambrian era are nevertheless as prone to weathering and erosion as any other series. Rain and wind and frost had loosened the surface; the gnarled roots of sage and thyme had continued the process; and now the decomposed stone at the top of the cut was slippery with moisture as well. Moving a yard at a time, venturing a brief flash from the shielded torch whenever his foot warned him of an obstacle or a fissure ahead, Javel found it hard not to dislodge flakes of rock with every step. The men following him, feeling their way in the blackness, were less lucky. Despite his muttered warnings, sometimes a boot scraped; there were stumbles followed by a patter of small stones dropping to the track below; once he heard a stifled curse. Then suddenly cloud over the sea thinned and the moon's position was discernible behind a veil of translucent gray. In the wan half-light they could see that the rock walls transformed themselves into steep, scrub-covered banks in another fifty yards.

But although they would be able to scramble down there easily enough, they would be no more than a quarter of a mile from the viaduct. Javel paused to listen: around a curve in the track, he could hear the voices of German guards in the blockhouse. Worse, stifled by a guttural command but unmistakable, there was the yelp of a dog.

Javel held his breath. The mist was condensing on his mustache. He mastered a compulsive urge to sneeze. "Twice as much care from now on. Pass it back," he muttered to the man behind him.

It took them twenty minutes to make the bank and inch their way one by one down between the tufts of vegetation lining the scree. Javel laid the briefcase down on one of the ties, leaning the handle gently against a rail. The smooth steel was ice-cold against the back of his hand. As he straightened up, the last man stepped on a loose stone, fell on his back, and slid the final few feet of the bank in a shower of pebbles and rock fragments.

The six saboteurs froze. For an instant there was silence. Then the dog barked, impatiently, aggressively. It was joined by another and another. They heard the rattle of chains.

From around the corner, men shouted. Feet crunched on the ballast. The top of the bank was momentarily silhouetted against a misty glow. Staring at his own breath steaming in the reflected light, Javel realized that the guards must have a searchlight trained on the viaduct. Once they saw that it was not menaced, he hoped, they would investigate no further. The orderly German mind would not conceive of the idea of a minor sabotage so near a major target. Agonizingly, cramp locked the arch of his left foot. He flexed his boot against the rail, willing the painful contraction not to spread to his calf muscle.

The light vanished. The commotion around the corner subsided. One of the dogs whimpered as a rough voice yelled angrily. Then gradually the distant conversation recommenced. "Must have decided it was a fox or a badger," somebody murmured.

"Let's hope so," Javel said. "You two men climb the bank on each side of the tracks and keep watch. The rest of us'll head back and place the charge where she's running through solid rock again." He turned his back on the invisible viaduct and began tiptoeing toward the rendezvous. "It's too dark to see the ties," he whispered over his shoulder, "so keep off the cinders, well out to the side—but look out for the semaphore wires."

They had retraced their steps for about seventy-five yards when he stopped and flashed the light briefly to one side. The two sets of tracks were now fenced in by near-vertical rock walls about fifteen feet high. "This should do," Javel said. And then, turning to the quarryman: "It's over to you now."

"Give us the light for a second," the quarryman said. He took the torch and held it close to the crystalline red stone. In the brief spurts of light that he allowed to escape from the lens, they could see that the moist, glistening surface was crisscrossed with the marks of bore holes that had been drilled when the cut was originally blasted. The quarryman edged along until he found a diagonal seam running beneath a slight overhang. "This might do the trick," he said. "It'll bring down a couple of tons if we're lucky. Let's have a look at what we've got."

Javel took back the flashlight, opened the briefcase, and shone the light inside. "Jesus!" the quarryman said. "That won't exactly let the sea in!"

"It's all we can spare. So long as we cut the line, that's all that matters. Think of it the way you'd think of a cheap Christmas gift."

"Come again?"

"It's the thought that counts," Javel said.

The quarryman sighed. "We'll split it two ways," he decided. "Pack the larger portion between the rail, the tie, and the cradle here . . . and the rest in this fissure beneath the overhang. We don't have to cut both tracks, do we?"

"No, no. Just the down line—direction Marseille–Nice. Now that the Italians have quit, this is the way Hitler sends supplies to the troops facing the Americans across the Rapido."

"We'll do the best we can," the quarryman said. Under his direction the explosive was divided, packed, fused, wired. The moon had disappeared again. The damp chill of the air in the cut numbed their fingers to the bone. Sometimes, faintly, they heard the sound of the sea washing up the *calanques** far below, but mostly the silence was broken only by the rasp of breath and the tiny clinks and scraping noises inseparable from the job they were doing. The Germans in the blockhouse seemed to have run out of subjects of conversation.

It was almost four o'clock when the quarryman at last rose to his feet and stretched himself to ease his cramped muscles. Javel gave a low whistle to summon the two lookouts. They came one on either side of the cut and stood looking down into the darkness. "You're from Le Trayas, aren't you?" he whispered to the one nearest the highway. "Right. As soon as she goes up, you cross the road and make for home. There are cliff paths leading down to the ocean, aren't there? Well, get to one of those as quick as you can." He turned to the man standing next to him. "And you're from Miramar, just beyond? Right. As soon as we reach the bank, you go and join him. You'll never be able to cross over otherwise: the place'll be thick with huns until daybreak."

"But what about—?"

"Me and the explosives expert here have bicycles. We'll have a hard grind up into the hills from the bridge, but it's a downgrade

* *Calanque:* A Provençal term for a miniature creek or inlet between fingers of rock stretching seaward.

after that until we hit one of the forest trails. The other two are from Théoule. It's almost nine miles, poor bastards, but they can make it this side of the highway—and it's forest all the way."

Javel shone the thin beam of the flashlight upward, locating the lookout on the upper side of the cut. "Catch this and hang on to it until we arrive," he ordered, tossing a coil of wire accurately into the man's hands. The quarryman checked the terminals at the lower end of the wire for the last time, and then they returned to the bank and climbed silently to the higher level. By the time the quarryman had regained possession of the coil and paid it out to its fullest extent, they were almost back at the bridge.

He was busy with batteries and a pair of pliers, some time after the two men from Théoule had been sent home, when he asked Javel, "How did you know there would be no night trains passing while we prepared the explosive?"

"I work in the freight yards at La Bocca. None were scheduled," Javel replied.

"But how did you know the Boche wouldn't put through an unscheduled run?"

"I didn't."

The quarryman whistled through his teeth. "I'm glad I didn't think to ask you that before!" In the flashlight beam that Javel was shielding with one hand, he held up two lengths of wire from which the insulation had been stripped. "Away you go," Javel said.

The quarryman touched the naked wires together.

A livid, greenish-orange flash, less brilliant than Javel expected, accompanied the double explosion, but the detonation itself stunned him with its thunderclap force. They lay face downward, hands laced over their heads, while rock fragments, cinders and pieces of wood splintered from the ties showered from the night sky. Before the echoes of the blast had died away, there was a heavy, rumbling thump followed again by a patter of stones on the iron-hard ground. "Ha! Brought down a section of the wall, as I hoped!" the quarryman enthused. He clapped Javel on the shoulder. "Let's go, huh?"

Javel was pedaling laboriously uphill before the singing in his ears died away and he could hear the shouts, the tramp of feet, and the barking of dogs that heralded the searchlights sweeping through the trees below him.

Flashback II

Autumn, 1940 – Spring, 1942

I

TWO INCIDENTS shortly after France's capitulation had strengthened Miniconi's determination to avoid at all costs the defeatist line adopted by Pétain and his followers. The first, just before he was demobilized, was when he saw French officers at Fréjus actually toasting the German victory in champagne; the second, not long afterward, took place at the railroad station in Nice. Miniconi was standing in line, waiting to buy his ticket from the clerk. There were two men in front of him: a thin one and another Miniconi described as "a great fat fellow with a watch chain stretched across his vest and a belly so big that he had difficulty getting the change from his pants pocket." Said the fat man conversationally to the thin, "Thank Christ we lost the war—otherwise we might still be governed by those left-wing motherfuckers of the *Front Populaire*."

There were many who shared this view which so enraged Miniconi. The specter of a Communist takeover was easy to raise in

France in 1939 and 1940. A great number of Frenchmen, particularly among the middle classes, were acutely aware that the rapidity with which their governments had come and gone in the 1930s had become a subject for ridicule among their European neighbors.[1] They saw in the order Hitler had brought to Germany—and the paler copy Laval and Pétain proposed in their own country—a blueprint for the future that met with their approval.

Such people, typified by Miniconi's enemy Commandant Giammet, shared one reaction with those less scared of "a takeover by the Reds." Numbed by the military disaster, bewildered by the speed with which it had happened, they did not at first realize the full implications of the armistice terms imposed on them. With disbelief, with resignation, and finally with apathy, the majority of Frenchmen saw the occupation of three-fifths of their country,[2] the suspension of parliament, preparations for the rationing of food, the rupture of diplomatic relations with almost all the Allies, the expulsion of their fellow countrymen from Alsace and Lorraine (which Germany had annexed), and the introduction of the first of Hitler's infamous laws discriminating against the Jews.

Those destined to become collaborators or at best acquiescent in Pétain's betrayals drew on a natural chauvinism to blame anyone but themselves for the debacle. The British military effort had been halfhearted; Roosevelt had turned his back on France's cry for help; the Royal Air Force had refused to release enough planes from home defense to protect French troops in the battle areas. The list was long, and those parts of it which were anti-British were heavily underscored by Churchill's ill-advised order to the Royal Navy to attack units of the demilitarized French fleet harbored at Mers-el-Kebir, near Oran.[3]

In metropolitan France, even those inclined to dispute the armistice and the acceptance of its terms were at a loss to know how they could express their opposition. General de Gaulle had broadcast his famous rallying cry—"France has lost a battle; she has not lost the war!"—on June 18, the day after Pétain had pleaded for a ceasefire. Four days later, as the act of capitulation was being signed, he amplified his appeal—"The flame of French resistance must not be extinguished and shall not be extinguished!"—inviting fellow countrymen who wished to continue the struggle to join the Free French forces he was being permitted to recruit in England.

For those who had escaped with the remnants of the British expeditionary force, those already in England, or those living in French colonies overseas, it was a stirring call to action. But for men and women imprisoned in conquered France the grand words had little meaning, even if they had been heard. There was certainly no such thing as a resistance *movement* in the hot summer of 1940. The French in fact were faced with a situation for which neither their education nor their experience had prepared them. Their country was a democratic republic, whatever its electoral shortcomings. No political party was banned. There was thus no existing "underground," no organized revolutionary apparatus, no machinery for fomenting revolt: there had been no need for any. And the occupiers were quick to eradicate organisms whose structure could have been modified to canalize anti-German feeling or lend cohesion to what was still merely a generalized resentment. Trade associations, unions, business societies, freemasonry, even political parties were banned. The Pétain-Laval puppet administration in Vichy would govern by decree; its officials would be nominated and not elected. So far as the Church was concerned, despite the individual heroism of many priests, monks, and nuns, the hierarchy—because of Pope Pius XII's refusal to condemn the Fascist tyrannies in Germany, Spain, and Italy—was at best neutral.

The Resistance had therefore to start from zero, creating its own systems, inventing its own methods as it spread. Paradoxically it was the severity of the new laws that gave the initial boost to the movement designed to flout them: the first *réseaux* (networks) came into existence because there was an urgent need for them.

In the early summer, northern France had suffered the chaos of what became known as the Great Exodus, when a large proportion of the population* quit their homes and fled before the advancing Germans, choking the routes and paralyzing the civil administration with demands for food and shelter. Many of the refugees who escaped the attacks of Goering's Stukas filtered south to what was to become the unoccupied zone. Now, once the demarcation line had been established, a second exodus began. Jews in occupied France suffered immediate persecution. Their property was confiscated, they were denied radios, forbidden to go to theaters, cinemas, and

---

* To give one example: Lille, near the Belgian border, had a population of 200,000 in 1940. When the Germans took over the town only 20,000 inhabitants remained.

certain stores, obliged to wear the yellow star, frequently deported to concentration camps. A great number therefore sought refuge in the unoccupied zone. Friends were thus forced to improvise means of getting them past the Nazi guards strung out along the frontier separating the two zones.

Once clandestine means existed, others made use of them: Communists, foreigners, gypsies, and other persecuted minorities; French volunteers who wanted to escape and join de Gaulle; refugees; criminals; and, later, Allied aviators who had been shot down or bailed out over France. The pool of "illegal" persons in the southern zone then created its own problems. French with suitable papers could fairly easily be transported across the Mediterranean to North Africa; the others had to be spirited across another frontier into neutral Spain—and for this more *réseaux* had to be created.

The existence of these networks, few and unrelated though they were at the beginning, nevertheless engendered the need for ancillary services. False identity papers, forged ration tickets, and other spurious documents were required. The foundations were laid for what was to become a nationwide chain of "factories" producing these clandestine necessities.

Of armed resistance, at first there was none, such isolated acts of violence as occurred being individual expressions of defiance, outrage, or despair.[4] Before patriots organized themselves into groups, the occupiers had to contend only with what was called "the Whispering Resistance." This consisted of innumerable petty acts of rebelliousness or subversion, none of them dramatic, none breaking any specific German regulation, but all contributing to a climate of contempt and dislike. In the words of a Parisian contemporary, "We laughed at the Germans, we pretended not to see them, we deliberately misdirected them in the subway, we boycotted their parades and concerts—and of course we defaced their notices and posters, ripped them down or plastered them with the victory 'V' or the Cross of Lorraine."

Not everyone supported this campaign. Among those who did, countless tracts, leaflets, and newsletters circulated secretly. Dropped into the mailbox with a request to make perhaps 20 copies and pass them on, these were handwritten, typed, duplicated, sometimes mimeographed. They protested, satirized, or simply informed, their repetition of Britain's BBC news bulletins helping to counteract the Axis propaganda pumped out by the German-controlled newspapers and newsreels. In the first cruel months of the occupation, the radio was in fact the rallying point of all those who were neither defeatists nor collaborators. "It is no exaggeration"—Henri Michel wrote in the first postwar edition of the Larousse encyclopedia—"to say that the resistance of the French people was born around a radio set. The loudspeaker became a kind of sacred altar gathering together, at fixed hours, a larger and larger number of families."

The radio, certainly, was Ange-Marie Miniconi's only means of knowing what was going on in the world outside Peille and the censored realm of France. And through him, the village got to know too, for he owned a multiwave Arcor 830 receiver made by the American Radio Corporation, and with this he was able to get London more easily, and far more clearly, than anyone else. It was a good set to begin with, but since his schooldays Miniconi had been passionately interested in radio; working on a theory of his own, he had made certain modifications to the selector and amplifier valves,[5] with the result that shortwave reception, especially of the British Broadcasting Corporation's Overseas Service, was improved one hundred percent.

Through the receiver, Miniconi and the nucleus of his group kept in touch with developments affecting De Gaulle and his Free French. There was as yet no two-way communication but familiar French voices beamed from Britain (one of them belonged to the actor Claude Dauphin) boosted their confidence and helped them realize that they were not alone in their opposition to Vichy. Peille in any case was fertile ground in which the seeds of dissension could flourish. The commune had since the middle ages maintained a stoic individuality as the southeastern corner of France passed from the house of Savoy to the kingdoms of Piedmont and Sardinia and then back again. Behind their fortress walls, the townsfolk had resisted all attempts by the powerful Counts of Provence to subjugate them. As a group, they were still reluctant to accept authority, which they regarded as interference by outsiders. So although neither Socialist nor Communist parties were officially represented there, the village was nevertheless known in the region as *Peille la Rouge* (Peille the Red). Its coat of arms, displayed over the building which had housed the courts of justice in the middle ages, was a red Templars' cross on a Mediterranean blue shield, surmounted by a crest comprising three battlemented turrets in a fortress wall. The supporters were sprigs of rosemary, and the motto curling beneath read *Vivere Liberi aut Mori*—live in freedom or die.

Miniconi found plenty of friends who shared his views in such an atmosphere. Among his closest associates were Pierre Simondi, out of the army now and without a job; Octave Nikolai, a dark, fresh-faced little man who owned the village grocery store and also ran the butcher's; Honoré and Marius and César and a dozen other stalwarts whose children attended his school; and—perhaps surprisingly—the Curé Fabron, a gentle man who spent much of his time gathering wild herbs on the mountain slopes. These he dried, packaged, and sold by mail, the sachets of thyme and rosemary, sarriette and serpollet, sage and basil and verbena providing a modest revenue which he devoted to the restoration of Peille's slender, pyramid-capped, twelfth-century church tower. There was no physician in the village, but sometimes Dr. Roux would drive up from l'Escarène in the little black Peugeot with the headlamps hidden behind its swept-back radiator grill and join fervently in the discussions.

If they were not gathered around the Arcor radio, they met at *Le Cercle*. This was a local institution—not exactly a café, although drinks and refreshments could be obtained there, not exactly a club, although a stranger would scarcely have felt at his ease. Subsidized by the municipality, who paid a manager to look after it, *Le Cercle* was a long, low room off one of the arched and cobbled alleys that passed for streets in Peille. It was also, because of its total privacy, an ideal setting for plots and plotters.

Nikolai, Simondi, Miniconi, and their friends could hardly be said to have been plotting in the late summer of 1940. The full extent of Pétainist collaboration and the horrors of deprivation and occupation in the northern zone were yet to be realized. They were at first simply crystallizing their opposition—and most of their outrage and concern centered on the fear that their village might be placed under the control of Mussolini's Fascists. As the crow flies, Peille is only five miles from the Italian frontier. A ten-mile "demilitarized" strip had already been agreed along the entire length of that border. There was an armistice commission in Nice, which had itself been returned to France only in 1860 after the Treaty of Turin.* Now there was news that the armistice terms permitted the Italians to retain the territory in the upper reaches of the Roya Valley that they had occupied in the closing days of the war. This was less than twenty miles northeast of Peille, and it looked suspiciously as though history might be about to repeat itself.

Miniconi thought it prudent to have a private word with the Curé Fabron. One day not long before the fall semester began, the two men left the village at dawn and headed for the high ground where the priest gathered his herbs. The Curé was back at dusk, but Miniconi did not return for three days. With the aid of upland shepherds who knew the mountain paths, he had made a preliminary contact with the Italian partisans: after all, they had been fighting fascism underground since 1923; in the days to come their experience could prove invaluable.

For the moment Miniconi and the other members of *Le Cercle*— already referred to as the Groupe Jean-Marie—contented themselves collating information on Italian troop movements and passing it on to certain left-wing contacts in Monte Carlo.

Despite the armistice commission, despite a nominal garrison here and there, the Italian troops actually in the area could hardly be taken seriously as a menace: one would have a cousin in Antibes, another an aunt who had married a shopkeeper in Monte Carlo, a third would visit in-laws at Villefranche every Sunday. It was against Frenchmen that the initial shafts of the insurrection were aimed. It was necessary, it was essential, to start a "de-mythification" of Pétain, who was followed so blindly by so many simply because, as the victor of Verdun in the First World War, he represented the "glory" of France.[6]

II

MINICONI'S CONTRIBUTIONS to this new "Whispering Resistance" were typical of a great number. With the start of the new school year, rewritten history textbooks, hastily rushed through the print-

---

* The plebiscite which was the condition of the treaty's ratification could be said to be conclusive: 25,743 votes in favor of returning to France; 260 against. The population of Nice has increased tenfold since then.

ers, were decreed for all grades. The period 1914–1918 had to be represented as a colossal mistake, Teutonic achievements in the arts were stressed, the Spanish Civil War must be seen as a victory for right as well as for the Right. There was nothing he could do about this, not if he wished to keep his job, which was at the discretion of the administration. But with the new books came a jumbo-sized portrait of Pétain, designed for display on the schoolhouse wall. When Spinelly, the school inspector, made his first visit at the beginning of the semester, the 4-by-5-foot picture was nowhere to be seen.

"The portrait of the Marshal?" Spinelly asked. "You haven't put it up?"

"Er . . . no," Miniconi replied vaguely. "No, I'm afraid I haven't gotten around to that yet."

"Well, see that his picture is on display the next time I come around," the inspector warned.

A week later he was back. There was a picture of Pétain on display —on a postage stamp, gummed in the center of an empty wall. Spinelly repressed a smile and went away. He would be able to report that the Marshal's likeness was on view.

A second incident involved the newly created *Légion Française des Combattants.** It was some special day on the Vichy calendar. There was to be a parade, followed by a ceremonial salute as the tricolor was hoisted—except that the schoolmaster had shinned up the flagpole at night armed with a razor blade, and when the officer in charge tugged on the rope, the flag stayed on the ground and the severed halyards fell around his head and shoulders.

The third episode saw Miniconi back at the scene of his first public protest in 1938: the war memorial on its rocky spur overlooking the ravine. It was November 11, 1940. A squad of LFC veterans from La Turbie were drawn up around the monument. The mayor of La Turbie and his two *adjoints* had driven the six miles around the back of Mont Agel for the Remembrance Day ceremony. Lieutenant Gallet, the local recruiting officer for the *Légion*, was there. So were Commandant Giammet, the mayor of Peille, and most of the inhabitants. It was the perfect opportunity for some kind of gesture—but

* Inaugurated by Pétain himself at the end of July, 1940, this paramilitary organization, designed to re-establish national pride, was an association of veterans not unlike the American Legion—but with a strong right-wing, collaborationist slant. It was followed three months later by the *Chantier de la Jeunesse,* a cadet formation suspiciously like the Hitler Youth.

this must on no account involve ridicule: the last thing he wished to do was insult the memory of the fifty-six fallen patriots whose names were engraved on the stone, or outrage their relatives' feelings. He was not displeased with the solution he found.

He had been asked for the occasion to have the schoolchildren sing a "suitable" hymn after the two minutes' silence in honor of the departed. At precisely eleven o'clock, the final sad notes of *The Last Post* quavered into silence. The tail end of a mistral blowing up the valley from the coast stirred the hair of the dignitaries standing bareheaded by the poppy wreaths. A soldier scraped his boot on the gravel and someone coughed. Then Miniconi raised his arms.

Forty children's voices burst into a spirited rendering of the old anti-German patriotic song *You Shall Not Have Alsace-Lorraine.*

"It's not a tune that I particularly like," Miniconi confessed later in *Le Cercle.* "But since Hitler has just annexed the two provinces and thrown out the French population, you can hardly say it's not suitable."

By the time the song was finished, there had once again been a hasty retreat from the small *place* surrounding the monument, and he was alone with the scowling legionnaires and his children.

Such pinpricks, multiplied by a thousand all over the country, achieved no specific aim. They served simply to make the point that there *was* resistance against the occupier, there *was* opposition to the policies of Pétain, in the hope that at least some of those who followed him so loyally and so blindly,[7] some of those who had been plunged into apathy by the defeat, might be encouraged to manifest their disapproval as well.

The movement, spontaneous rather than planned, began to show dividends in 1941. It started with the railroad workers (with some of whom Miniconi was later to work so closely). Suddenly there was chaos in the transport planning departments because the tickets attached to freight cars, marking their eventual destination, seemed mysteriously to become switched. Trains were delayed by unaccountable signal failures. Faulty switchgear or badly maintained rolling stock caused holdups and derailments. None of this could be blamed on individuals: each incident could have been accident, carelessness, even a genuine mistake. Later the Germans multiplied the guards on all rail installations, instituted a system of reprisals against controllers whether they were responsible or not, and patrolled the tracks between stations with armored trains. But the *cheminots* remained in the forefront of the Resistance throughout the war.*

In the late spring of 1941 there was a miners' strike in the north. When a Vichy official cried to a mass meeting, "We've given you shorter hours, better pay, improved conditions—what more do you want?" the strikers shouted with one voice: "Guns!"

The strike was followed by a limited number of demonstrations, mainly in Paris, Lyon, and Marseille. They were small and they lasted a very short time—perhaps a forbidden march through a single city block, with the *Marseillaise* playing and a tricolor flying, before the police arrived and the demonstrators fled. But they showed again, to the French as much as the Germans, that the spark of resistance was alive.

It was to curry favor with their Nazi masters that the Vichy authorities in both zones tried to quench the spark before it could be fanned into De Gaulle's flame. At the same time—in July of 1941, shortly after Hitler had declared war on Russia—Pétain broke off diplomatic relations with the Soviet Union and declared that he had "no objection to the formation of a legion of Frenchmen to fight against Bolshevism." Soon afterward, the *Légion Voluntaire Française,* recruited from among French Fascists and "super-collabos," dispatched its first brigade to perish alongside the Nazis on the eastern front.

These actions unleashed an anti-Red witch-hunt beside which the McCarthy era in the United States would pale into insignificance. Communists, Jews, and foreigners—especially the British—were presented in newspapers, in magazines, on film, and at public meetings, as the enemies of France, sabotaging what Pétain called the "National Revolution" and "preventing us collaborating with the Germans in the formation of a New Europe." Laval broadcast a speech in which he stated unequivocally: "I want a German victory; I look forward to a German victory." And persecution of Jews and suspected "Communists" in the northern zone was hotted up to a pitch of ferocity that far surpassed anything the Germans had actually asked for.

The French, however, assumed the excesses to be due to the occupiers, and it was then, in retaliation, that the assassination of in-

* *Cheminot:* one who works on the *chemin-de-fer,* the iron road. Railwaymen formed their own Resistance network, one of the widest-spread, bravest, and most active in France. The organization was known as the FER (iron) *réseau.*

dividual German soldiers began. Even among the most anti-Vichy elements there was opposition to this policy—mainly because of the savage reprisals which could be expected in the areas where the killings occurred. But the leaders of the growing resistance movements argued that it was essential, whatever the cost,[8] to prove to the occupiers that the spirit of the French could not be extinguished by atrocities alone.

In the "free" zone, it was decided to try persuasion before repression. It was this that led to the series of advances made to Miniconi in the winter of 1941. Lieutenant Gallet made the first approach. He had driven up to Peille to give an address on Pétain's so-called "National Revolution." The lecture was sparsely attended—together with l'Escarène, Peille had the worst record in the whole of the Alpes-Maritimes for recruitment to the LFC. On the principle that it is always better to know your enemy, Miniconi had nevertheless gone along to listen. After it was over, the lieutenant approached him and said, "Why don't you join the *Légion,* Miniconi? We need men like you."

"You know why," the schoolteacher replied. "I disagree with its aims. I dislike what it stands for. I just can't go along with it, that's all."

"You don't have to agree," said Gallet. "Not with everything. We're all entitled to our opinions. But you're a veteran; you'd be welcome. You might find it would be a help in the . . . advancement . . . of your career."

"I'll take a chance on that," Miniconi said, and he left the hall.

"I know why they want me to join," he said later in *Le Cercle.* "My views are not exactly secret; I have a certain local notoriety; I'm not lost in the crowd. Also, the schoolteacher in a peasant community is in a special position. You're supposed to be the one who knows; they look to you for a lead. So, if I was to join the *Légion* . . ." He shook his head. "They'd all think: if it's all right for him, it's all right for us. The whole point of our opposition would be lost."

The pressure was nevertheless strong. The next approach, subtler and more insidious, was made at the beginning of 1942. He was offered a specific job within the *Légion.* He was to travel around the area, much as Gallet did, but lecturing to the *Chantier de la Jeunesse* and explaining to them the mystique of the "National Revolution." He would have the rank of a three-star captain, with uniform supplied, and there would be a car and chauffeur, with unlimited gasoline, at his disposal. For a man with a wife and two children, the offer was tempting. At that time, in addition to free accommodation, Miniconi received a personal salary of 1,250 francs (about $25) a month. His wife received slightly less. The pay he was offered as a captain in the *Légion* was 13,000 francs (about $260) a month.

Miniconi turned it down.

The next time around, the attack came from a different quarter. Spinelly, the school inspector, happened by one day just before Easter when the village was lost in low cloud which had formed inland over the Mercantour massif and rolled down toward the sea past the Pic de Baudon. Miniconi escorted him to the door when he had completed a somewhat perfunctory inspection. Spinelly stood staring out at the mist swirling across the roadway. "It would be a great help to everybody," he said, "if you would only consent to join the LFC."

Miniconi was silent for a moment. Moisture dripped from the iron railings on either side of the gate and ran down the cream stucco walls of the schoolhouse. "I thought I had made my position clear on that point," he said at last.

"You don't have to *believe* in it," the inspector urged. "If you'd just sign the forms . . ."

"I am not in the habit of signing anything that's shoved under my nose."

"It would make things much easier for me. I do try to do my best for you. But you must know that your actions—and your attitude —have upset . . . certain people. If it wasn't for the fact that you have an excellent record as a teacher . . ."

Miniconi sighed. "Naturally I am grateful for your consideration. But I cannot possibly bring myself to—"

"Look," Spinelly cut in, "I'm a Freemason. But if it was necessary, I would happily officiate at a Mass."

"If it was necessary."

"Exactly. And in your case, you may find that it *is* necessary."

"I'm sorry I cannot agree with you," Miniconi said. "I have never been in favor of compromise."

A few weeks later, Spinelly made another attempt to persuade him to join. Miniconi, again, was adamant. Then the inspector called unexpectedly one evening—as a friend, he said, rather than in his official capacity. He stressed the advantages that membership would bring, the way it would be received by his superiors, the example it

"Commandant Jean-Marie"—a photo taken soon after Miniconi emerged from the shadows to don the uniform of a lieutenant colonel in the FFI.

An eagle's-nest village perched on a mountainside a dozen miles from Nice: Peille in wintertime. Le Cercle was in the block of houses below the tiled dome of the town hall.

The old schoolhouse where Miniconi's Resistance activities first came to the notice of the authorities. Since World War II it has been transformed into a hotel-restaurant.

The World War I memorial at Peille. On the far side of the ra-vine: the village church with its twelfth-century pyramid tower.

Le Suquet as seen from the old port in Cannes. The Mont Chevalier school is among the group of buildings below and to the right of the ancient clock tower.

The only existing portrait of "Curtel." This pass-port photo was used on the false ID papers pre-pared for Commandant Jean-Marie's Number Two on the night they saved Cannes from destruc-tion.

Sam Kadyss in 1940: a resistant in Occupied France. Behind him at right: two Wehrmacht men in uniform. (COLLECTION SAM KADYSS)

Even guerillas have to relax: a rare photo of Léon Noël (left) and Sam Kadyss sunbathing on the Croisette before the Germans invaded the southern zone. (COLLECTION SAM KADYSS)

"A solitary Sten, inherited from the Marie-Raymond network"—Kadyss with the famous and temperamental weapon that members of the Groupe Jean-Marie nicknamed Caroline. (COLLECTION SAM KADYSS)

After the Liberation: Kadyss receives the Resistance Medal from General Koenig. (COLLECTION SAM KADYSS)

Sam Kadyss today.

Francis Tonner, tragically killed by a shellburst just before the Liberation: an amateur portrait of the hero whose family farm became both a rallying point and a "safe house" for the whole Resistance in the Cannes area.

Francis Tonner, circa 1939.

The viaduct at Anthéor. Beneath the central arch: a German blockhouse; in the center foreground: part of the underwater defenses.

A page of Miniconi's notebook: one of the numerous rough drafts from which he built up the organizational structure of the Groupe Jean-Marie. Most of the active members of this underground army appear in these three columns of names and numbers.

40ᵉᵐᵉ Compagnie

Commandant : ÉMÉRINI Alexandre (Curtel) matric. 4940
Lieut: adjoint : RICATTO Gaston (Raymond) matric. 4801

Groupe JEAN-MARIE   40ᵉ Cⁱᵉ FTPF.   1ᵉʳ détachement (MAUREL dit Sanglier 4451)

1ᵉʳ Gr.	ABLETTE (3100) (ROMANO J.) 3116 - 3117 (Bob)	Le HÉRON 4422 CARPE (3101) BRIENZA 2 3118 . 3119	BROCHET (3102) CATANO 3120 3121	GOUJON (3103) LAMBERT. C. 3122 - 3123
2ᵉ Gr.	BORÉAL (3104) RICHAUD . L. 3124 - 3125 (SERGE)	LA RESSE 4423 ELBE (3105) PAROLA.L. 3126 - 3127	GAROTTE (FLAVIEN (3106) BALMET. M. 3128 - 3129	RACINE (3107) FERTEY 3130 3131
3ᵉ Gr.	GASPÉ (3108) SALIGNON 3132 - 3133 PLACIDE - MARIE	30 NOVEMBRE 4424 ZODIAQUE (3109) CLAUZIER A 3134 - 3135 GUÉRINI (2)	CIGÜE (3110) ANDRÉS 3136 - 3137	SEXTANT (3111) SMILEVITCH 3138 - 3139
4ᵉ Gr.	ÉPHÉMÈRE (3112) BARZILEL R. 3140 - 3141	JANOT 4425 FLOUVE (3113) DE CARO. G. 3142 - 3143	CALIFORNIE (3114) SCHIANO.R. 3144 - 3145	St JUST (3115) ROSSI.M. 3146 - 3147

Groupe JEAN-MARIE —   40ᵉ Cⁱᵉ FTPF   2ᵉ détachement (KADYSS dit Sam 4802)

OTELLO (3148) Richaud M. 3164 - 3165 (Olivier)	GUÉTARY (4427) PANDA (3149) Menato O. 3166 . 3167	PANURGE (3150) CAPANNI 3168 - 3169	PAOLI (3151) Garro 3170 - 3171
CIGALE (3152) VASSIAUX . A. 3172 - 3173	BEC FIN (4418) PEZENAS (3153) BERNARDI J. 3174 - 3175	PLATINE (3154) BRUSCHI.J. 3176 - 3177	ANGUILLE (3155) ARNAUD 3178 - 3179
PASCAL (3156) COLLATO .R. 3180 - 3181	ROUGEOLE (4419) PRÊLE (3157) FAISSOLE .L. 3182 - 3183	BELETTE (3158) GIANNI J. 3184 - 3185	QUÉBEC (3159) FOURMOND J. 3186 - 3187
ÉQUIPE (3160) GIRAUDO 3188 - 3189	PÉTUGUE (4420) GORIOT (3161) GARINO.A. 3190 - 3191	ÉSOPE (3162) HENRI.G. 3192 - 3193	ARLES (3163) JACQUET.L. 3194 - 3195

A document the Gestapo would have given a great deal to see. Hidden beneath a barrel in Davaille's wine store, the schema of the 40th FTPF Company showed how the organization was protected against betrayal under torture by the "cell" structure subdividing it into Detachments, Groups, and finally "Triangles." The two base members of each triangle knew each other—and were known—only by their numbers; their chiefs were identified by code names. Since the war, Miniconi has added the real names of those he has been able to locate and identify, although even today many remain blank. This sheet, detailing only the first two Detachments of the Company, bears the names of many of the principal actors in the drama (Curtel, Sanglier, Kadyss, Arnaud, Smilevitch the Pole, M. and Mme. Placide, the schoolmaster Salignon, etc.). The Cross of Lorraine franking stamp was cut from a square of linoleum.

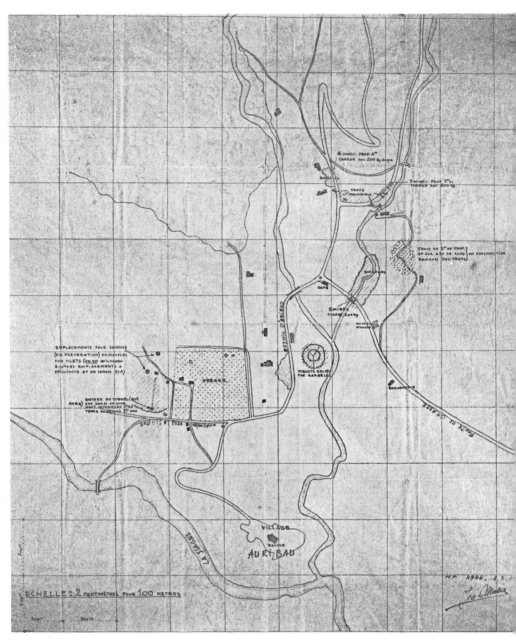

One of the secret maps of German defenses prepared by Miniconi's 3rd (Exterior) FTPF Company and passed to the Allied High Command shortly before the invasion. The map, dated August 8, 1944, and countersigned by "Jean-Marie" himself, shows the position of barbed-wire entanglements, the site—and strength—of minefields, and the location of two groups of mysterious holes in the ground. These depressions, three feet wide and six feet deep, might have been intended as individual snipers' emplacements, or they could have been designed to receive some kind of anti-airborne-troop obstacles. Also to be noted: the gun emplacements and suspected antiaircraft battery approached by a 600-foot tunnel to the northwest of the village of Auribeau.

MILICE FRANÇAISE

UNION DÉPARTEMENTALE
ALPES - MARITIMES
33, Boulevard Victor-Hugo
NICE

TÉL. : 840.27 - 840.28
CH. POST. MARSEILLE 980.20
AD. TÉLÉG. : MILIFRANCE-NICE

NICE, le
CANNES le 27 MAI 1944

N/Réf.
V/Réf.
Objet :

A dater de ce jour, Chaque Franc-Garde doit prendre ses dispositions en vu d'un départ précipité.

Il faut donc : Mettre ses affaires en regle dès aujourd'hui; preparer pour l'evacuation des familles un minimum de bagages.

Preparer pour soi même un sac avec chaussures de marche, couvertures, linge de rechange et arme individuelle.

Toutes dispositions sont prises en vue d'une evacuation precipitée des familles. Un lieu de repli est prevu.

Chaque Franc-Garde devra se presenter chaque jour à la Permanence de la Milice.

Un brassard Special lui sera Remis.

En cas de bombardement aerien ou d'alerte côtiere, rejoindre d'urgence la Permanence de la Milice ou le point de rassemblement qui peut être Fixé.

En raison de la gravité de l'heure, le Chef DARNAND compte sur la discipline absolue de ses FRANCS-GARDES, De la Stricte observance de ces directives depend le Salut de tous.

Le Chef de CENTAINE
ROUX Maurice.

A warning of the impending Allied invasion circulated among Darnand's French fascists as early as May 1944. The notice, a nearly illegible fourth or fifth carbon copy, appears on a form not unlike a present-day air letter. It instructs militiamen to prepare their arms and a minimum of baggage in case a "hurried evacuation" of the region becomes necessary. Assembly points for them and their families have already been organized, the circular says. Thanks to the efficiency of the Resistance, this rearguard action never took place.

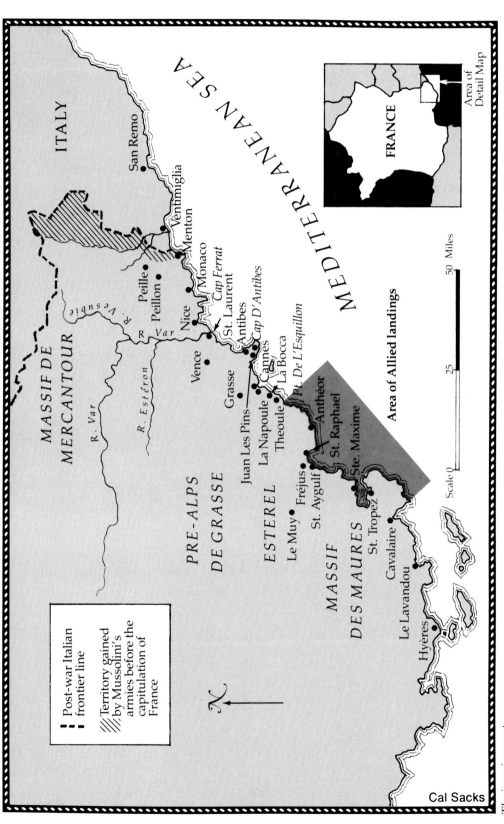

ITALY

San Remo

MEDITERRANEAN SEA

Ventimiglia
Menton
Monaco
Cap Ferrat
St. Laurent
Antibes
Cap D'Antibes
Cannes
La Bocca
Pt. De L'Esquillon

Peille
Peillon
Nice

*MASSIF DE
MERCANTOUR*

R. Var

R. Vésubie

R. Var

R. Estéron

Vence

Grasse

Juan Les Pins

*PRE-ALPS
DE GRASSE*

La Napoule
Theoule
Anthéor
St. Raphael
Ste. Maxime

ESTEREL

Le Muy
St. Aygulf
Fréjus

St. Tropez

*MASSIF
DES MAURES*

Cavalaire

Le Lavandou

Hyères

Area of Allied landings

Scale 0   25   50 Miles

FRANCE

Area of
Detail Map

N

Post-war Italian
frontier line

Territory gained
by Mussolini's
armies before the
capitulation of
France

Cal Sacks

The invasion coast.

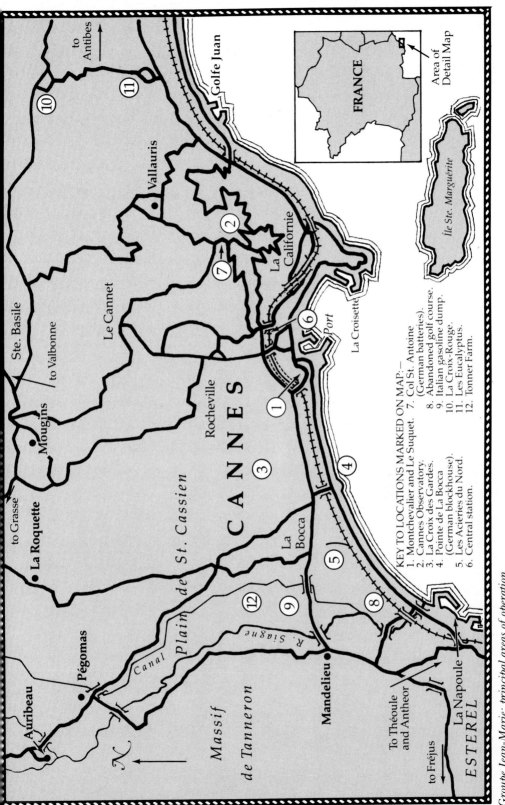

KEY TO LOCATIONS MARKED ON MAP:—
1. Montchevalier and Le Suquet.
2. Cannes Observatory.
3. La Croix des Gardes.
4. Pointe de La Bocca.
5. Les Acieries du Nord (German blockhouse).
6. Central station.
7. Col St. Antoine (German batteries).
8. Abandoned golf course.
9. Italian gasoline dump.
10. La Croix-Rouge.
11. Les Eucalyptus.
12. Tonner Farm.

Groupe Jean-Marie: principal areas of operation.

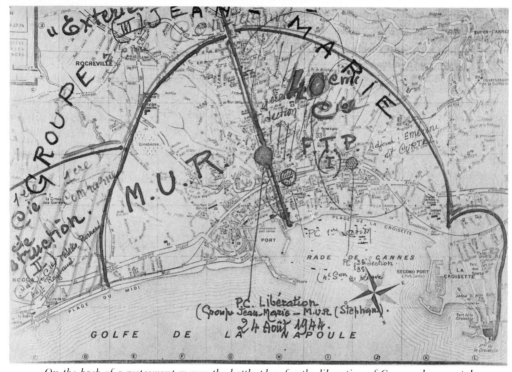

On the back of a restaurant menu: the battle plan for the liberation of Cannes drawn up by Miniconi and Vahanian, showing the neighborhoods assigned to the FTPF and the MUR. The thick line bisecting the map in the center runs down the Boulevard Carnot.

A modern view of the Croisette. All the buildings lining the world-famous tree-shaded promenade would have been blown up by the Nazis if Miniconi's bluff had not fooled the German commander.

History in handwriting: the pages of *Claire Miniconi's* diary for August 15 and 16, 1944, the days of the Allied invasion of southern France. The first page notes "very strong formations of aircraft" passing over Cannes and the pounding of coastal batteries by medium bombers. At 0430 hours the alert is sounded, and then "all day long the sirens scream, as we learn that the Allies, French, English, American, are landing between Nice and Marseille: 800 ships, 14,000 aviators, 12,000 parachutists." (In fact the invasion fleet was 1,200 strong.)

The entry for August 16 reads: "Quiet. We are allowed 100 grams (about 3½ oz.) of bread or flour. No vegetables. Still a little fruit. False news relayed by American, French and German radio says that Cannes is in the hands of the Allies. Not true. Warships cruising off Cannes fire ceaseless broadsides at the batteries; we hear the whistling of shells, the machine-gun fire of diving airplanes. The Germans are blowing up the port. Happily our neighborhood is calm and the children are not terrified."

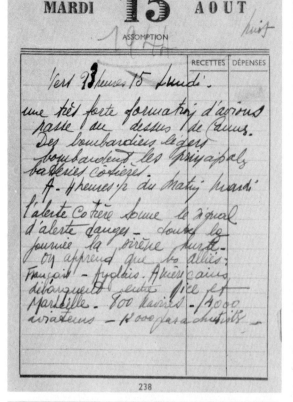

"A jeep speeding along the coastal highway from La Napoule"—the first Americans arrive in La Bocca.

"Tens of thousands of men, women and children—laughing, cheering, weeping, embracing, singing the Marseillaise—*jammed the broad tree-lined avenue as far as the eye could see" —the Boulevard Carnot not long before the arrival of the warning that German tanks were on the way.*

United States infantry from the 36th Division of General Patch's Seventh Army march into Cannes after it has been liberated by the Resistance.

Luckily—although he is shooting straight into the sun—there is an amateur photographer with film in his camera there to record the event. Leading the parade is the proudest kid in town; at right, a resistance fighter on a bicycle gives directions to an American soldier.

Soon afterward (it happened all over France) the girls come out with a warm welcome for the "invaders."

Victory parade of the Resistance forces in Cannes on Liberation Day.

Miniconi and the author today: the wartime Resistance leader explains the operation of a clandestine radio receiver and transmitter, the first to be parachuted to the British secret agent Peter Churchill. (PHOTO: JERRY BAUER).

would set. Before he left, he extracted a promise from Miniconi that he would at least consider the idea. And he left behind him the membership forms, filled in and ready for signature.

Miniconi was beginning to be worn down by the constant pressure, the veiled moral blackmail. He was preparing seven pupils for the *Certificat d'Etudes* and the last thing he wanted was an argument over ethics. For a moment, he thought seriously of signing the forms. It was, after all, simply a matter of writing his name: he would not be expected to do anything. It was in no way comparable to the job he had refused, which would have involved taking money in return for propagating the Vichy ethos.

A radio news bulletin broadcast that night by the BBC's French Service caused him to change his mind. Through the Arcor receiver, Miniconi and his friends had learned of the RAF's victory in the Battle of Britain. A year ago, it had cheered them with details of the Italian army's defeat by the British in Cyrenaica. Later, after the arrival of Rommel's Afrika Korps, they had listened with growing concern to the ding-dong progress of the desert battles. Now, according to the distant voice from London, Rommel was on the attack again; he had taken Tobruk and stormed over the border into British Egypt. Ritchie, the British general, had been relieved of his command. It sounded suspiciously like a Middle Eastern version of the Sedan breakthrough which had led to the fall of France. In the same newscast, it was revealed that U-boats had sunk 627,000 tons of Allied shipping, 114 vessels in all, during the past ten days.

Miniconi switched off the radio. The news was depressing but it had helped him come to a decision. If, as now seemed horribly likely, Europe and the Mediterranean were to be overrun by the Fascists and their collaborators, he wanted no part of it, however indirect. He tore up the papers Spinelly had left and threw them in the trashcan.

Soon afterward he was denounced as a "menace" for the second time.

III

IT WAS in July of 1942 that Miniconi was summoned to the Nice *Commissariat Spéciale*—a branch of the police created to perform certain counterintelligence duties and deal with political offenders.

There are two ways of reaching the city from Peille: down the zigzag road leading through olive groves to the valley and l'Escarène, or via La Turbie and the coast. He chose the latter: the summer heat was stifling and there was a chance that there might be an onshore breeze once he was past the bulk of Mont Agel and heading toward the ocean. Route D.22 leaves Peille below the ruins of a medieval keep, skirts the landward side of the mountain, plunges through three short tunnels, and then switchbacks over a pass before it twists its way down to La Turbie. But, to the schoolteacher's disappointment, the downgrade brought no cooling wind: the shuttered millionaires' villas on Cap d'Ail, the irregular shape of Cap Ferrat sprawled across the bay of Villefranche, even the Victorian confections of Monte Carlo immediately below were all obscured by the heat haze unifying sea and sky.

The humidity turned Nice into a steambath. Already there were signs of wartime neglect: peeling stucco above the colonnades around the Place Masséna, cracked basins surrounding the dry fountains, threadbare lawns, and weeds among the flowers in the public gardens. The city was like an old dog with its tongue hanging out in the heat.

Shabbiness and decrepitude were underlined by the presence of swarms of refugees from the north. They were the ones dressed in black, the men and women whose clothes looked too big for them, cramming the sidewalk cafés, crowding the parks, spilling over onto the beach—"the homeless in their hot Sunday best, sweating, pushing, shoving in the scramble to find a place to sleep and something to eat."*

By the big hotels along the Promenade des Anglais there was nevertheless money at work. The people who make fortunes out of the misfortunes of others, the hustlers who bribe their way into the best seats, the selfish, the indigent, and the plain rich had also flooded south to forget the inconveniences of what, after all, was somebody else's war. Black marketeers and their women sipped imitation coffee and under-the-counter highballs on the terrace of the Hotel Ruhl. There were still Delages and Darracqs and Delahayes for the liveried flunkies to park beneath the pink dome of the Negresco. Miniconi had never seen so much heavy gold jewelry in his life.

* *Extenuating Circumstances,* by Eda Lord, Hodder and Stoughton, London, 1972.

He walked beside the colorless sea, shouldered his way through the alleys of the old town, and managed to buy himself a beer in a jam-packed bar on the Boulevard Jean Jaurès. If a mild remark about the "phony war" could prompt a denunciation before the battle had even been lost, he reflected, it was hardly surprising that his present opinions, frequently and forcefully expressed, should have come to the ears of the authorities and confirmed their belief that he was not exactly the ideal citizen as defined by Commandant Giammet and Marshal Pétain.

The Commissariat was near the central station. It smelled of dust and sweat and disinfectant. The official who questioned him sat behind a desk in his shirtsleeves, his collar loosened and dark patches under his arms. Another man sat in the background, taking notes. From their accents, Miniconi judged them both to be Corsicans.

As he had expected, the interrogation was along predictable lines. What were his political affiliations? (He had none.) Which of the following people did he know? (He had never heard of any of them.) Why had he said this? Why had he done that? What did he think of such-and-such? He could guess from the dossier open on the littered desk that they had it all there—from the Armistice Day speech after Munich to the failed exam for the officers' training school, from the incidents concerning the song, the flag, and the posters at Peille to the school inspectors' evaluation of his teaching career. They would also have his military record as a volunteer and his academic record as a hardliner who cracked down on trouble-makers. So far as he could, he confined his answers to Yes or No, only amplifying his replies when the question involved motive and he could plead patriotism as the reason for his actions. If, as seemed likely, they were trying to catalog him as a Communist conspirator, a harborer of renegade Jews, and therefore an enemy of the state, they were welcome to infer it from the evidence . . . but they wouldn't do it through any answers he was going to give.

He was signing the *procès-verbal* encapsulating his replies when the official behind the desk picked up a photo and said, "Do you know this individual?"

Miniconi looked at the picture. A man of medium height, with hair slightly thin on top, walking along an anonymous promenade. Judging by the skirts of women in the background, there was a wind blowing. It was the kind of shot taken by street photographers at tourist resorts. For the first time since he had come into the room, Miniconi lied. He shook his head. "No," he said. "I never saw him in my life."

The man's name was Mertens. He lived in a small house in Beausoleil, on the border of the Monaco principality. Someone had brought him to *Le Cercle* once, and Miniconi had seen him there several times since. They shared a number of views on the war, the capitulation, and the attitude of Vichy. More recently, he had visited Mertens at his home, under cover of darkness. It was said—although Mertens himself had never mentioned it—that he was in fact the Communist party's secret organizer for the whole of the Nice area.

It was late in August when Miniconi received his second summons to the city—this time to the Inspectorate of the Academy of Nice. He was stunned when he heard what Davoine, the Chief Inspector, had to say.

His "case" had been considered by the Préfet, the Departmental Committee and the Inspectorate itself. It had been decided that "his activity was of a nature to harm or prejudice the work undertaken by the Marshal [Pétain]." He and his wife were therefore to be relieved of their posts at Peille. Without hearing the charges, without a chance to bring evidence or defend themselves, without even knowing they were on trial, they had been judged and found guilty. They were fired.

There was no appeal from this decision. The Préfet, his police, and the counterintelligence service had in fact argued that Miniconi should simply be sacked. There were suggestions that he should be jailed. But in view of his school record the Inspectorate—largely influenced by Spinelly—had opposed such solutions as too harsh and suggested a *déplacement* and demotion instead. It was agreed then that he should be transferred as a junior teacher to a school in Cannes; that his wife, similarly downgraded from headmistress, should go to another school in the same town; and that they must both live in the *résidence surveillée* category. This meant that they would be, or might be, under official surveillance all the time, that they must report to the police at certain times, and that they were obliged to notify authorities of any and every journey, however short, that they intended to make outside the boundary of Cannes.

Miniconi walked out of the building in a daze. The city was sweltering in subtropical heat. Melted tar gleamed on the roadway; the red, white, and green Italian flag hung limply from the mast outside the Armistice Commission, and it had just been announced that the Avenue de la Victoire must be renamed the Avenue Mussolini. The worst thing of all, he realized, waiting on a bench for the bus that would take him home, was the time element. The fall semester began in a few days; his replacement at Peille had already been appointed and was due to move into the schoolhouse. He had little more than forty-eight hours in which to make his farewell to the village, pack up his furniture and all his possessions, and move them, together with his family, to Cannes, more than twenty miles away. And that wasn't the most difficult part of the problem: at Peille, the apartment above the school went with the job; the junior posts to which he and Claire had been transferred carried no such benefits. He would have to find accommodation in Cannes within the same forty-eight hours—at a time when the whole coast was crowded with black marketeers, wealthy refugees from Paris and the north, and those fortunate enough to be able to escape the rigors of life nearer to Vichy. Even if he was lucky enough to find a place, there remained the near-impossible task of locating a moving company with the time—and the gasoline—to transport them there.

The sheer mechanical difficulty of the problem was enough to subdue his humiliation and his rage as he stared unseeingly out the window of the ancient bus while it wheezed and groaned its way up the steep grades leading to La Turbie and the village. It could of course have been worse. The Préfet of Nice, imbued with the puritan spirit of Pétain's "National Revolution," had already rounded up 2,000 prostitutes and homosexuals and incarcerated them in an internment camp near Sistéron, in the Basses-Alpes. There were ugly rumors that, in accordance with the wishes of the Nazis, a list of Jewish families was being compiled and the yellow star system was under consideration. Miniconi supposed he was lucky that liberal schoolmasters were not classified quite so far down the list as prostitutes, homosexuals, foreigners, and Jews.

He was luckier still in his choice of friends. At dawn the following day, Octave Nicolai rode down to Cannes on a bicycle in search of an apartment. Other habitués of *Le Cercle* attempted to locate movers, supplied crates and packing cases, and helped Miniconi and his wife clear the schoolhouse of the evidence of six years of family life.

Thirty-six hours later, Octave returned, triumphant. Miraculously, marvelously, he had found an apartment. It was some distance from the schools to which Miniconi and Claire had been transferred, but it was spacious, it was spotlessly clean, and it was not too expensive. He had paid a deposit on Miniconi's behalf, and a lease would be ready for signing the following day.

Somebody else, meanwhile, had chanced to meet a friend who knew a man in Sospel, back in the mountains, whose brother had a truck.

The following day Miniconi himself went to Cannes and signed the agreement. By the time he returned, arrangements had been made for the truck to transport the family and all their possessions to their new home. He walked for the last time up the winding path leading to the war memorial. It was almost dusk and the mountains encircling the village were solid with shadow. Beyond the series of valleys dropping away to the coast, the ocean lay like a sheet of molten metal in the rays of the setting sun. He stared at the Cap d'Antibes, the distant silhouette of the Esterel massif, and the two dark streaks marking the islands which lay off the point at Cannes. By this time tomorrow, he would be less than two miles from those islands, looking out across the roofs of the town from the windows of a strange apartment. He shook his head and walked back down the rue Lascaris, past the four spouts of the twelfth-century Gothic fountain, under the vaulted arches spanning the rue Centrale and into *Le Cercle* for a farewell *pastis* with his friends.

They started loading the truck early the next morning. By ten o'clock they were ready to leave. Miniconi packed Claire and the two boys into the cab with the driver and clambered over the tailgate to stow himself among the chairs and bookshelves. The Arcor radio, carefully wrapped in a rug, was balanced on his knees.

It seemed as though the entire village had assembled outside the empty schoolhouse to see them off. Unforgettably, the men as well as the women were in tears as they waved goodby.

IV

THE VILLA Thébrilou was halfway along the rue de Grignon in Le Cannet, the suburb which lies on the high ground to the north of Cannes. Like many small houses on the Côte d'Azur, it was divided horizontally into two apartments—the owner, Madame Faga, living on the garden floor, the Miniconi family in the rented quarters above.

It was a pleasant enough place, with a wide balcony and separate stairs leading to the entrance door. But the Miniconis were so exhausted on the night of their arrival that they slept on makeshift beds on the floor, and several days later Claire had still not started to unpack the crates.

Her husband was surprised. Usually she was adamant on the necessity of getting things in their right place in the quickest possible time. "I don't know," she said when he voiced his astonishment. "Somehow . . . somehow I can't see us staying in this house."

"But . . . why ever not?"

"I don't know. I just can't."

"There's plenty of room. It's not uncomfortable. The rent's not outrageous—considering what some people have to pay." Miniconi was puzzled. "I'm sure Madame Faga will let the boys play in the garden," he said.

"It's such a long way from the school," Claire said. "And there's something about the way that woman looks at us . . ." She shrugged and lapsed into silence.

The villa was certainly inconvenient geographically: the Montfleury school, where Miniconi was to report, was more than a mile and a half away; the Maurice-Alice, to which Claire had been assigned, was almost two miles. So far as their landlady was concerned, although she was perfectly polite, it was true that she gave the impression of being wary, almost furtive, each time they happened to come face to face with her.

It was not long before they found out why.

A certain Madame Lecourtois, hearing that the apartment in the Villa Thébrilou was for rent, had been to view it after Octave Nicolai had seen it. Madame Lecourtois was a widow who lived in Grasse, a market town a few miles inland on the lower slopes of the Pre-Alps. Finding the social life of Grasse too dull for her, she was envious of mixing with the monied, cosmopolitan world still existing on the coast. And the apartment suited her very well.

Yes, Madame Faga said, but unfortunately—it was most regrettable—a man had already taken the apartment on behalf of some schoolteacher from the mountains. He had paid a deposit and the lease had been signed. Otherwise she would have been only too delighted to have so charming a tenant . . .

No problem, said Madame Lecourtois, reaching for her purse. All Madame Faga had to do was swear that Miniconi and his friend had threatened her, that she had signed the lease and accepted the deposit under constraint. And, of course, that Madame Lecourtois had viewed the apartment and paid *her* deposit days before Octave Nicolai had even rung the bell. She had a son who was a director of one of the Vichy youth movements, the lady from Grasse said. These things could always be arranged. And, naturally, if Madame Faga had been put to any extra expense . . .

Within a few days of his arrival, Miniconi therefore found himself —to his stupefaction—appearing before a Justice of the Peace, accused of uttering threats with a view to obtaining accommodation. The attorney he had been forced to retain was not even allowed to plead. Having heard the Lecourtois complaint, which was an exact reversal of the facts, the judge, evidently well briefed on Miniconi's background, said, "Madame, you have made out your case and I find in your favor. Luckily for you, they were good Frenchmen who made the law in this country."

Miniconi was served with an eviction order and given two days to remove his possessions and quit the apartment.

Her husband went to the Mairie. The local education authority had transferred him to Cannes, he said. It was up to them to find accommodation for him and his family. Where was the *logement de fonction* to which he was entitled?

"You've got a nerve!" the bespectacled woman who interviewed him said. "Coming here with a request like that! With your record? Please close the door as you leave."

Miniconi knew nobody in Cannes. The few apartments the real estate agents could offer were far beyond his means. He was obliged to store his furniture and move the family to a modest pension, the Hotel de Bourgogne—and even there the weekly bill was more than his own and his wife's salaries combined.

To make an impossible situation even worse, it seemed at first as though there might not be any salary, at least as far as he was concerned. When he reported for duty at the Montfleury school on the first day of the semester, Carabalona, the principal, met him at the top of the steps and barred his way. "You are not to come in here, Miniconi," he said.

"Not to come in?" Miniconi's bewilderment showed on his face. This was the school where they had once been so grateful to him for taking on extra classes. "But . . . I've been appointed here. The education authority in Nice . . ."

"I have the right to overrule their decision, to refuse the appointment."

"But . . . ?"

"At a staff conference last night," Carabalona said, "it was decided —and I quote—'Monsieur Miniconi's activities can do nothing but harm here.' I therefore forbid you to enter and I must ask you to leave."

This was virtually the last straw. Miniconi didn't know where to turn. Friends in official positions had already appealed to the Bishop of Nice in an attempt to have the decision to expel him from Peille revoked. His Lordship had graciously let it be known that, in his considered opinion, "a change of air could not be other than beneficial to Monsieur Miniconi."

Fortunately help came from an unexpected quarter. Salignon, the director of the Mont Chevalier school in the old town, had a post vacant on his staff, and he applied to the authority to have Miniconi fill it. "I have no idea why," Miniconi said to Claire. "I never met the man. I suppose he must have read my dossier or seen my marks.* But he just about saved our lives!"

Even then, the annoyances resulting from Miniconi's liberal views were not at an end. On the second day of the semester, Carpentier, the local inspector for the Cannes area, came by the Mont Chevalier school to visit his new class. All teaching materials at this time were supplied, and strictly controlled, by the municipality. And because of wartime shortages, the Cannes authorities had not yet gotten around to furnishing these necessities to every school in the region. Miniconi's classroom was bare of textbooks, paper, pencils, pens, ink, and exercise books. There wasn't even a stub of chalk with which he could write on the blackboard. At the end of the inspection (which had been prompted, Miniconi discovered later, by a letter from Madame Lecourtois), Carpentier wrote in his dossier: *The class is not in the state in which I would have wished to find it. I expect to see an*

---

* At this time schoolteachers, like French schoolchildren, took with them from job to job and school to school an exercise book in which their career was summarized. To comments from the director, if they were juniors, were added those of the visiting inspector—who marked them on a scale of 20 each time he had observed the compartment, standard, and handling of their class.

improvement next time. In addition, Miniconi, who customarily scored 15 or 16, had the humiliation of seeing himself marked only 5 out of 20.

Finally there was the matter of Claire Miniconi's employment. A colleague who knew something of Miniconi's views drew him aside one day late in October and said, "Look, it's not my business, but your wife's at the Maurice-Alice, isn't she?" And when Miniconi nodded, he went on: "The thing is, the *Légion*'s very hot at that school, and its influence is . . . disagreeable. Your wife would be much happier here. Why don't you try and get her a transfer?"

Miniconi thanked him and went to see Carpentier. He might as well have saved his time. Not only did the inspector refuse to consider a transfer (the reason he was given for the request was of course purely domestic); "he put me outside his office," Miniconi told Claire furiously, "like a dog. Like—a—dog!"

It was these further examples of the Vichy mentality at work— and the thought of what hell life must be for people less fortunate than himself—that determined him to continue, and increase, his opposition to the regime in Cannes. Only this time the disagreement would be expressed in action rather than words.

Scene Three

THE FIRST active operation carried out by the Miniconi group was the attempted derailment at La Bocca on November 2, 1943; the second, the successful blasting of the railroad track at Anthéor exactly two months later. Thirty-one days after that, once more on the second of the month, they struck again. Then less than a week passed before the fourth assault was mounted, on February 5, 1944. The last two—at Mandelieu, near the scene of the first, and La Source, a heavily built-up area between Cannes and La Bocca—were more daring in their execution. So was a raid on a secret gasoline dump in January. None of them would have been possible if it had not been for an unexpected and extraordinary piece of good fortune which had come their way in the New Year.

It was in the middle of the morning on January 15. Javel, the two men from Théoule, and three other resistants, from Cannes, were on their way to a rendezvous at Auribeau, a tiny hilltop village five miles inland from La Napoule. Miniconi had already recruited two companies, each more than 200 strong, from patriots living and working in Cannes and La Bocca. But as the rigors of the occupation became increasingly more severe, the difficulties of operating away from home multiplied daily. It was to discuss the possibility of forming a third company, drawn from resistants living in the outlying areas surrounding the town, that the meeting had been called . . . first, because sabotage operations were easier in the country; and second, because, clearly, the quicker the saboteurs could go to ground after their attack, the safer they would be. It was, Miniconi thought, too much to expect men to cover nine or ten miles on foot—as some of them had after the Anthéor operation—and then turn out for a day's work as though nothing had happened.

Javel and his companions were bicycling up a dirt road that ran through fields between the Siagne river and a canal. In peacetime, the broad valley produced flowers and fruit, but now the rectangular strips of cultivation were planted with beans, potatoes, cabbages, and even sugar beets. On the far side of the river the land rose steeply to the Massif de Tanneron and the forest of mimosas which would turn the countryside lemon yellow in a few weeks' time. It was a cold, clear day with the sky bright blue above the rim of snow outlining the mountains in the interior.

The six men were pedaling past a bamboo thicket growing along the far bank of the canal when Javel heard the unmistakable *thock!* —*thock!*—*thock!* of a woodman's axe biting into a tree. There was nothing unusual in this: anyone with timber on his property might be chopping or sawing wood to burn when coal was unobtainable and the southern nights were unseasonably cold. But the noise of the axe was accompanied by voices, and the voices were speaking German.

Waving the others on, Javel dismounted and walked across a plank bridge spanning the canal. The sound was coming from the far side of the bamboo screen. Cautiously, he slid in among the ten-foot-high stems and edged his way to the other side of the thicket. What he saw then made him catch his breath.

Beyond the bamboo, a small meadow rose to the edge of a wood. And beneath the trees, a squad of German soldiers were at work under the direction of a *Feldwebel.* They were felling and trimming holm oaks and pines, some of which had already been sawed into lengths and stacked. A smaller group of men were digging, a little farther into the wood.

The NCO was in uniform, with a carbine slung over his shoulder and a pistol at his hip. But the men wore fatigues and most of them were stripped to their singlets. Their jackets were draped neatly over a log at the bottom of the meadow.

And—this was what had made Javel gasp with surprise—their small arms were piled within a few feet of his hiding place.

Like shocks of iron corn, the three pyramids of rifles stood unguarded among the tussocks of grass. Parting two of the bamboo stems to give himself a broader view, Javel surveyed the meadow and its surroundings.

The detachment had evidently arrived by the minor road linking La Bocca with Pégomas. Javel could see the windshield of the truck that had brought them, shining in the sunlight beyond the trees. Just as clearly, the *Feldwebel* was unaware that there was a trail on the other side of the bamboo screen—and sensibly enough he had ordered his men to pile their arms, as he thought, as far away from the road as possible.

Rattling the dry canes as little as he could, Javel pushed his way excitedly back to the track and signaled to the other five men, who had stopped some distance farther on.

"A dozen rifles!" he enthused when they had returned. "Piled in three stacks of four. There are cartridge belts slung over a log with the jackets. I think there may be pistols in holsters, too."

"But . . . that's incredible!" one of the men from Théoule said. "You mean they've simply dumped everything they've got and there's just this one sergeant . . . ?"

"That's what I said."

"You're absolutely certain," another man queried, "that there's only—I mean they don't have lookouts posted in the wood or anything?"

"Come and see for yourself," said Javel. Together, the two of them plunged back into the bamboo thicket.

"He's dead right," the man said when they returned five minutes later. "Christ, the bloody guns are only about six feet away! You wouldn't need to take more than two steps to get your hands on them!"

There was a sudden chorus of voices. "What are we going to do?"

"Go get them, of course!"

"But suppose—?"

"Suppose nothing! How often do we get an opportunity like this?

A dozen rifles with ammunition? Maybe revolvers as well? Virtually unguarded? Be your age, Palmier!"

"What about the rendezvous? We're late already. The Auribeau—"

"Fuck the rendezvous!" Javel broke in harshly. "If we don't show within three minutes of the scheduled time, the others will know something has happened and disperse anyway. They know the rules as well as we do. We'll make another rendezvous some other time. But we won't have another chance to get these guns!"

The second man from Théoule said, "All right. How are we going to work it? Should I make my way to the road through those bushes and attract their attention? Throw a stone at the windshield of the truck, maybe? Decoy them away from this end of the field while you step out and grab the guns?"

Javel shook his head. "As soon as they see or hear anything unusual, the first thing they'll do is go for those guns."

"Then how . . . ?"

"Stealth," Javel said. "That should be the keyword. Now here's what we do . . ."

Soon afterward, he was standing hidden among the bamboo canes opposite the log across which the German uniforms were draped. Now that he was nearer, he could see that there were holstered revolvers among the webbing belts and bandoliers. One of the Théoule men stood next to him, staring up the slope of meadow at the soldiers among the trees. "What are they doing, for God's sake?" the man whispered. Some of the Germans were maneuvering the cut logs toward the excavations inside the wood.

"Giving themselves a clear view down to the ocean," Javel said. "Using what they cut down to revet dugouts and foxholes. You know they're shit scared there'll be an Allied landing along this coast."

"We should be so lucky!" the man interrupted bitterly. "There was supposed to have been an Allied landing in October of last year, but they went to Algeria instead."

"There'll be one sometime. And this must be the Boche's second line of defense; they'll fall back here if the Allies break through the fortifications they're building along the shore."

"And what do we do? Stand and watch as usual?"

"That's the time we come out of hiding and attack the Germans from behind," Javel said. "That's why we have to get our hands on those guns."

The *Feldwebel* had disappeared among the trees. Perhaps he was inspecting the dugouts. "All right," Javel said, "let's try." Dropping to their hands and knees, they crawled to the edge of the thicket.

In the winter months in the South of France the sun's trajectory is so low that even at midday long shadows are cast. The log lay within an irregular band of shade beyond the bamboos, and Javel was counting on this to minimize any movement they made if one of the Germans happened to look in their direction. Once away from the shelter of the canes, they lay flat on their faces and wormed their way toward their objective. The grass was still moist from the previous night's frost and the ground smelled of earth and wet leaves.

As soon as they were hidden from the fatigue squad by the bulk of the log, they reached up to grasp belts and bandoliers, drawing the heavily charged webbing down on their side with infinite care lest the jackets be disturbed. Since they were only three or four yards from the thicket, it was easier to unflap the holsters and toss the Mauser pistols back in among the bamboos from their concealed position. But the weighty cartridge belts were a different matter; they were obliged to make several journeys each, hearts thudding and breath rasping in their throats as they backed up on elbows and knees dragging one or two with them each time.

When finally they were safely hidden in the thicket once more, Javel wiped one sleeve across his brow and gave a low whistle as he began gathering up the belts and guns. He had left one man to guard the bicycles. The other three were standing among the bamboos, each one opposite one of the rifle stacks. When they heard the signal, they were to count up to fifty and then emerge from their shelter, smoothly and unhurriedly, walk the three paces to the weapons, pick them up, and return to the trail on the far side of the canal.

"But they'll see us! Supposing they see us?" one of the men had protested when Javel outlined his plan. "We'll be *loaded* down with four rifles each, and you'll be even worse off, with a dozen handguns between two of you! To say nothing of the cartridge belts! The krauts'll be able to move three times as fast as we can."

"They'll be able to, but I don't think they will—even if they see us," Javel had replied. "Think, man. There'll be thirteen of them with just one rifle and one pistol—the sergeant's—between them. Against them they'll have a dozen of each . . . and for all they know, there may be forty or fifty of us! My guess is that they'll expect an attack as soon as they miss the stuff. And they're going to drop into those foxholes so quick you won't see them for dust!"

Palmier said, "Yes, if they don't know there's a dirt road behind the bamboos, they'll probably think it's some kind of ambush. But they won't keep their heads down forever. What about our get-away?"

"What do you mean? We have bicycles, don't we? Even if they knew about the dirt road, they couldn't get their truck to it, not through this thicket."

"I don't mean that," Palmier said. "I mean we'll be lumbered with two rifles, two big pistols, and a cartridge belt each. That's a clumsy enough load for a man on a bike anyway. I mean we'll be kind of conspicuous, won't we?"

"I think we *should* turn it into an ambush," another man put in. "Shoot as many of the bastards as we can."

"And have half the population of the valley butchered as a re-prisal?" Javel said. "All right, there are people working in the fields. They'll notice us when we ride away. We hope they're friends, in which case they'll see nothing. If they're collabos—well, that's just a risk we have to take. They won't know us by sight anyway."

"All the same," one of the men from Théoule said, "a posse of six cyclists each carrying three guns—no, *four* guns, for God's sake!—that's a bit much, isn't it?"

Javel sighed. "Look," he said. "We'll split up. We'll go like hell. We'll junk the stuff as soon as we possibly can. You two guys from Théoule, head back toward the sea: the Tonner farm's only half a mile down the trail. Hand the guns in there; Francis and his brother will know what to do with them. Then go on home. You, Palmier, and Musa—you ride on toward Auribeau. There's a stream running into the Siagne below the village—"

"You mean by the old mill?"

"Right. The mill's abandoned, as you know. But the stream is still channeled beneath the building . . . and it's hidden behind trees in a steep-sided valley. You could wade in there and stash the guns on one of the stone shelves above the water level, and nobody'd suspect they were there in a hundred years."

"What about you and Lama?"

"There's a culvert runs under the trail this side of Pégomas, in case of an overflow from the canal. It'll be dry at this time of year. We can stow ours in a niche I know about in there."

"And then?"

"Then we all come back separately, at night, and we dismantle the weapons and over the next couple of weeks we take them in pieces to Jean-Marie's depot."

Miniconi had found the hiding place for his small armory through a tipoff from one of his men who was a chef in a big, rich house on the avenue Fiésole. In the grounds of the place next door, the chef told him, there was a bluff running along the rear of the property —and about ten feet up in the bluff there was a cave or grotto. The place next door was called the Villa Fiésole. It belonged to the painter Jean-Gabriel Domergue, whose pictures of swan-necked beauties had graced the pages of glossy magazines before the war. Domergue was not in residence now—he was thought to be still in Paris—and the villa was shuttered and empty. But in time the grotto in back became very full indeed: without the knowledge of the artist, but with the connivance of his gardener, the entire Groupe Jean-Marie used it as their secret arsenal from then until the Liberation. The only person embarrassed by this clandestine storage was the gardener, who was never able to give his boss a satisfactory explanation for what looked very like a bald pathway worn across one corner of the back lawn when the villa had been untenanted for so long.

In January of 1944, however, the quantity and variety of arms stored in the cave were insignificant. This was why Javel's unexpected haul from the German fatigue squad near Pégomas was so important. And in fact, despite the objections, as so often happens with tasks which seem at first to bristle with difficulties, the completion of the operation was absurdly, ludicrously easy.

As Javel and his companion lurched through the thicket toward the plank bridge, their arms full of handguns and their shoulders bowed beneath the weight of bandoliers, the three other men emerged from the bamboo. Moving smoothly and unhurriedly, they stepped to the piled rifles, picked them up, and tucked them under their arms. Then, as openly and casually, they turned around, retraced their steps, and disappeared among the canes. Nobody saw them. Nobody noticed any movement. Nobody missed the weapons.

The *Feldwebel* went on shouting at his men—admittedly, his back was turned to the thicket—and the men continued chopping and digging and maneuvering logs in the wood at the top of the slope of meadow. By the time the alarm was finally raised, the resistants had vanished in their several directions and there was nothing left to show that they had been there but the snake-tracks of bicycle tires in the dust at the side of the trail beside the canal.

Because of the importance of this heist, Miniconi was able to plan two more attacks on the railroad in quick succession—and in places where, without enough weapons to beat off a possible assault from a German patrol, he would never have dared to operate before.

The Mandelieu attack, on February 2, took place near a bridge where the railroad crossed the Argentière river not long before it ran out into the ocean at La Napoule. The bridge itself was policed by two sentries, and there were private gardens and commercial yards running down to the tracks all along the sector Miniconi had chosen. Even more audacious was the operation at La Source, for it took place by a level crossing on a busy street, less than half a block from the central telephone exchange, which was guarded by the Germans night and day.

In each case the raid was carried out by six men and a section leader. In each case the leader summoned the saboteurs by coded flashlight signals from the walls and alleys and stacks of lumber and platelayers' huts that had concealed them since they arrived singly at the rendezvous earlier in the night. In each case only four men worked on the line, while the leader and the two others—heavily armed now, thanks to Javel's good fortune—kept watch above or beside the permanent way.

At Mandelieu the steel tracks were sprung away from the ties the way they had been at La Bocca in the first operation, three months before. Members of a section gang from the FER network operating out of the La Bocca freight yards had left suitable tools for Miniconi's crew by the crossing at La Source. Using the big T-shaped keys, they unscrewed fishplates, loosened cradles, and then simply lifted out a 12-foot section of rail, carried it away bodily, and dumped it among supplies in a building contractor's yard.

Neither operation resulted in a derailment: searchlights on the locomotives enabled the engineers to stop the trains before they arrived at the breaks in the line in each case. But there were of course delays. It took the Nazi wrecking crew an hour and a half to replace the missing rail at La Source. Two hours and fifty minutes passed before the track at Mandelieu was repaired. It wasn't much —but there would be other delays, Miniconi knew, organized by patriots at Cagnes-sur-Mer, Beaulieu, and Cap Martin, and the trains held up were carrying supplies to the German forces defending Monte Cassino.

It was the cumulative effect of such minor operations, Miniconi's chiefs believed, that could in some small way lessen the hell the Americans were suffering below that seemingly impregnable fortress.

Flashback III

Autumn, 1942 – Spring, 1943

I

MINICONI'S DETERMINATION to transform brave words into brave deeds once he was installed at the Mont Chevalier school in Cannes had taken some time to show results. And time, like almost everything else, was a commodity in short supply when he was transferred to the town in 1942—especially for a teacher who was conscientious. French education then was something of a conveyor-belt affair: so much information to be packed into so many heads in such and such a period. Correcting homework, marking essays, setting and evaluating tests, left little free time during the semester, even after the pupils had gone home. What there was, Miniconi used in an attempt to get to know the place. The picture was very different from the one he had been used to at Peille. The population of the village was less than 1,000; that of Cannes 70,000 in the center alone. If outlying residential and commercial areas such as Le Cannet, La Californie, and La Bocca were included, the figure was almost trebled.

There was another difference even more marked. In Peille, folks tended to speak their minds, whichever side of the fence they were on. In Cannes, people seemed afraid to speak at all.

Miniconi spent more—and drank more—than he could afford, quartering the center bar by bar in the hope of hearing something, anything, that might bring him into contact with some of the inhabitants who shared his views.

Cannes is arranged in a half-circle around a sandy bay—one of the few eastern Riviera resorts not to have a shingle beach. At the western extremity is the port, the customs house, and the casino; at the eastern end, the snob Palm Beach peninsula, with the offshore islands a few hundred yards away. Between the two curves runs the palm-shaded promenade called the Croisette, lined with expensive hotels, glittering in peacetime with the automobiles of the rich, the famous, or the merely beautiful. A little way along the Croisette and a couple of blocks inland are the railroad station, the market, and the fashionable end of the rue d'Antibes, the resort's principal shopping street. From here the die-straight avenue Carnot runs northward to the high ground around Le Cannet, cutting the town in two.

Miniconi knew it would be useless trying to find fellow spirits in the ritzy Croisette district: the bars and sidewalk cafés in the neighborhood of the Majestic, the Carlton, the Martinez, and the Grand Hotel would be more likely to harbor those trying to buy meat or coffee, or sell gold rings and diamonds. But there were bars near his school on the promontory overlooking the port, bars in the ancient cobbled streets where fishermen drank. There were bars along the rue d'Antibes and up the avenue Carnot, brasseries near the market, taverns throughout the poorer quarters of the town. In particular, there was the Taverne Royale, a noisy and popular rendezvous across the street from the railroad station. He tried them all, striking up conversations wherever and whenever he could, discreetly exposing his views in the hope that someone would agree with his opinions or take him up on them. But he drew a blank all along the line. They evaded the issue, or ignored it, or changed the subject. It was the same if he helped his wife with the marketing. In Peille, wartime shortages due to the blockade and the demands of the Germans had scarcely affected them. Sugar might be short, and coffee and rice nonexistent, but a mountain village in an agricultural area would never lack fruit and vegetables, butter and milk and eggs, the meat from an illegally slaughtered sheep. Shopping in Cannes was a different matter. You drew the minuscule entitlement due on a ration ticket and that was that.* And so far as unrationed foodstuffs were concerned, you could stand four-deep in a 200-yard line-up, only to find an hour later, when you were a few feet from the entrance to the store, that they had sold out of whatever it was and were putting up the shutters. Nevertheless, although he heard plenty of complaints and grumbling, and hard-luck stories by the score, not a whisper of actual resistance, not a word about opposing the régime reached Miniconi's ear.

Yet there must, he knew, be resistants working somewhere in the town. Either their security was one-hundred-percent efficient—or they were too scared to commit themselves in case he turned out to be an agent provocateur. The only thing to do, he decided, was to find a specific contact. And for this he had to return to Peille.

He went during the two-day school holiday over *Toussaint* (All Saints' Day, or Hallowe'en), dutifully reporting to the Commisariat of the 2nd Arrondissement that he was going back to his old home to visit relatives. He took the train to Nice, changed on to the Sospel line, got off by the cement works at La Grave de Peille, and finished the journey in the pint-sized bus running a shuttle service up to the village. From there he went to see Mertens at Beausoleil. Mertens advised him to go and talk to a man in a Nice haulage contractor's office.

Yes, he was told. There was a contact. But any approach must be made very discreetly. The existing *réseau* in Cannes had been *brûlé* (blown): almost all the members of the network had been arrested by Vichy police and sent to internment camps; the few remaining at liberty were wary of any approach by strangers, lest it should be the result of a confession and lead to the decimation of the rest of the organization. However, if he went to a certain antique dealer near the railroad bridge on the Boulevard d'Italie, he could be put in touch with the survivors. No names were to be mentioned. He was

* Under the French rationing system certain products classed as luxuries—including croissants, brioches, cakes, pastries, chocolate, preserved meats and certain confections—were forbidden altogether. The bread ration was 50g (less than 2 oz.) per day. A monthly ticket entitled the holder to 400g (less than 1 lb.) of fats, including butter, margarine, lard and oil. The meat ration was derisory and 200g (not quite ½ lb.) of cheese was allowed per month. An adult not in a special category, able to obtain his full rations, was assured of 1,150 calories per day—rather less than half the amount considered necessary by dieticians.

simply to ask if he could see an Oriental chest in Japanese lacquer. The antiquarian would have been forewarned of his visit.

Miniconi went home well pleased with the excursion. At last he was on to something definite; now there should be a chance of some real action! He was consumed with impatience, waiting for an opportunity to make the contact. But French schools worked Saturdays at that time, leaving their pupils a free day every Thursday, and it was not until the following week that he was able to make his way to the shop during business hours.

It was a big double-fronted store with grimy windows and furniture stacked on either side of an aisle leading into the gloomy interior. A bell jangled as he pushed open the door and went inside. There was an elderly couple in back, haggling over the terms for some chaise longue they were trying to sell. Miniconi affected to study cabinets and commodes, brass-railed Empire occasional tables, and Louis XVI chairs with threadbare upholstery until they had gone. Then he walked briskly to the office at the rear of the store. A man of about his own age came to the door.

"Good morning," Miniconi said. "I wonder if you can help me?" The man was dark, of less than medium height, with handsome Latin features. But his sunken eyes were feverish and his skin sallow and unhealthy.

"Anything I can do . . ." he said politely.

"I was looking for something in the line of *chinoiserie*."

"Then I'm afraid I cannot help you. We deal only in French period pieces."

Miniconi stared. "You don't have, for example . . . an Oriental chest in Chinese lacquer?"

The dealer shook his head. "Nothing like that at all."

"But . . . ?" Miniconi was nonplussed. "Are you *sure?* An Oriental—"

"Absolutely certain," the man cut in. "I regret, Monsieur." He held open the door as the schoolteacher went out. The bell clanged again as it closed behind him.

Miniconi couldn't understand it. What had gone wrong? Was he mistaken in thinking that the dealer had looked suddenly apprehensive when he made his code request? Had he too been blown and were there police spies concealed somewhere among the rows of dusty furniture? Or had Mertens' contact in fact been arrested and a ringer left in his place to put the finger on anyone who tried to make contact? No, that was hardly likely: if the man he had seen had been a double agent or an impostor, he would surely have encouraged Miniconi to say more, rather than choking him off like that. Maybe, then, he knew he was being watched and was warning everyone to stay away from him?

Remembering that he himself was officially under surveillance, too, he hurried through a network of narrow streets behind the Croisette, went in one entrance of the post office and immediately out the other, and then loitered beneath the plane trees in the deserted garden in front of the town hall while a small coastal steamer maneuvered into position by the customs house quay. When he was certain that he was not being followed, he walked to the railroad station and telephoned Octave Nicolai in Peille. The only thing to do was check back with Mertens in Beausoleil—and he hadn't the time to do that personally, nor would it be wise to call Mertens direct.

The following day, he called Octave again. "I have a message for you, Ange," the little groceryman announced. "I hope it makes sense to you. The message is: 'In far eastern affairs, never confuse the Chinese with the Japanese.' "

Miniconi laughed aloud with relief. "Message received and understood," he said. "Over and out."

What a fool he had been! Imagine making a mistake like that! In his eagerness to get things moving, he had behaved like the greenest amateur! No wonder the antique dealer had looked worried! On the following Thursday, he went back to the store and walked straight to the office. "I made a stupid mistake, the last time I came here," he said frankly. "It was a *Japanese* lacquer chest I was interested in. By some slip of the tongue I said Chinese."

The dealer's face was suddenly smiling. He held out his hand. "André Emerini," he said. "Code name Curtel. I'm glad to know you. You'd better come inside."

The network, Miniconi learned, had indeed been virtually destroyed. The men especially had suffered. It was feared that some might have been handed over to the Germans rather than interned, and for this reason most of the women had been instructed to lie low. Even the strongest characters had been known to break once the Gestapo torturers had gotten their hands on them, and nobody was safe until it was known whether or not the captives had talked.

Apart from Curtel himself, the only members of the *réseau* still active were a man code-named "Raymond" and two women. Both of the women were foreign. "Tatiana" was a Rumanian, and "Clara," whose real name was Goldenstein, was the widow of a Jewish businessman. "This is principally an information network," Curtel explained. "The bulk of our work has been printing and distributing tracts and newsletters, telling the truth about the Vichy betrayal, and counteracting Nazi propaganda. It's necessary, too, to put the record straight about our comrades fighting in the north—you know the way the Vichy press always presents them as 'Jewish terrorists' or 'Communist spies.' "

Miniconi nodded. "Is there any more active work to be done?"

"We have managed to pass a few refugees and a couple of Italian deserters to people who can look after them. There's an escape line organized by a farmer called Augier in Haut-de-Cagnes, and another in the Esterel."

"Your group isn't the only one working here, is it?"

Curtel shook his head. "There's a British group with a radio. We feed them information on Italian troop movements and so on. And at least one, probably two, other local networks, but we haven't succeeded in making contact. They're probably allied with Frénay's *Combat* organization. You can hardly blame them if they steer clear of a network that's been blown."

"What possibilities are there for sabotage?"

"We were completing a study of that when the arrests were made," Curtel said. "There are the railroad workshops at La Bocca, of course."

"*Les Aciéries du Nord?*"

"That's right. And the small boat-building yard between here and La Napoule. Apart from that, it's just electric transformers, pylons, water-supply installations—and of course the railroad itself. We have a map with all the vulnerable points marked."

"I think you've done a remarkable job," Miniconi said.

"The trouble," Curtel said, "is that I cannot go on doing it." He explained that he had only recently been released from an internment camp himself . . . on grounds of ill health. He was still a very sick man, obliged to live above the store with his mother. He didn't really feel strong enough to go on organizing the group; it wasn't fair to the others—especially as Raymond had located several prospects who sounded as though they would make admirable recruits.

They needed somebody more active as a leader. He would nevertheless be happy to act as a Number Two, Curtel went on, if somebody could be found to head the group. Mertens had spoken very well of Miniconi, stressing his courage, his organizing ability, and his passion for active resistance. Would he be prepared to take on the responsibility?

Miniconi didn't hesitate an instant. It was the opportunity he had been waiting for. He made a rendezvous to meet Raymond the following evening and returned home, for the first time in weeks, in an elated state of mind.

It was the second lucky break they'd had since the beginning of the month. They actually had a home to go to now. The parents of one of Miniconi's pupils—perhaps out of sympathy, perhaps out of good-heartedness, maybe because they admired his score of six out of seven *Certificats d'Etudes* at Peille the previous year—whatever the reason, these parents had offered the family an apartment at a reasonable rent. They were now comfortably installed on the first floor of No. 5 *bis,* avenue du Grand-Pin, which was much nearer the center of town, and far more convenient for their schools.

An additional advantage was that they could listen to the radio again. Miniconi had not considered it advisable to signal the fact that they possessed one at the Hotel de Bourgogne, and in any case it would have been impossible to tune in to London there. But now, though reception might be more difficult in a heavily built-up area, they could once more get the BBC and the Free French broadcasts on the 31, 40, and 50 meter wave bands. Since the United States had entered the war after Pearl Harbor, a year previously, they had also gotten into the habit of listening to the Voice of America on the 13 meter band—and it was a VOA news flash early the following day that tipped them off to the Anglo-American landings in North Africa.

French patriots were delighted to hear that at last the Allies were in a position to start hitting back, outraged to learn that Vichy had ordered French troops to resist the disembarkment, relieved when a ceasefire was agreed upon two days later—and then indignant beyond words when the invaders, instead of dealing with the Resistance in Algeria and Morocco, left the civil administration in the hands of Admiral Darlan, the arch-collaborator they had all been fighting against. That was on November 10. Before then, Miniconi had met Curtel and Gaston Ricatto, the man whose code name was Raymond, in a café near the port. Raymond was small, muscular, taciturn—a dynamic little man who believed in action rather than words. His hair was thick and dark, and there was a dark fuzz covering his forearms and the backs of his fingers. "Start operating again," he said. "That's what we must do. Enough for the nucleus of a group already."

"You've sounded out some people?" Miniconi asked.

Raymond nodded. "Got some good ones lined up. Couple of hard men. Frossart—they call him 'le Teck,' the man of teak—and Sam Kadyss. He's big, dark, tough. Jewish, I think, but we don't ask. Then there's Bouthier and Maurel, and both of them have more prospects in mind. Maurel's an inspector on the SNCF, a *cheminot*. He should be able to put us in touch with plenty of railroad workers who share our views. Could be useful."

"I thought Maurel was attached to the FER *réseau* at La Bocca," Curtel said.

The little man shrugged. "Maybe. What does it matter, so long as he helps us?"

Miniconi asked about the other resistance groups working, or thought to be working, in the area. Although security was strict, he was told, certain overlaps were inevitable—and the picture that emerged from these was complex. Since the beginning of the year, the British secret service had been operating a clandestine radio transmitter from a property on the Cap d'Antibes, under the direction of an officer landed from a submarine. Curtel's group, which was named Marie-Raymond, had been furnishing information to them on German and Italian activities—including the use, in the unoccupied zone, of Gestapo detection trucks.* Another transmitting "station" was later installed at the Villa Val-Désir, in the rue de Rome, Cannes. The service was managed by Captain Henri Frager,

---

* The use of these vehicles, with the approval of Vichy but in flagrant breach of the armistice terms, resulted in the arrest of the entire headquarters staff of the Alliance *réseau*, headed by Marie-Madeleine Fourcade, on November 7, eve of the Allied landings in North Africa. In radio liaison with London, the *réseau* had organized General Giraud's escape by submarine the previous night. A second group of officers, due to rejoin him in North Africa, was due to be embarked at Le Lavandou on the 7th. But the rendezvous—betrayed by an informer—was changed to Cros-de-Cagnes, and it was to make sure that the British were aware of this unexpected alteration that the Alliance radio operator, imprudently, continued transmitting long enough for the premises to be located. When Hitler invaded the southern zone, French police set Marie-Madeleine and her companions free while they were being moved from one prison to another.

assistant to the painter André Girard, who was better known under the code name Carte. Girard himself was at that time controlled by the British agent Peter Churchill. A father and two sons named Audouard owned a third property that was at the disposal of resistants. This was the Villa Charles-Edith, in the avenue de Windsor —the "safe house" used for many months by all the British and French agents parachuted into the South. "Like a beehive, that place is," Raymond said to Miniconi. "I'm surprised the neighbors don't complain!"

Whether they arrived by parachute or submarine, the British and French agents were sent, respectively, by the SOE or the BCRA. Special Operations Executive was a small branch of British military intelligence charged with the infiltration of agents and radio operators into occupied Europe. It was commanded by Colonel Maurice Buckmaster, whose name identified the *réseau* run by Peter Churchill. The *Bureau Central de Renseignements et d'Action* was directed by the famous Colonel Passy, whose real name was Dewavrin. Attached directly to General de Gaulle's personal staff, the BCRA intelligence unit functioned on an elitist plan (as might be guessed from the fact that its chief chose to identify himself with the name of Paris's most ritzy district). It was accused of ignoring the left-wing elements that made up the greater part of the Resistance in France in favor of Christian-Democrat organizations such as *Combat.* Passy was alleged to have been a prewar member of the Cagoule (an extreme-right-wing secret society with certain resemblances to the Ku Klux Klan: its members, the *cagoulards,* were "the hooded ones"). What seemed to be nearer the truth was that *réseaux* received arms, equipment, and financial aid from the BCRA in direct proportion to their declared support for de Gaulle.

The situation was further complicated by the fact that arrangements for the delivery of these supplies had to be made through SOE—and there was of course rivalry between the two organizations. But, to de Gaulle's fury, the British had insisted on retaining control of "Radio Patrie" and its *Frenchmen Speak to the French* broadcasts, through which secret messages were transmitted. Later, there was more confusion still, when the United States Office of Strategic Services began establishing its own *réseaux* in France. But until American bases were more firmly installed in Europe, submarine deliveries continued to be made by the Royal Navy, *parachutages* by

British night bombers, and the transfer of key personnel to London by Lysander airplanes of the RAF.

Because of the basic inefficiency of these arrangements—and because it was impossible to obtain a clear picture of the conditions throughout occupied Europe—anomalies and irregularities proliferated. These in turn were exacerbated by jealousies and disagreements between different resistance movements, and by the Anglo-American dispute over who was to lead the Free French. The British were the hosts and reluctant champions of de Gaulle; Roosevelt preferred Giraud, because he was less personally ambitious, less of an official "rebel," and therefore more likely to retain the support of the great mass of Frenchmen faithful to Vichy—from which Ambassador Leahy had only been withdrawn in June of 1942. The key to Roosevelt's policy had always been to remain friendly with *all* Frenchmen, and to do this he had to avoid the appearance of forcing any particular leader on the country once the war was over—which was why he was unwilling to "underwrite" de Gaulle.

Such niceties of State Department etiquette were lost on resistants in France in 1942. To those of them who were anti-German but still loyal to Pétain because of the rule of law, Giraud was the man to follow; for those whose sympathies lay with—or who had been part of—the demilitarized army, Giraud again was the natural choice. But for everyone else de Gaulle, whatever his faults, was the country's savior. And it was de Gaulle, and de Gaulle alone, who was able to communicate with the Resistance because of the link between the BCRA and the SOE.

Carefully worded broadcasts inspired by London therefore went some way toward appeasing the wave of indignation provoked by the American rapprochement with Darlan in North Africa. But a great deal of suspicion remained. The mood of euphoria created four days earlier by Montgomery's victory at El Alamein was soured. The American image was tarnished. "It's all very well for them to tell us that the arrangement is temporary," Raymond said furiously to Miniconi. "We've heard that one before. We hear it every time some fresh liberty is lost. And it's exactly the kind of thing we've been hearing from Vichy for the past three years. Darlan signed that ceasefire *as a representative of Pétain*. Those are the bastards we've been fighting, for Christ's sake! And the Americans leave them running the show instead of handing it over to the patriots who've been risking their lives preparing the ground for their damned landings!" He shook his head angrily. "It stinks! The whole thing stinks!"

"Plenty of things stink," Miniconi said. "Laval actually *congratulated* the krauts on beating off the Canadians in the Dieppe raid. That smells to me. So do the Vichy speeches praising them for 'mastering' the commando raids on Boulogne, Le Touquet, and St. Nazaire. It's the worst kind of sycophancy: those raids were never intended to be anything more than probes to see how the Germans reacted in defense. As for the bishops and cardinals in the occupied zone making a declaration of loyalty to Pétain—to me that's the worst of all."

Raymond spat. "Load of shits!" he said.

"Maybe. But there's no sense wasting energy calling names. What we have to do is make sure the same thing doesn't happen here. The Allies may deal with Darlan in Algeria, but they're not going to deal with Pétain and Laval here—and it's our job to tell the people the truth, to let them know what goes on, so that they'll leave the British and Americans in no doubt when they land here that they can't pull the same thing a second time. Our job in the next few months is going to be information and not sabotage; it's going to be political, if you like, rather than military."

In this Miniconi was mistaken. On the following day, November 11, seventy-two hours after the Allied landings in North Africa, German and Italian troops broke the 1940 armistice agreement and invaded the unoccupied zone.

II

VIOLATION OF the armistice terms by the Axis armies provoked a series of dramas which were materially to affect the horrors—and the dangers—of life in the southern zone. Like the units which had at first resisted the Allied landings in North Africa, the remnants of the army still operative in Vichy France were pledged to resist invasion of their limited territory by *any* forces. This "Army of the Armistice," as it was called, had in fact secretly been maintaining camouflaged arms dumps ever since the capitulation. It was planned to use these weapons if the Germans crossed the border between the two zones, and the General Staff, receiving intelligence reports that such a move was imminent, had actually issued orders for a general mobilization. But Pétain and Laval heard of this through a collaborationist officer and persuaded the German High Command to delay their entry by one day—from November 10 to November 11, ironically enough the date commemorating the armistice which terminated World War I. During this critical 24 hours, the plan to resist was effectively spiked.

Senior officers were ordered back to their barracks, with the threat that armed force would be used against them if they refused to obey. Vichy police surrounded the arms dumps, which were later handed over to the Germans. Detachments of Vichy gendarmerie set up roadblocks, made arrests, and inhibited any troop movements. Only General de Lattre de Tassigny, who was stationed at Montpellier in command of the 16th military district, found it "incompatible with military honor" to stay put when the Nazis marched in.

De Lattre had at his disposition three infantry regiments, a regiment of cavalry, and one of artillery. His plan was to withdraw along the coast to the Corbières region between Perpignan and the Spanish frontier, gather around him in that hilly, wine-growing redoubt as many of his fellow soldiers as he could, and then hold off any German attacks while the majority of his force was evacuated by sea to North Africa from the tiny harbor of Port-Vendres, at the eastern margin of the Pyrenees. At 1100 hours on the morning of the 11th, he set off in his staff car, followed by nine officers, 180 men, and two 75mm. antitank guns. One battalion of the 8th Infantry was entraining at Montpellier railroad station; others were to follow or rendezvous along the route.

The plan was effectively sabotaged by Vichy. High-ranking officers arrived in Montpellier and informed the regimental commanders that de Lattre had been relieved of his command; the officers at the various assembly points were arrested by gendarmerie; even the loyal infantrymen already in the troop train were betrayed—the stationmaster gave orders for the locomotive to be detached and the train was immobilized. Finally the 180-strong escort with its two guns was forced to turn back by formations manning Vichy roadblocks. "There was a great deal of talk, that day, about stopping de Lattre," Honteberry, the local *préfet,* remarked drily, "and none whatever about stopping the Germans."

Stranded with a car, a driver, four aides-de-camp, and no army, de Lattre walked into the police station at Toulouse at 6 o'clock the following morning and gave himself up. "In his cell that night," writes Henri Noguères,* "he must nevertheless have been one of the very few officers in the French army to have slept the sleep of the just."†

On November 13, General Weygand, Pétain's chief link with North Africa and the only man capable of persuading the Vichy regime to resist, was arrested by the Gestapo.

Hitler then ordered the total dissolution of the Army of the Armistice because of its "anti-German bias." The death penalty was prescribed for anyone who knew of the existence of an arms dump and failed to report it. The cost of the occupation, paid by the French, rose to 5 million francs ($100,000) a day.‡ The entire merchant shipping fleet of the port of Marseille, nearly 600 vessels with a combined tonnage of 645,000, was demanded as a contribution to help beat the Allied blockade. The Gestapo [9]—already illegally operating in the southern zone with their "inspectors" and their detection trucks—now required facilities to install headquarters in every sizable town in France.

Pétain and Laval gave in to all these demands, and agreed in principle to a plan under which all able-bodied Frenchmen under sixty were to be sent to Germany as slave labor. Once again Hitler's sole concession related to the French fleet at Toulon, which was to be allowed, with a handful of infantrymen, to defend the port against all comers. But the soldiers were withdrawn, rumors (subsequently confirmed) circulated suggesting that the fleet was to be handed over to Mussolini, and during the night of November 26–27 tanks of the SS 1st Armored Corps under the command of Obergrüppenfuhrer Hausser began a pincer advance on the town. Admiral de Laborde, who had already refused an invitation to join the Free French in Algeria§ and had been prepared also to resist an

---

* *Histoire de la Résistance en France—Volume 3* (with Marcel Degliame-Fouché), Robert Laffont, Paris, 1972.

† Sentenced to ten years' jail by a Vichy state tribunal for insubordination, de Lattre was subsequently rescued by a Resistance action squad and flown in an SOE Lysander to North Africa, where he formed the victorious French 1st Army, later to invade Provence.

‡ The sum is calculated at the prewar rate of around 50 francs to the dollar and 200 to the pound sterling. To help local trade in North Africa, Eisenhower later devalued the franc (to 75 and 300 respectively).

§ The admiral's signal replying to the offer was terse. It consisted of the single word *merde* (shit).

Allied invasion of the southern zone, gave the order to scuttle. More than 235,000 tons of naval craft, 100 warships in all, capsized, sank, blew up, or were otherwise destroyed.

The effect of all these events on the Resistance was profound. One of the most immediate results was a certain rationalization in the organization of anti-German activity. Broadly, this now resolved itself into four main groups. These were (1) a fusion of the main right wing, or Christian Democrat, elements into a single network known as the MUR (United Resistance Movements); (2) an underground military formation created by disillusioned ex-members of the disbanded Army of the Armistice, now calling themselves the *Organisation de Resistance de l'Armée* (ORA); (3) a partisan movement directed by the *Front National*—the clandestine political organization that owed much of its impetus to the banned Communist party—which was known as the FTPF or *Franc-Tireurs et Partisans Français;* (4) the *maquis* proper.

To make the rash of initials more confusing still, the Free French headquarters in London, which was more closely in touch with the MUR than with any other network, insisted that the movement's civil and political activities should be separated from the military. Those engaging in the latter were known as the *Armée Sécrète* (AS).

The organizers of the AS and the ORA believed with the intelligence chiefs in London that their members should be trained—but that they should refrain from any military activity until the Allies had landed on French soil. "Imprudent" guerilla activity, they felt, would only result in savage reprisals and the consequent alienation of the civilian population. It could also provoke an extra influx of German troops and thus make the planned invasion more difficult still.

The FTPF chiefs disagreed. They believed the occupiers should be hit as often as possible, however puny each individual blow might be. There was thus a considerable amount of overlapping between the various movements. Kaltenbrunner, the Nazi police overlord, estimated the AS fully at around 80,000 men, for example. But many of these had agreed to join because there was no risk of immediate action. Others again, the more daring and impatient, became members of FTPF units in addition to their AS affiliation, attracted by the more spectacular aspects of sabotage, assassination and other acts of defiance. In the same way, railwaymen in the FER network often joined the AS, officers in the ORA carried out administrative work for the MUR, women whose domestic ties were with one organization might find themselves politically or emotionally drawn to another. It was therefore impossible at any one time to calculate the total number of people actively involved. There was, however, one thing they all had in common which was not shared by members of the *maquis.*

Operatives in the MUR, the AS, the ORA, and the FTPF were ostensibly living "normal" lives: they lived in their own houses or apartments, they had jobs, they possessed ration tickets and genuine ID papers. It was only during clandestine operations that they assumed their "guerilla" identities. The *maquisards,* on the other hand, were true outlaws. They lived a nomad existence, mainly in mountain areas, fighting to live and living only to fight—the hunted, the homeless, the persecuted, and those who were refugees from slave labor in Germany.[10]

For all these elements of the underground, recruitment, training, and any other activity became doubly and trebly dangerous now that the troops of Hitler's Third Reich were in the southern zone. They had to contend not only with the attentions of the French police and gendarmerie, not only with the reactionary mentality of Vichy officials and the risk of denunciation by scared or malicious fellow countrymen; they now had to fear the spot check in the street, the scrutiny of papers by armed military patrols, the knock on the door before dawn. And of course the knowledge that detection of their illegal activities almost certainly meant torture and death.

Like Nice and Monte Carlo, Cannes was officially in the zone of occupation assigned to the Italians.* But members of the German security services were everywhere, frequently in plain clothes or with cover identities. They already had a network of informers, fifth columnists, and Vichy spies recruited by the Gestapo "inspectors" illegally permitted by Pétain to roam the southern zone before it was invaded. Now they demanded an official "presence," and the Hotel Montfleury, on the lower slopes of the ridge sheltering the town to the north and east, was requisitioned as their headquarters.

---

* Mussolini, said to be enraged at the "humiliation" of being treated always as the junior partner in Axis affairs, had insisted on this. The Italian High Command remained in Menton, which was as far as Italy could penetrate during the mini-invasion just before France capitulated. A division was based on the old Armistice Commission headquarters in Nice, another in the Alpine foothills near Chambéry, and a third in the neighboring *département* of Isère. There was also an Italian contingent in the Drôme and at Hyères, near Toulon. Italy, in fact, had been given the south-eastern corner of the country.

Ange-Marie Miniconi was at the Mairie, making some routine inquiry in connection with the school, when he heard the loud-speaker patrol wagons announcing that the Italians were coming—and appealing to the population to remain calm. It was a sunny day, with a light breeze blowing whitecaps toward the deserted beaches. Most of the inhabitants living in villas along the Croisette came out on to their balconies to watch the parade as an infantry regiment marched in with band playing, flags flying, and plumes nodding in the wind. The following day, the red, white, and green ensign of the House of Savoy hung above the portico of the Hotel Gallia. That evening Miniconi received a message from Curtel asking him to be at a certain table in the basement of the Café de la Régence, in the Boulevard Carnot, at 21 hours 20.

The man who slid into the seat opposite him and gave the correct password was a cabinetmaker named Poujol. It was he who had set up the first radio contact with London under the direction of Captain Henri Frager of the Carte network on the Cap d'Antibes. And it was Poujol and Frager, together with Peter Churchill, who later moved the transmitter to the Villa Val-Désir, where Poujol was living, when the first site had proved unsuitable. That had been the previous February. Now the SOE and their French colleagues in Britain wanted every available scrap of information on the strength and disposition of the Axis forces in what had been the unoccupied zone. Could Miniconi and his small group help collect this material and assist the members of the Buckmaster *réseau* with the coding and decoding of messages?

Miniconi agreed at once. "We have friends working on the railroad at La Bocca," he said. "A great deal can be deduced from the movements of freight trains and the supplies they carry. Even the children in school, repeating what they heard their fathers say, can provide useful clues. And of course the Italians are—shall we say? —a voluble people. All we have to do is be around and listen."

"So long as the Italians remain here," Poujol said.

"Yes. So long as they stay here." Miniconi nodded soberly. The Gestapo had already installed a second unit in the Hotel Gallia, as both men knew. So long as the Italian flag hung outside that hotel, their task would be dangerous but not impossible. If it should ever be supplanted by the swastika, and the men at the Hotel Montfleury given their head, the odds against them would be lengthened immeasurably and the task rendered infinitely more perilous.

For several weeks, Miniconi, Curtel, Raymond, and the other members of the group made their way secretly to the Villa Val-Désir in the early hours of the morning, helping to code the information they had brought and decode the replies from London demanding more and more details of the German and Italian troop movements along the coast. It was hard and tedious work, sitting among the rafters in the attic above Poujol's workshop, for each message was in a double cipher and required maximum concentration if it was to be understood or transmitted correctly. The Nazi jamming, moreover, was so intense that it was never possible to receive before midnight, and the best time of all turned out to be between 6 A.M. and 8 A.M. in the morning. Miniconi learned in those weeks to live a schizophrenic existence, remaining with his wife and children for the evening, stealing out into the darkened streets soon after 11 P.M., and frequently bicycling straight to school after a busy night at the villa in the Rue de Rome. Fortunately, like many men whose singlemindedness is equaled by their determination, he was able to make do with two or three hours' sleep a night, snatched whenever and wherever it was possible.

Inexplicably, the Gestapo detection apparatus never pinpointed the SOE transmitter at the Villa Val-Désir. True, it was moved at regular intervals to a property belonging to the Baron Malval in the Californie residential district on the high ground behind Cannes. But the "broadcasts" often exceeded the seven minutes that was considered to be the safety limit, and sometimes added up to as many as eight hours in twenty-four. It was a common occurrence when Miniconi first worked with the Buckmaster *réseau* for the operator to send and receive seventeen separate messages in a single night.

Sometimes they would be helped by Peter Churchill, a keen-faced young man with smooth, dark hair and shell glasses. The British agent was secretly housed and fed by Mme. Poujol when he was in Cannes, but his network extended north as far as the Jura and west to Arles, and he was not always there. A Nazi double agent had infiltrated the *réseau* in the north, and there were bitter arguments between Frager and Carte, who had now moved toward the Spanish border, fearing themselves no longer safe on the Riviera.[11]

Among other visitors bringing information to the clandestine radio station at the Villa Val-Désir was Colonel Vautrin, the officer in charge of the Nice subdivision of the AS, and Roger Renaudie, a local member of the Buckmaster network, with special responsibility for organizing the embarkation and landing of men and material from British submarines.

Renaudie was a short, dark, wiry man with an ebullient temperament and an unrivaled knowledge of the coastline, from the largest yacht basin to the smallest private jetty. His work was not without its dramas. On his very first mission—arranging Peter Churchill's initial disembarkation at Antibes—the submarine surfaced in the middle of a fishing fleet from Cagnes-sur-Mer. Fortunately, as the Englishman remarked drily when they were safely ashore, the natives were friendly.

On another occasion, Renaudie was rowing a dinghy laden with small arms and portable radio transmitters from a submarine to a private beach on the Cap d'Antibes when heavy seas capsized the small craft and washed him up on the rocks. He was forced to break into a gardener's hut in the grounds of a neighboring mansion and steal a coverall in order to get home without arousing suspicion—for the apartment block in which he lived also housed the local gendarmerie and he dared not risk being seen in clothes sodden with seawater. Relieved of its weighty cargo—which of course sank as soon as the boat was upturned—the dinghy meanwhile righted itself. It ran aground on the Cap two days later.

"What do you think," the commandant of the gendarmerie said to Renaudie that evening in the local café, "we found an empty rowboat in a creek below the lighthouse—and there were a couple of sub-machineguns jammed beneath the thwarts!"

"Extraordinary!" murmured Renaudie.

"We've arrested a number of people in Antibes and Juan-les-Pins who are known to sympathize with that bastard de Gaulle, but none of them seems to know anything about it. It's a bit of a mystery, in fact. Who would have come ashore there? Some kind of villains, clearly. So why didn't they take the guns with them?"

"Perhaps they were black marketeers," Renaudie said.

The most hazardous of his adventures took place not long after the Nazis marched into the unoccupied zone. As soon as it was clear that Hitler intended to fortify the Mediterranean coastline against the expected Allied landings, British and French intelligence chiefs in London decided that it would be too dangerous to continue the submarine "service" to and from the Côte d'Azur. Agents and material would in future be parachuted into France and taken out by Lysander aircraft. But first, before the watch along the coast had established itself, there was one more mission to accomplish. Renaudie was given a package containing secret SOE papers that were too lengthy and detailed to be transmitted by radio, and instructed to row them out to a submarine at a certain time on a certain night.

Renaudie and two friends waited on the seaward side of the Cap at the appointed time, but the mistral had been blowing the day before, and there was a gigantic sea running. Huge waves reared up in the dark and marched across the shallow seabed to fling themselves on the rocks in explosions of foam and spray. "Surely they'll never come?" one of the friends protested. "Not on a night like this. Not with this kind of breakers!"

"It doesn't make any difference below the surface," Renaudie reminded him. "They won't feel the agitation of the water until they're close inshore."

"But they'll up periscope before they surface. To check that it's safe. And when they see the conditions . . ." He shrugged and left the sentence unfinished. "It's already ten minutes past the time," the other man said.

"I think they'll come," Renaudie said. "We'll take a risk and give them half an hour, as it's such a filthy night."

They stood on the rock shelf, listening to the roar and hiss and suck of the waves. Every now and then a squall of wind blew out of the darkness, soaking them with spray, plastering their clothes to their limbs. Fifteen minutes passed. "Jesus, but it's cold!" one of the men said, shivering. "They're not coming. They can't be coming now. We'd better—"

"*Look!*" Renaudie shouted suddenly. They all saw it at once. Among the stars glittering above the invisible horizon, a brighter, yellower light shone intermittently. It rose and fell, now pricking the night with a pattern of dots and dashes, now vanishing behind the black bulk of a wave. "It's the right code!" cried Renaudie. He sprang up onto a boulder and began signaling his reply with the hooded, rubber-covered torch that was his most prized possession.

The other two hurried to a small inlet on the lee side of the point. The dinghy was drawn up on a shingle bank, out of reach of the waves. "He'll never make it through this," the first man said, shaking his head. He stared at the backwash creaming between the rock outliers framing the creek. The steep combers rearing up out of the sea looked twice the height of a man.

Renaudie was beside them, helping to manhandle the dinghy into the water. As they waded into the short stretch of foaming shallows, pebbles hammered against the ankles of their sea boots and they had to brace themselves to avoid being thrown off balance by the undertow. Once the boat was floating, Renaudie clambered in, seated himself on the thwart, and took up the oars. He looked over his shoulder. "Wait for this one," he shouted, "and as soon as she's broken, push like hell!"

The wave arched over and burst in a flurry of foam. Struggling against the pull of the current, the two men surged forward until they were thigh-deep in the rough water, shoving the dinghy out as hard as they could. Renaudie started rowing frenziedly. The frail craft lurched and then got under way, skimming the surface as it was seized by the backwash. But already the following wave was piling up ahead of it. The crest crumbled into white. The wave crashed down on the boat, slewing it around and half filling it with seawater. Renaudie was pulling on the oars like a madman, spinning the dinghy back to face the next one. But the great mass of water rose inexorably beneath him. The dinghy rode up the slope like an elevator. The bow canted upward as the crest folded over—and then the boat capsized and was hurled back toward the shore as the wave broke with a thunderous roar. They dragged Renaudie out of the shallows, righted the boat, and tried again. The same thing happened. The third time, they lost one of the oars. "It's no good," Renaudie panted. "We'll never get her through that first line of waves while the sea's running like this. There's nothing else for it: I'll have to swim."

"*Swim?* Roger, you're crazy!" one of the friends yelled over the pounding of surf. "You'll never make it. You'll be smashed to pieces on the rocks."

"Or you'll die of cold. I'm freezing already—and that damned sub is lying five hundred yards offshore. Don't be a fool, man."

Renaudie was stripping off seaboots and sodden pants. His teeth were chattering. "I've swum in rougher seas," he said stubbornly. "For longer distances. If they can brave depth charges and mine-fields, and then risk being blown out of the water by shore batteries after coming all the way from North Africa, the least we can do is carry a message five hundred yards."

"But Roger—"

"The message is vital," Renaudie snapped. "They're expecting it." He stared out over the whitecaps to the signal lamp that was still intermittently flickering. "Keep sending, so that they'll know I'm on my way," he ordered.

The papers were sealed into a waterproof oiled-silk envelope. Renaudie pulled his fisherman's jersey over his head and stuffed the packet between his T-shirt and his skin. Then he pulled the belt from his pants and buckled it tightly around his waist. Wearing only the T-shirt and his shorts, he strode into the water. "The only problem is that first line of breakers," he said when they made a last attempt to dissuade him. "After that it's just a matter of plugging away, up one slope and down the next." He raised an arm in salute and turned his back on them.

They saw him half wading, half running down the shelving beach with the undertow. They saw him pause fractionally and then dive into the center of a wave as it arched over before breaking. They thought they saw him as an indistinct blur, hurled about on the crest of the next. And then they saw nothing but the surf, the tumbling foam beneath the stars.

Drenched to the waist themselves, the two men stamped up and down to keep their circulation moving. Half an hour passed. Forty minutes. At last, sadly, they turned inland and started walking. "I told him," one muttered as soon as they were beneath the pine trees, out of the wind. "I told him."

They had gone about two hundred yards when they heard the footsteps. Drawing back into the shadows, they watched until the pale shape emerging from the dark was identifiable. It was Renaudie, trotting *toward* them with his whole body shuddering and his breath smelling strongly of rum. The sea had carried him to the beach of La Guaroupe, on the sheltered side of the point. "Bloody sight quicker . . . coming back . . . than going out!" he gasped. And all he would say of his astonishing exploit was: "I think they were happy to have the papers."

Miniconi, in the meantime, was expanding his own undercover group. It was slow and dangerous work, making the apparently casual contact, steering a conversation, posing here and there a significant question. Much of it had necessarily to be effected at second hand, through personal recommendations, after the passing of cryptic messages. Almost all of it depended, in the long run, on one person's judgment of another's good faith. And the enemy's agents would be trained to disrupt precisely that judgment, to betray exactly that faith. By the end of the year, however, a number of invaluable additions had been made. These included Gabriel Davaille, an older, gray-haired man who owned a liquor store near the Town Hall; Salignon, the director of Miniconi's own school; a *brigadier* (noncommissioned officer) at the Cannes police headquarters; and two couples whose premises were used as "mail drops" by members of the group wishing to contact one another. The latter couldn't have been more different, socially or temperamentally. Monsieur and Madame Placide, the manager and manageress of a *Bon Lait*** in the rue Georges Clémenceau, despite their name, were a lively and gregarious pair who liked nothing better than to gossip over the white tile counter of their little store; Monsieur and Madame Guernini, who lived in the rue du Maréchal Joffre, were on the other hand the archetypes of the dreamy intellectual. He was a professor of music, and she gave piano lessons in the cluttered living room of their first-floor apartment above the busy street leading down from the railroad bridge toward the port. From the point of view of security both couples were ideal: neither took part in any meetings or activities of the group; all that either of them knew, all they could ever tell, was that certain people whom they knew by sight but not by name sometimes left or collected letters there.

Georges Tranchant, who was only fourteen when Miniconi first recruited him, became one of the most useful members of the group under his code name, Toto. They had met originally because the boy was a wizard with anything concerning radio. Apart from his genius as a radio repairer and engineer, he was able to fabricate home-made batteries and accumulators—both virtually unobtainable by then—to drive the transmitters and flashlights used by the group.†

The news from North Africa continued to be good. The Russians seemed to be gaining the upper hand in the war of attrition fought

---

* *Le Bon Lait* (literally, "Good Milk") was the name of a chain of dairies.

† Today, Georges Tranchant is President–Director General of a multinational electronics corporation with headquarters in Paris.

over Stalingrad. Darlan was assassinated in Algiers, and his killer turned out to be a young fanatic from the right-wing *Chantier de la Jeunesse*. Despite an apparent swing of the pendulum of war in the Allies' favor, Christmas 1942 was nevertheless a sad festival in the South of France. The shop windows were empty, the lights burned low, good food was scarce and prohibitively expensive when available. Maiffret, the best pastry cook in Cannes, had gotten permission to sell a kind of "home cooked" candy made of almond paste each Friday and Saturday. The goodies were for regular clients only, and each customer was restricted to 100 grams (about three and a half ounces) every week. The rich started standing in line before dawn on Friday, and the stock was exhausted before noon.

As a parent, Miniconi found it difficult. Difficult to explain to children aged seven years and eight years why Santa Claus didn't come to visit them any more. Difficult to explain why the apartment wasn't bright with decorations and piled with gaily wrapped New Year gifts the way it used to be at Peille. Difficult, too, to explain the notices in heavy black type promising death to those sheltering refugees, when the nearest they had been to actual warfare was the scuttling of the French fleet at Toulon. (And the evidence of this, symbolically enough, had come through means that were literally underground. The 80-mile-distant explosions were inaudible in the open air. But Miniconi's class had been evacuated to the requisitioned Rothschild villa as a precautionary measure, since Le Suquet was in a very exposed position. And there, in the cellars used as air-raid shelters, the detonations were discernible as a faint vibration transmitted through the rock.)

Early in January of 1943, Miniconi encountered another resistant who was radically to change his life and alter the style of his clandestine activities. He came out of the Montchevalier schoolhouse after handing in a sheaf of reports at noon one day and stood looking across the red tile roofs of the town below. From the yard, he could see the port, the casino, and the whole curving stretch of the Croisette. It was a sunny day, and fishermen were mending blue, green, and violet nets stretched along the sidewalks around the harbor. The leafless branches of plane trees which should have been trimmed the previous year obscured the facade of the town hall. Further away, he distinguished squads of Italian soldiers in shorts and singlets exercising on the sandy shore. There were two destroyers anchored off the islands on the far side of the bay.

Miniconi sighed. It was time he made his way home to share his meager luncheon ration with Claire and the boys. He hurried down the steep zigzag path dropping to the rue Georges Clémenceau and called in at the *Bon Lait* for a promised half-pint of milk. With the bottle, Madame Placide handed him a coded message from Curtel fixing a rendezvous on a park bench in front of the Town Hall at ten minutes before two o'clock. Miniconi was there a little early. He sat reading a newspaper as though he were killing time in the few minutes before school restarted. At ten of two, a man sat down at the far end of the bench, lit the stub of a cigarette, and pronounced the agreed password as he shook out the match flame. Miniconi folded his paper, murmured the correct response, and rose to his feet. The courier, who was wearing a beret and a workman's blue coverall, told him to be in the back room of a hotel near the courthouse at 5:30. Miniconi nodded absently and strolled off toward the school.

The man who met him at the hotel was of medium height and heavily built, with a receding hairline and a determined jaw. His credentials were impeccable: from the style of his greeting Miniconi knew that he had been sent, directly or indirectly, by Mertens at Beausoleil. He introduced himself by the code name Lass, and announced that he had orders for Miniconi to expand his group into a full company of guerilla fighters, organized in a specific way so as to minimize the risks of detection and betrayal.

"The AS have the right idea," Lass said later as the two men paced the Croisette in the dusk, "using a basic unit of only six men, and then grouping those cells together in sections of thirty. But they don't go far enough. You need far stricter compartmentalizing than that. Damn it—all the Gestapo have to do is catch a couple of section heads and there's half a network gone."

"*If* the section heads talk," Miniconi said.

"*Anyone* can talk—given certain conditions," Lass replied. "And those bastards know how to make the conditions right. There are exceptions, of course, but nobody dare swear that they could hold out. The best protection is to minimize the risk, and the only way to do that is to use the triangle system."

"Triangle?"

"The basic unit is only three men," Lass explained. "Two men and a leader, if you like. Each of these men knows only his mate and his leader. The leader knows only his own two men and his immediate superior. To make it even more foolproof, the leaders and their superiors have code names, but the men are known only by numbers. That way a leader can give away only three people, his two men and his boss; and the men can betray only two. And if they do, it doesn't lead the Gestapo any place, because they only learn code names or numbers."

He went on to explain that the formation of a company on this model was hierarchic. Most of the other networks gathered together a crowd of like-minded people from among whom leaders were chosen. The triangle system started at the top.

A company commander chose a second-in-command and appointed four men whom he could trust absolutely to lead the detachments making up the company. Each of these men then recruited four people on whom *he* could rely to command the sections comprising his detachment. Finally the section heads in turn chose four leaders of triangles, each of whom was responsible for his own two men. A section thus comprised four triangles and a leader—thirteen men in all. A detachment of four sections and a leader added up to 53 resistants, and the full company worked out at four times that, plus the commander and his adjutant—a total of 214.*

From the point of view of security, this strict *cloisonnement,* or partitioning, meant that the maximum number of members a leader at any level knew personally was five: the four he had recruited and his immediate superior. Furthermore, 128 of the rank and file were identified simply by numbers, and the majority of the higher grades by their code names only. Except by coincidence or accident, there was no contact between the heads of different sections during the formation of the company, nor did the members of one triangle know those from any other in the same section. It was only when the time came for action that the various units might find themselves together, and as soon as the operation was over they would retreat into whatever was their natural background.

Miniconi was delighted with the simplicity of the scheme, and with its efficiency. The logical approach pleased his own sense of detail and planning. He was assigned a block of four-figure numbers ranging from 3100 to 5000 from which to select the *matricules* which

---

* The organization of triangles, sections, and companies counseled by Lass can more easily be understood with reference to the illustration in the picture section following page 64—a schema of the first two detachments formed by Miniconi himself.

would identify his men and women, and agreed to start organizing the company at once. Lass did not say from whom the orders to form it came, and Miniconi did not ask. He heard later that Lass had been a career officer with the rank of commandant, that he was now military organizer for the FTPF in the Alpes-Maritimes *département*, and that he was based in the Atlantic Hotel in Nice, which had become a kind of resistance stronghold. It was not until after the war that Miniconi learned Lass's true identity: his name was Liso Albertini, and he was the Communist mayor of St. Martin-du-Var, a riverside village at the foot of the mountains six miles inland from the site now occupied by Nice airport. At the beginning of 1943, the schoolteacher didn't even know that the company he had been instructed to recruit formed part of the FTPF. The members of such groups customarily referred to themselves as the "patriotic militia," and that was good enough for him. The essential thing was to act.

The instruction Miniconi had received at the Hyères officers' training school proved useful. He took the risk of calling a meeting at his own apartment. Under cover of a social lunch one Sunday, he explained the basic structure of the company to the six men closest to him. Then he appointed Curtel the company commander and Raymond his second-in-command. The first detachment was to be led by Maurel, the railroad inspector who had supplied so much useful information for them to pass on to the radio operators at the Villa Val-Désir. His code name was *Sanglier* ("wild boar"). Big Sam Kadyss would head the second detachment, and Frossart, "the man of teak," the third. The fourth detachment was to be commanded by Gabriel Davaille—code name *Roseau,* or "reed"—the older man who ran the wine store near the Town Hall.

Miniconi himself would retain overall command and occupy himself with organization and administration as his four lieutenants built up their sections and triangles. He adopted the code name Jean-Marie—and from then on, the network as a whole was known as the Groupe Jean-Marie. Meanwhile, it was necessary to arrange for the concealment of such arms as they had, and also for the safeguarding of papers—for Miniconi could not be expected to keep in his head the details of so complex an organization; somewhere there would have to be progress reports and a coded list of volunteers enrolled.

Such documents, it was decided, would be kept beneath an upturned barrel in Davaille's wine store, where the regular passage of a number of different people would cause no comment. As for the weapons, Miniconi gave instructions that, for the moment, each man took care of his own pistol—if he had one. He would himself hide in his cellar any larger guns, explosives, detonators or grenades. At that time, a year before they were told of the grotto at the Villa Fiésole, the only arms qualifying for this second category were a solitary Sten gun, inherited from Curtel's Marie-Raymond network, and a 7.65mm. Belgian FN automatic that Miniconi had acquired on the black market to supplement the 6.35mm. weapon given to him by his father.

One of the most vital tasks facing the group in the immediate future was the expansion of this "arsenal" to reasonable proportions.

Scene Four

BIG SAM Kadyss was not particularly tall, but he was broad-shouldered and solid and he gave the impression of height. His hair was dark, his eyebrows thick and straight, and his features so regular that the word handsome seemed inadequate as a description. Like many strong, tough men, he spoke rather quietly.

Kadyss had been a card-carrying member of the Communist party at the outbreak of war, and when the party was outlawed after the capitulation he had been jailed in the small town of Combles, in the Somme. Nine months later, toward the end of 1941, he escaped and headed for the unoccupied zone. After many weeks of alarms and escapes, hiding by day and traveling by night, he managed to cross the frontier secretly and made his way to Cannes, where he found work at *Les Aciéries du Nord*. On the factory floor he soon discovered plenty of fellow workers who shared his political convictions and his will to resist, but it was in fact through a member of the Tonner brothers' action group that he was eventually recruited for Resistance work by the MUR.

As an enthusiastic member of AS.24 (the local branch of the *Armée Sécrète*, the MUR's military arm), he spent much of his free time organizing social club outings—rambles along the valley of the River Loup or the Siagne; bicycle rides among the cork oaks and the pine trees of the Esterel. On Saturdays and Sundays when the weather was fine, the people of Cannes and La Bocca became accustomed to the sight of a dozen or twenty young folks setting cheerfully out with a bottle of wine and as much of a picnic as the rations would allow in their haversacks. What was less well known was that beneath the sandwiches of gray wartime bread there would be bundles of clandestine leaflets, forbidden publications, or working parts of dismantled weapons being moved from one cache to another or delivered to *maquis* units in the back country.

"I'd been doing this kind of thing for some time before I was able to contact local representatives of the Party," Kadyss said in an interview twenty years later.* "The fact that they were hunted down as much by the French police as by the Germans, quite apart from the Party itself being outlawed, explains why it took me so long to get in touch. Once I had, I found myself with a double Resistance duty: in addition to my work for AS.24, the Party asked me to organize local groups of FTPF." It was with the nucleus of friends that he had collected in this way that Sam Kadyss joined Miniconi's newly formed company and became leader of its second detachment.

At first they confined themselves to such minor acts of defiance as the distribution of tracts, the posting of seditious stickers, and an occasional sabotage—running a machine without oil, sand in the axle box of a freight car—that could not be traced to a particular individual. Then, in December of 1943, they learned that a stock of gasoline that had been hidden from the original Italian occupiers was still buried in the back lot of a transport depot on the outskirts of Cannes.

While this would be of limited use to resistants in town, since gasoline-powered cars were permitted only for those on official business, the *maquisards* in the interior would find it invaluable: there were plenty of minor roads on which automobiles could be driven without the risk of running into a roadblock. There were, however, difficulties in the way of delivering it. The gasoline was in 50-gallon drums, and there were several dozen of them. The number of men required to disinter these, the labor of transferring them to a truck,

* Published in *Le Patriote*, August 26, 1964.

the noise this would inevitably make, and finally the problem of transporting the clandestine load secretly—each of these factors had to be considered before a workable plan emerged, and it was not until the night of January 19–20, 1944, that the raid actually took place.

Five days earlier, Miniconi and Kadyss had been on the point of giving up the idea; it was, they decided, too difficult and too dangerous. And then Javel and his men had the good fortune to happen upon—and steal—the carbines from the German detachment near Pégomas. With these weapons and ammunition, a much stronger guard could be posted, and it was agreed that the operation should go ahead as speedily as possible. The hell with the noise: if a Nazi patrol arrived before the job was done, there would be enough fire power available to pin them down while the men with the fuel got away.

"Yes, but what about the getaway?" Kadyss asked. "Finding a truck's no problem. We can get enough black market gas—or siphon enough from kraut vehicles in the transport pool—to take us as far as the Esterel. But won't every roadblock in the area be manned to stop us?"

Miniconi shook his head. "You're forgetting one thing, Sam," he said. "We know about the gasoline stocks, but the Germans don't. And if they don't know it's there, they won't suspect it's being stolen. We'll load up as many drums as the truck will take—and then we'll broach the rest and set fire to them. They'll be so busy figuring out how the blaze started, and trying to put it out in case it acts as a beacon for Allied bombers, that they'll pay no mind to the noise of an isolated truck on the outskirts of town."

As it turned out, Miniconi was right. Kadyss coopted fellow workers who belonged to AS.24 to supplement the members of his own FTPF squad, and the action unfolded exactly as planned. The transport depot was some way from the nearest Wehrmacht post, and by the time local collaborators, alerted by the noise of picks and shovels, had warned them that something unusual was taking place, half the drums had already been rolled up the planks leading from the ground to the rear of the truck. The truck was parked in back of the depot; the German armored cars and motorcycle patrols were approaching from the front. Under the supervision of Kadyss, the guards manhandled two of the 50-gallon containers toward the entrance gates and broached them. As the gasoline gurgled out from the open bungholes, half a dozen more were brought up and left parked in the volatile flood. Kadyss signaled the resistants to disperse. He slammed shut the tailgate of the truck and walked forward with a box of matches in his hand.

As the first *whoomp!* of igniting gasoline shook the windows of the neighborhood, the truck driver started his motor. Kadyss sprinted up and swung himself into the cab just before the vehicle turned into the street. They made their way along narrow lanes through the working-class quarter of La Bocca and then out toward the Esterel on the farm tracks webbing the plain of St. Cassien. Over the clatter of the motor they could hear the distant shrilling of fire bells and then the thumping detonations as the sealed drums exploded like land mines one by one. They dropped off one drum at the Tonner farm and headed for the hills. A huge column of black smoke marbled by flame was still billowing into the night sky when the truck pulled in beneath the pines and bumped along the trail leading to the Pic de l'Ours.

Flashback IV

Summer, 1943

I

THE FORMATION of the first FTPF company in the Groupe Jean-Marie was completed by September of 1943. As the organization improved and the number of triangles increased, so the obstacles that had to be overcome proliferated and the forces ranged against them multiplied.

The Abwehr (German military security police) and the Gestapo intensified their anti-Resistance measures throughout France with a ferocity and callousness that surpassed any of the atrocities perpetrated the previous year. Detachments of the SS carried out merciless reprisals in localities where Nazi personnel had been attacked or acts of sabotage committed.[12] The taking—and the shooting—of hostages absolutely at random became a daily occurrence. At the same time, the *maquis* were ruthlessly pursued and slaughtered. Women taken prisoner with a *maquisard* unit were raped, flogged, mutilated, sometimes buried alive. And for anyone even suspected of harboring or helping resistants it was the torture chamber, the execution post, or the cattle train to a slow death in Auschwitz, Mathausen, Dachau, Belsen, or Buchenwald. In a single day in the Autumn of 1942, 113 patriots were shot.

It was at this time that Pétain and Laval created the infamous French Militia under the leadership of Joseph Darnand, who had been head of the *Légion Français des Combattants* in the Nice area. Darnand, who had pushed collaboration to the point of serving on the eastern front with the Waffen SS, had been the man who formed the notorious LFC "action groups" to harry patriots opposed to the occupiers. The Militia, recruited from among the toughest of these SOL* squads, were armed and wore black battle dress with a beret. In hunting down resistants and handing them over to the Germans, in hounding the Jews and persecuting refugees, they exceeded the demands of their masters and "displayed a stupefying zeal in antic- ipating the wishes of the Nazis."† Miniconi put it more crisply: "They are the French Gestapo," he said.

In the early days of 1943, the plight of Jews and other non-Aryans became the most acute problem facing both the Vichy French and the Resistance on the Côte d'Azur. When the country was divided into two zones, non-French Jews in the northern half were deported to the extermination camps in Germany, while those of French na- tionality—through a shabby bargain negotiated by Laval‡—merely lost their rights and were obliged to wear the yellow star. Not un- naturally, the majority fled to the unoccupied zone. There was, therefore, a panic among these outcasts when the Germans broke the armistice agreement and marched south. As soon as the new zones of occupation were delineated, they fled once again—to the area occupied by the Italians, who were notably less manic in their racialist policies.

Within a few weeks almost 30,000 Jews had flocked to the regions administered by the Italians, many of them still possessed of consid-

---

* *Service d'Ordre Légionnaire*—a kind of posse or private police force.
† Philip Erlanger, *La France Sans Etoile*, Librairie Plon, Paris, 1974.

‡ To retain as much support as he could in France, while satisfying Eichmann's demand for a certain number of Jews to feed the ovens at Auschwitz, Laval agreed to deport the children of non-French Jews with their parents. "It is not the policy of the French government," he said piously, "to separate children from their parents." In return, he was promised that Jews of French nationality would not be sent to the extermination camps.

erable means. Schools, synagogues, and centers of documentation supplying false papers were set up at Barcelonette, St. Martin-de-Vésubie, Vence, and the ski resort of Mégève.

Ribière, the préfet of the Alpes-Maritimes, was horrified to see this invasion flooding his already overcrowded domain. Even the BOFs* had been forced out of the smart hotels along the Promenade des Anglais and on the Croisette in Cannes! He issued an order consigning all foreign Jews to forced residence either in the Ardèche *département,* in the German zone, or the Drôme, which was half German, half Italian. French Jews in the Alpes-Maritimes would wear the yellow star.

Fortunately, there were other authorities in Nice who disagreed with this harsh move. Jean Médecin, the mayor, for instance. When General Vercelli, commanding the Italian IVth Army, had paid his first official visit after the armistice violation, Médecin had been warned that he would be asked to move against Freemasons, who were particularly unpopular in Rome. Quickly, he obtained busts of Garibaldi and Masséna (who, being Niçois, were Italian according to Mussolini's theories), and placed them on either side of his desk. Seeing these two illustrious Freemason compatriots, Vercelli took the hint and refrained from raising the subject.

A similar delicacy obtained in discussions of the Jewish problem. Calisse, the Italian consul-general, cabled Rome to point out that the préfet's orders had been given without prior consultation with the Italian Armistice Commission—but that the results would nevertheless, in the eyes of the world, be blamed on the Italian government. The reply, dictated by Mussolini himself, was specific. The Italian forces themselves would take such measures as were considered necessary in their own zone. The préfet's order was countermanded —and if the French attempted to obey it, they would be stopped by force. There was no longer any question of deportations, no longer a problem of yellow stars.

Later, Ribbentrop tried to persuade the Duce to reconsider. He had almost succeeded when a Vatican official pleaded with Mussolini not to take a final decision before he had read a complete report on German atrocities against the Jews in Poland. Could Italy afford, at this stage of the war, to make herself an accessory to such acts?

* The letters stood for *Beurre, Oeufs, Fromage* (Butter, Eggs, Cheese)—in other words, black marketeers.

Mussolini read the document, was horrified, and refused to accede to the Nazi's request.

Many Jews nevertheless made preparations to leave—or to do their best to leave. If Hitler could break one zonal agreement, he could break another. There was no knowing when the Wehrmacht might be asked to march again. In anticipation of such a move, Miniconi made contact with *maquis* groups in the Esterel massif to the west of Cannes, and with Madame Delar, the wife of an aviator, who was prepared to put at their disposal her villa on the heights above the town. Such escape channels would be useful too in other respects: the Germans had started to fortify the Mediterranean coastline; many of the Todt Organization workers were prisoners of war from Poland and the low countries, and it was likely that a number of them would want to desert.

They would not be the only ones swelling the ranks of the *maquis*. In the spring of 1943, the Vichy government promulgated a law requiring all men to register for war work in Germany. There were already 240,000 Frenchmen slaving in Nazi factories, and a further 923,000 working as prisoners of war. Now Sauckel, the gauleiter who gave Pétain and Laval their orders, demanded an extra quarter of a million before March 15. The effect of this *Service du Travail Obligatoire,* if fully implemented, would be to deport every man in the country who wasn't employed on some essential job.

Not surprisingly, a vast number of young men who had never before felt particularly strongly either for or against the Resistance became fervent converts to the cause of freedom. Anything was better than being herded into a train at gunpoint and sent off to face the Allied air raids in a German labor camp. As soon as their STO call-up papers arrived, thousands and thousands of them simply left town and got lost. Most of them ended up in the *maquis,* renouncing home, family, and identity to live an underground existence, with a new name, under conditions of strict discipline and extreme hardship.

The flood of recruits brought unforeseen problems to the *maquisard* chiefs. In the first place, bitter experience had shown that the ideal number for an outlaw unit was between 30 and 50 men. More made the outfit unwieldy and difficult to move in secrecy; less undermined the team spirit and engendered a feeling of isolation with consequent loss of morale. To accommodate the influx, it was therefore necessary to create many new formations and find trained leaders for them. In the second place, all these men had to be supplied with false ID papers and, if possible, ration documents. Welcome though they were, their appearance made trouble too for the *réseaux* that fabricated forged documents. The vastly increased amount of paper required, the heavier traffic, the multiplication of clandestine meetings, all aggravated the risk of detection.[13] This in turn meant more frequent raids by the security forces, which made the *maquis* unpopular with Resistance units already established elsewhere. (To cite one example, the Germans became so exasperated by the opportunities for evasion offered by Marseille's old port neighborhood that they ordered the evacuation of the whole area. Then the warren of ancient, interconnecting buildings was demolished and bulldozed to a level stretch of rubble.)

The FTPF had an additional problem to deal with, and it arose from their own side rather than the occupants'. This concerned the scarcity of arms, explosives, and other war necessities, which had to be parachuted into France now that total occupation of the coast made submarine landings impossible. Because of the Nazi security services' efficiency, 80 percent of the dropped matériel fell into German hands, simply because the Resistance had neither the mobility nor the means to distribute it quickly enough, to get it under cover. Of the remaining 20 percent, very little was destined for the FTPF. Feeling that they were being discriminated against, the leaders of the *Front National* sent an emissary to London at the end of 1942 with a letter setting out their aims and objectives, affirming their allegiance to de Gaulle, and asking for more positive aid in arms and equipment. As it was, the letter said, FTPF units spent most of their time organizing special operations just to steal weapons from the enemy.

The letter remained unanswered. In March 1943, therefore, another messenger made his way to Britain and repeated the plea at a meeting of de Gaulle's planning chiefs and the BCRA. Something of the "official" attitude toward the FTPF and its actions can be gauged from Colonel Passy's memoirs. In his description of the courier and his request, the gallant colonel wrote:

> For a good twenty minutes he outlined for us the prowess of his guerilla fighters and partisans—how they had assassinated a

sixty-year-old reservist at Armentières, blown up a newspaper kiosk at Epernay, retrieved two dozen grenades and six holsters at Mézières or at Sédan, and so on.

These "litanies," the French intelligence chief sneered, reminded him of nothing so much as "those stories about dogs killed by hit-and-run drivers featured in mass-circulation newspapers before the war."*

The BCRA's hostility could be accounted for under three headings. First, alone among the major networks, the FTPF refused to lose their autonomy and work with the unified *réseaux* directed from London; second, they insisted on the concept—deplored by the Allies—of "immediate action" against the enemy; third, although there were numerous well-known non-Communists on the central committee of the *Front National,* the organization was considered as a whole to be Communist-inspired, and de Gaulle's advisers (with an eye to the political situation after the war) wished to avoid any chance of their chief being tagged "the Red General." It was therefore better that the FTPF should be associated with them as little as possible.

Passy's sarcasm is rightly condemned by the historians, who point out that these "immediate actions"—later officially approved by de Gaulle himself—cost the lives of many patriots. But, perhaps not surprisingly, the FTPF saw no improvement in the deliveries of arms. They were forced to continue raiding arsenals and quarries for explosives, to kill soldiers in order to take their weapons. Worst of all, when such raids involved reprisals against the civilian population, they saw themselves described in French newspapers as "terrorists" and criminals—and all too often they saw the population agree with the description. Apart from profiteers who worked for the occupiers, there were plenty of farmers, shopkeepers, small manufacturers, and artisans—people for whose products there was always a sale—who wanted no part of any movement that threatened their livelihood, and who would be the first to report or denounce any activity they thought might put them at risk. The raids continued nevertheless. The "two dozen grenades" retrieved at Mézières or Sédan were put to good use. In Paris, one FTPF detachment, within a space of three weeks, mounted seven separate and

* Quoted by Henri Noguères and Marcel Dégliame-Fouché, *op. cit.*

successful attacks on the enemy. Working in pairs or groups of three only, they:

—Threw a grenade into a restaurant in the place Clichy which was reserved for German officers, killing some and wounding others;

—Attacked a bus full of Nazi soldiers returning to their barracks on the Pont de Neuilly, killing a number with a grenade;

—Lobbed a grenade into a truck full of German soldiers at Bicêtre, killing 11 and wounding 16;

—Created a "scene of carnage" by dropping a bomb into an autocar full of Germans as it passed under the Porte d'Orléans;

—Left a delayed-action charge in the window of a German garage in the 15th Arrondissement, blocking the street for days;

—Bombed a requisitioned hotel in the rue Dupleix, setting fire to the building, causing considerable damage, and wounding a number of the occupants;

—Threw a grenade into the middle of a Nazi street patrol, killing most of its members and wounding the rest.

None of the partisans was captured, killed, or wounded in any of these operations. The action groups that sabotaged electric transformers, mined bridges, derailed trains, and halted the work of factories were not always so lucky.

It was therefore with the greatest caution that Miniconi and his lieutenants were obliged to complete the enlistment of the first company in the Groupe Jean-Marie. No candidate was considered unless he or she had been vouched for by at least two others already accepted. After that, discreet inquiries were made, the "prospect" was interviewed, and his or her friends quizzed before even the existence of the group was admitted. Darnand's Militia—in uniform and out—were everywhere. Mussolini's OVRA were operating. The Vichy police and gendarmerie were being pressed to act. And there were always informers ready to talk, either to deflect attention from themselves or to curry favor with the occupants. There was, too, the ever-present risk that there might be a traitor in the ranks, that someone whose arrest was still unsuspected might have broken under torture, allowing the Gestapo to infiltrate an agent in the guise of a prospective "candidate."

Fortunately, as an auxiliary to the company, Miniconi had been able to recruit a separate section among the Cannes police. Commanded by the *brigadier* Fauré, this comprised six "triangles" headed by the *agents* Salinx, Ottalini, Teyssier, Prisla, Hugues, and Edmond Pierrazzi. The information these men were able to pass on—about impending raids, about names on the police files, about future policy—was invaluable. Together with details supplied by three Mairie employees, named Goumot, Ordan, and Moraccini, it was among the most important contributions to the relative immunity of the group during its formation.

By the early summer of 1943 there was also a military adviser, Lieutenant-Colonel Petréquin, and an intelligence officer, Commandant Duvallon, who acted as liaison between the group and the Free French clandestine information service in Cannes. Daringly situated in the Villa Petit-Clos, just behind the Gestapo headquarters at the Hotel Montfleury, this was organized by an air force captain named Ardouin, who was in daily radio contact with General Koenig in Algiers.

Among other useful contacts that Miniconi had made were a Captain Maurice Derché, the commander of AS.24 (the local branch of the *Armée Sécrète*), and a group of men at the head of the MUR in the Cannes-La Bocca area. These included Stefan Vahanian and Tony Isaïa, the chief and his adjutant, a young man who ran a bicycle repair service in the center of Cannes, and the brothers Tonner. An action group led by the Tonners specialized in the smuggling of arms and the spiriting away of refugees and resistants on the "Wanted" list, many of whom were hidden—sometimes for months at a time—in the barns and haylofts of the Tonner farm. Their most spectacular operation had been to arrange the escape of Allied agents from an internment camp at Dernay, near Toulouse, over 200 miles to the west. Miniconi coopted Francis Tonner as liaison between his group and the MUR.

The owner of the bicycle store couldn't have been more of a contrast, visually, to the ebulliently Latin Tonners. He was twenty-four years old, smooth-faced, with features as bland as an Oriental's. Born at Châtellerault, in the center of France, he had escaped from a prisoner-of-war camp soon after the armistice, regained his own country, and then made his way to the unoccupied zone to avoid embarrassing questions from the Vichy authorities. He had been an active member of the Resistance since 1941, serving as an instructor in Derché's AS.24 in addition to his work with the Tonner group. Now he became an important addition to Miniconi's FTPF company as well. His name was Léon Noel, and he adopted as his nom-de-guerre the pseudonym *Grand Duc*.

With these allies, Miniconi continued collecting and then transmitting information on troop movements, fortifications, railroad schedules, munitions shipments, and the establishment of enemy supply dumps. To those of his recruits who questioned the usefulness of such work and craved more positive action, he would say, "Everything is useful. The peasant who is late delivering his produce to the market, the freight car that arrives in Briançon instead of Brest, the semaphore that jams in the *Stop* position, the Town Hall clerk who goofs on his paperwork or goes home early—they all help to act as a drag, to slow down the Nazi war effort. And every scrap of information we dig up, however trivial it may seem, assists the Allied planners to get an overall picture of the terrain—and therefore increases the chance of a successful landing when the time comes."

At this stage of the struggle, the long-awaited "Second Front"— which Stalin had been calling for to relieve pressure in the east— was confidently expected within a few months (Duvallon, fresh from the radio at the Villa Petit-Clos, told Miniconi privately that the date was set for October, 1943). The war seemed to be going well for the Allies at last. After their disastrous defeat at Stalingrad, which cost them 24 generals and 300,000 men, the Germans had been pushed out of North Africa and vanquished in Sicily. American and British bombers pulverized the Reich's industrial centers by day and by night. In Italy, Mussolini had been deposed and arrested.

II

IN CANNES, Miniconi received a summons to meet Lass in the basement bar of La Régence. "How far have you got with the formation of the company?" the FTPF organizer asked when the two men had drunk a couple of glasses of wine, exchanged banalities about the food shortage, and then begun to walk in an apparently casual way toward the railroad station.

"It is complete."

Lass seemed impressed. "But that's excellent," he said. "You had better start another one at once. We shall need a team of trained saboteurs in this area to cut the Boche communications before the landings." The existing company, he told Miniconi, would be known as the 40th Company, FTPF. The new one, with the accent on saboteurs, was to be the 1st Company of Destruction. In keeping with the paramilitary nature of the organization, and in accordance with the number of men he commanded, Miniconi himself—or "Commandant Jean-Marie," as he was known on the FTPF books—would be given the acting rank of captain.

"One more thing," Lass said as they approached the lower end of the Boulevard Carnot. "I'd like some idea of how the completed company is organized."

"In that case," Miniconi replied, "we had better see if we can buy a bottle of wine." And he turned right up a side street and led Lass to Gabriel Davaille's liquor store.

In the dank, winey atmosphere at the back of the *cave,* where the gloom was redolent of wet seasoned wood, Davaille tilted the upended barrel to one side and slid out a waterproof envelope containing a thin sheaf of papers. Miniconi removed a schema he had made of the four detachments and handed it to his superior.* Lass took the document over to the door and held it up to the sunbeams slanting in through the dusty panes. "This is first class," he said. "Admirable. I'm going to take it with me . . . as a model for the other commanders in the region!" He folded the paper and stowed it in an inside pocket.

"Isn't that dangerous?" Davaille asked when Lass had gone. "Walking about with that list on him? Suppose he was caught by a patrol? The Gestapo would give a lot to lay their hands on a thing like that!"

"Everything is dangerous," Miniconi said. "He's less likely to be stopped in broad daylight. He's going straight to the station and then home to wherever he lives. In any case, all he has is a lot of code names and numbers—even if he was caught, they wouldn't mean anything to the Gestapo."

"But if they tortured him . . . ?"

"There's nothing he could tell them, because he doesn't know. That's the advantage of an organizer from another town. He doesn't

* See illustration in picture section following page 64.

know the true identity of a single person on that list; he doesn't even know *my* real name—I'm simply Captain Jean-Marie so far as he's concerned."

"But don't *we* need the list? There's no copy, after all."

Miniconi smiled. "Fortunately I have a good memory. And I still have the rough that I made out when I was assigning the *matricules*."*

Lass and the secret document arrived at St. Martin-du-Var unscathed. Not everyone was so fortunate. At the beginning of July—nobody knew whether it was detective work or the result of a denunciation—Roger Renaudie was arrested by the Militia and handed over to the OVRA. They heard later through a contact at the Préfecture that he had been transferred to the gloomy fortress prison at Fresnes, outside Paris, where the Gestapo had access to prisoners. In accordance with normal practice, the local branch of the Buckmaster *réseau* immediately split up, lest the captive might have been "persuaded" to talk. Transmissions from the Villa Val-Désir ceased temporarily and the radios were hidden.

Captain Frager, who had set up the station originally, passed through Cannes that week, with the news that lighter, smaller, improved versions of the receivers and transmitters would be available soon, concealed in the false bottom of an innocent-looking valise. While he was in town, there was a fresh wave of arrests among the personnel of the *Armée Sécrète;* if the Allies were in the ascendency from a strictly military point of view, the Axis seemed for the moment to be triumphing underground—for it was less than two weeks since the Gestapo had arrested Jean Moulin and other members of the National Council of the Resistance near Lyon.† And ten days before that, it was General Délestraint, the overall head of the AS, who had been betrayed by a double agent and kidnapped by the Sicherdienst (the German secret police) outside a Paris métro station. Miniconi thought it was time he made his own arrangements for the forging of false papers. Fortunately, a member of his group named Buffet worked in the Mairie at Le Cannet and could lay his hands on the necessary blank forms and rubber stamps. Miniconi himself took the photos: it was impossible—and dangerous—to ar-

---

* See illustration in picture section following page 64.

† Moulin, responsible—with help from London—for amalgamating most of the southern networks into the MUR, was murdered by the Gestapo soon afterward.

range the proper lighting at his apartment, but there was an unfrequented lane nearby with a conveniently anonymous wall as background.

During the month, the Resistance chief held preliminary conversations at La Bocca with Léon Raybaud and Bernard Tosello of the FER network in connection with the formation of the "Company of Destruction" that Lass had demanded. A great number of the effectives of such a group, it was decided, could be drawn from the work force at *Les Aciéries du Nord*.

It was at this time that Miniconi met Hélène Vagliano, who worked for an auxiliary SOE network code-named "Tartane." Daughter of well-to-do Greek parents who had emigrated to England and then to France, she was a voluntary helper at the Mutual Aid Center for prisoners of war—a slender, fair, rather shy girl often seen bicycling through the streets of Cannes on her way to help or comfort the families of absent soldiers. What neither these families nor the police knew was that Hélène also acted as a courier. Under cover of her official activities, she organized the escape to Spain of Allied aviators who had been shot down over the continent; sheltered and fed refugees; and also operated a clandestine radio to maintain contact with her controls in Algiers, Gibraltar, and London.

Tartane and the many others like it were soon to be strained to their utmost. At the beginning of September, a secret armistice was signed between Italy and the Allies, but in one of the most tragic blunders of the war, Eisenhower refused to delay publication of its terms as requested by Marshal Badoglio, the new Italian head of state: the "unconditional surrender" of the Axis satellite—as demanded by Roosevelt and Churchill at the Casablanca Conference the previous year—was officially announced from his headquarters only five days later.* As a result, the invasion of Italy, instead of a

---

* Badoglio wanted the announcement held up until the end of the month. During the delay, he offered discreetly to withdraw Italian divisions from France and from the south of Italy. An attempt would be made to dislodge the Germans from airfields they occupied, and a ring of armor would be placed around Rome. Then, once the armistice was announced, Badoglio's troops would immediately change sides and turn their guns on their former allies. There were two reasons why Eisenhower refused to comply with this request. First, as a professional and loyal soldier, he was shocked by the "turncoat" factor; secondly, Badoglio had sent several emissaries to different Allied chiefs, each of whom appeared to be offering different sets of terms. The near-farcical situation resulting from this persuaded Eisenhower that the Italians must be both unreliable and irresponsible. He therefore decided to act unilaterally, or (in the phrase of a famous British newspaper editor) "publish and be damned."

walkover, turned into one of the bloodiest and most protracted struggles of the war. Warned of the Italian defection almost as soon as it was decided, Hitler occupied the whole of northern Italy, seized Rome, and sent his crack Panzer divisions south to contest the Allied landings at Naples and in Calabria. Nazi paratroopers rescued Mussolini from his prison and established a puppet Fascist state in the north. At the same time, all Italian armed forces were treated as hostile, and German troops marched into the Italian zone of France —which had been reduced only two weeks previously to the sector between Nice and the Italian frontier.

The effect on the Côte d'Azur was catastrophic. The swastika was already displayed outside the Hotel Gallia in Cannes; now it was to hang from public buildings in Nice as well. There was panic among the Jewish refugees who had crowded into the city from Mégève, Savoy, and the area west of Cannes when the zone was reduced. With the 30,000 Jews already living in the region, they saw their security threatened yet again. Secret negotiations had in fact been completed between Resistance chiefs and the new Italian authorities for the transfer of all these people, together with a further 17,000 from Yugoslavia, to North Africa. Special passports had been printed, which were to have been available even to those convicted because they had had no proper papers. The Italians had promised a fleet of 85 trucks to transport the evacuees to Genoa, where four ships were already waiting in the docks. But all these arrangements were contingent on there being a gap between the signing of the armistice and its publication. Once Hitler moved, the operation was stillborn. Blocked in northern Italy, the trucks never arrived. The ships fell into the hands of the *Kriegsmarine*. A great number of the refugees were captured and sent to concentration camps.

Eisenhower announced the armistice on September 8. That night there was music and dancing in the parks and squares of Nice. Italian soldiers were embraced in the street. The celebrations continued long after midnight. At dawn on the 9th, the Wehrmacht marched over the Var River, which was now the frontier between the two zones. Five busloads of fleeing Jews fell into their hands while they were still on the bridge. The Italians had been ordered to cease fighting the Allies but "to resist any other attack." In fact the Germans took over the whole region without a shot being fired —despite the Italians' superiority in numbers and, especially, in artillery. This was partly because General Vercelli had received no orders from Rome, and partly because, knowing their ex-allies' cyphers, the German intelligence chiefs had swamped the zone with conflicting radio and telegraphic signals.

A great many Italian officers had jettisoned their uniforms as soon as the armistice was announced, seizing what civilian clothes they could find and attempting to get home as soon as possible. Large contingents of troops straggled toward the frontier with the same idea. Still others sought the help of the Resistance or fled into the mountains in search of the *maquis*. But many thousands were captured and put to work at menial tasks by their Nazi masters— repairing roads, building fortifications, collecting garbage.

The Germans established a "forbidden zone" along the coast and started at once to hunt down the prey which the intransigence of the Italians had denied them so long. Two SS officials, Bruckler and Brunner, were charged with the mission. It was not a plan formulated on the spur of the moment. On September 4, the day after the signing of the secret armistice, they received a top-level directive on the handling of "the Jewish danger" on the Côte d'Azur. It was headed: *Object—Preparation for the Application of Anti-Jew Measures in the Italian Occupation Zone.* The text read in part:

> If the action envisaged is to have a satisfactory result it must be applied *without exception.* Given that the majority of police forces at our disposal are incapable of distinguishing if this Jew or that Jew—according to his nationality, which is more or less due to chance—should be affected by the anti-Jew measures, it would be extremely inconvenient from the propaganda point of view if exceptions of all kinds were once again made. . . . Jews will be arrested with all members of their families. Once captured, they will be transferred, 1,000 to 2,000 head at a time, to the Jewish camp at Drancy, from which, after a thorough investigation of their nationality, they will be evacuated as soon as possible toward the east. . . .
>
> The *total* flushing out of Jews from the former Italian Zone is necessary not only as part of the final solution of the Jewish problem in France, but also for reasons of security affecting German troops. This is an argument which should be put to the French government if, as expected . . . it intervenes on behalf of Jews of French nationality. *It will be necessary for us to associate with anti-*

Semitic Frenchmen in order to run to earth and obtain the denunciation of those Jews who have gone into hiding and of the people sheltering them. Suggested offer: 100 francs [$2.00] per Jew."

Bruckler and Brunner, like the twin ogres of some horrific Teutonic fairy tale, carried out their unsavory task with merciless efficiency. The SS detachment working for them was composed of experienced men who had performed similar duties in Belgium and Holland. Aided by Vichy police, who threw cordons around suspect areas and blocked off streets, they invaded hotels, lodging houses, and pensions, arresting with savage brutality any and all persons suspected of being Jewish. Those who resisted were ferociously beaten. Those who tried to escape were mowed down with machine guns. Neither the old nor the infirm nor the blind were spared. Pregnant women, even women in labor, were taken. The SS amused themselves searching hospitals, asylums, churches, nursery schools. They took particular pleasure in tormenting—and frequently killing—children. Babies were disposed of by having their skulls cracked against a wall. In Nice, more than 40 children, the offspring of Jews who had been succored by Christian families, were murdered by lethal injections.

Once rounded up, to the hotel Excelsior in Nice, the Montfleury in Cannes, suspects were screened for "Jewishness." The Gestapo did not even bother to examine papers: they knew these would probably be false. Instead, men were obliged to lower their pants. If they were circumcised, they were Jews; if not, they were Aryans. In consequence, certain agnostic Jews escaped and many Christians and Muslims who had been circumcised as a matter of hygiene were sent to the death camps. Selection among women was more arbitrary still. Thick lips or a prominent nose were sufficient to put a woman on a cattle truck bound for Drancy. One Catholic nurse was deported because she had been baptized Esther.

The ruthless searches of buildings were supplemented by Gestapo spies patrolling the streets in private automobiles, on the lookout for anyone with supposedly Jewish features. One patrol arrested an entire funeral procession because an informer had told them the dead man was Jewish. Passersby unwise enough to expostulate or even exclaim in horror were immediately arrested and added to the convoy.

For several months, collaborators, informers, and Vichy spies were in clover. The SS frequently offered rewards far in excess of the sum quoted in the directive received by Bruckler and Brunner. If the information could not be obtained by bribery, prisoners were tortured pitilessly in an attempt to wring from them the whereabouts of their families. Members of the Militia responsible for a particularly good haul sometimes received as much as 5,000 francs ($100) per Jew. "It must however be emphasized, to the credit of the Niçois," Philip Erlanger wrote,* "that the majority among them, redeeming the ignominy of Militiamen and other collaborators, set about hiding the Jews as soon as possible. Catholic organizations did what they could to protect the children. The Gestapo lost in this way a good part of their booty. Nevertheless, the toll—unavoidably approximate—was terrible: hundreds of dead and seriously wounded, around 5,000 [from Nice alone] deported, of whom very few returned. . . . At the same time, similarly horrifying scenes were being enacted in Italy. Jews, anti-Fascists, officers and soldiers who had attempted to resist the German invasion, were massacred or deported left and right. Such was the price of Badoglio's tergiversations and the obstinacy of Roosevelt."

For some months therefore the determination of the Resistance in the area to harry the new occupants and collect as much information on military movements as they could was inescapably tempered by the need to look after this new flood of refugees. Some remained hidden, others escaped the net and started a new life with a false identity, a limited number made their way through Resistance channels to Switzerland or Spain. But many of the younger men opted for the rigors of life among the Maquis, where they could learn to hit back at their oppressors.

* *Op. cit.*

Scene Five

IT WAS not until March of 1944, when the group had carried out four sabotage operations against the railroad, salvaged gasoline from the transport depot, and stolen arms from the German detail near Pégomas, that Miniconi's guerillas were able to lay their hands on a really important haul of weapons.

It was Curtel who heard about the cache. He was sitting in the office in the back of the Emerini antique store at dusk on the first of the month, doing his accounts. The mistral had been blowing all day and the air was clear and cold. The bell above the entrance door jangled; footsteps hastened toward the office between the stacks of furniture. He looked up, surprised to find a late customer at this time of year. It was probably someone who had been tipped off that the police or the Gestapo were after him, someone who needed cash in a hurry and hoped to raise a stake on a couple of Louis XVI armchairs that would turn out to be fakes. Curtel sighed and rose to his feet.

But the man who faced him was not a customer. He was a member of the 1st Detachment of Curtel's own 40th FTPF Company—a Pole named Smilevitch, who had been recruited some months before by

131

the Detachment chief, Sanglier. Smilevitch had a job with the OPA (*Office de Placement Allemand*), which was concerned with the transfer of Frenchmen to slave labor camps in the Reich. He had proved a useful contact, tipping off resistants when they were about to be drafted. Curtel frowned. "You know that you are forbidden to approach the Company Commander except in an emergency," he said sharply.

"This is an emergency. At least it's urgent—something that needs attending to right away." Smilevitch was out of breath. He had evidently been running. "I just came from the station. I wanted to catch you before you closed the store."

"Sit down and relax," Curtel said. He went to the door, opened it, and looked up and down the street. Already a star glittered coldly above the rooftops to the east. The wind had scoured papers and empty cigarette packs from the deserted sidewalks. A loose shutter banged and banged on the first floor of the house next door. He closed and locked the door, pulled down the blinds, and lit an oil lamp in the office. "All right, tell me about it," he said.

"Arms," Smilevitch said. "Pistols and grenades. Dozens of them. Kind of an auxiliary store stocked by the Boche."

"Where?"

"In an empty house in Antibes. A man who works for the electric company saw them go in and contacted me at once. I just came from there now."

"When you say an empty house . . . ?"

"I mean really empty. Nobody lives there. The Germans requisitioned it, but they don't seem to have done anything with it. Except store arms."

"They put a guard on it, though, surely."

Smilevitch shook his head. "That's the whole point. So far as I can see, nobody ever goes near it. And certainly there's nothing like a sentry."

"The extraordinary thing," Curtel said to Miniconi three days later, "is that he was absolutely right. I had the place watched for forty-eight hours. There's nobody billeted there and not a single German came near it."

The two men were sitting in the basement bar of La Régence. "Where is this house?" Miniconi asked.

"It's a small villa in the Croix Rouge neighborhood. A quiet street in among the market gardens and the greenhouses."

"You've checked out the entrances and exits? An escape route?"

"Sure. I was given a conducted tour by Sextant." Curtel used the code name by which Smilevitch was known. "I think we should have those arms. Do I have your permission to go in and get them?"

"Who would you take with you?"

"A Section from Sanglier's 1st Detachment. I think three triangles should be enough—Sextant's own, and those led by Gaspé and Zodiaque. With Sanglier and myself, that'll give us a couple of lookouts and nine people to deal with the weaponry."

Miniconi nodded. Zodiaque was a patriot whose real name was Andreé Clauzier; Gaspé was the code name used by Salignon, the headmaster of his own school. "As soon as you have it all worked out," he said, "get in there and go!"

It was in fact not until March 9 that Curtel felt ready to act. There had been an additional two days' surveillance, to make doubly sure that the villa was unguarded at all times. Then it was simply a matter of working out the approach and exit routes, briefing the triangle leaders, and waiting for the moon.

The Croix Rouge sector of Antibes lies on high ground to the northwest of the town center, where departmental Route 35 twists between pine trees toward Valbonne and the hot-toweled members of the pricey Cannes Country Club. More than three million square yards of the surrounding country is under glass—much of which had been broken in 1944 by air raids on La Bocca and the marshaling yards in Nice—and wartime shortages had forced the local gardeners to abandon their hothouse flowers for vegetables destined to garnish the tables at Nazi officers' messes. This was of interest to Curtel only insofar as it affected the frequency of German patrols in the area. Perhaps because the food shortage in occupied France was so acute, these had been doubled and then redoubled in an attempt to halt the thieving of produce, which ranged from the snatching of a ten-pound sack of potatoes to the hijacking of whole truckloads intended for the black market. Although the house where the arms were stored was itself unguarded, it was nonetheless necessary to plan the operation with great care.

Curtel himself walked the length of the quiet street twice before he slipped in through the side gate of the neglected cypress hedge that fringed the property. The villa next door was shuttered and silent. On the far side of the weed-choked garden was a vacant lot overgrown with brambles and mastic trees. Behind, there was a pinewood and then one of the smaller horticultural businesses. Sextant and the two other members of his triangle should be hidden in the boiler house which had once fired the steam pipes that heated the greenhouses there. Sanglier would approach via the wood and the vacant lot. Gaspé was to park his bicycle at the corner of the street and walk up openly with his companions once he saw the coast was clear, and the others were to arrive singly over the walls and fences that separated the garden from Route 35. They were not, however, due until after dark, and it was not yet dusk. Curtel crouched behind the spines of a yucca and surveyed the building he was to burgle. Blank windows on the upper floors were filmed with dust. Clumps of grass sprouted among the granite chips covering the driveway, and weeds grew waist-high between the roses. It was easy to imagine that the place had been uninhabited since before the war. Curtel looked up at the shallow pyramid roof surmounting the square tower above the entrance. Below it, a tiled frieze decorated with glazed fruit snared the last rays of the sun. He had more than an hour to wait.

As the light faded, he heard the sounds of the neighborhood separate themselves from the almost indistinguishable hum of the town as a whole. A man shouted and was answered by another. A group of workers cycled past, whistling, on their way home. Someone was sawing wood in a nearby yard. When it was almost dark, a *gazogène** labored up the grade and parked farther along the road. Soon afterward, Curtel flattened himself behind the bush when a snarl of motorcycles swelled in volume and stopped suddenly on the far side of the cypress hedge. He held his breath. German voices hectored, questioned. A woman spoke in French. And then abruptly the bikes roared to life again and the patrol rode away. Evidently they had been asking some passerby for her papers. Curtel shivered and drew his thin jacket more tightly around his body.

A little later, he started and smothered an exclamation as a hand fell gently on his shoulder. Sanglier had approached silently between the weed-choked flower beds. "Sextant and his two men are

---

* The gasoline shortage produced many bizarre alternatives to the petrol engine. Most popular was the *gazogène,* which fueled the motor with gas obtained by burning wood, charcoal, or coke. Its disadvantages were a heavy, cumbersome installation (usually at the back of the vehicle) for producing the gas; the amount of space necessary for storing the wood or charcoal; and the fact that the boiler had to be heated for 20 minutes before the engine would start.

waiting in back," he whispered. "Maybe we should go on down and start work on the door?"

"What about the others?"

"They'll be here as planned. Only I didn't brief the triangles led by Gaspé and Zodiaque because of the women. Six men from the First Section will be coming instead."

"What do you mean—'because of the women'?"

Sanglier explained, as the two men stepped warily around the graveled path to the back of the house, that the triangles led by Zodiaque and the headmaster of Miniconi's school each included a married couple—in fact the Guerninis and the Placides, who provided mail drops for the group. "I figured it would be crazy to put them at risk when there were others available," Sanglier said.

"You did quite right," Curtel replied.

The moon was rising above the mountains behind Nice as they descended the three steps leading to the back door. The door was locked and barred, but there were two frosted-glass panels in its upper half. Curtel took from his pocket brown paper and a small bottle filled with molasses. As Sanglier vanished into the shrubbery to post lookouts and collect the others, Curtel spread the molasses on the paper, plastered it to the glass, and engraved an irregular circle around it with a diamond ring. A sharp tap was then sufficient to dislodge a disk of glass, which he lifted silently out of the panel, still adhering to his paper. After that, it was an easy matter to thrust an arm through the hole, unlock the lock, and shoot the bolts. He turned the handle and opened the door.

They had already made sure that no burglar alarm or warning system had been installed, but it was nevertheless with a feeling of guilt and a fear of imminent discovery that the nine resistants tiptoed through the unoccupied villa. In the wan moonlight filtering through the grimed panes of the windows, they saw sheeted furniture pushed to one side of a large living room stacked high with German army bed rolls. There were steel helmets and dozens of pairs of boots neatly stored in another room. But it was in the cellar that they found what they had come for. Sanglier used his flashlight and whistled with surprise.

Ranged like iron fruit on the wooden shelves were a dozen grenades, a number of submachine guns, and more than fifty long-barreled Mauser pistols.

"Now that," Curtel murmured with satisfaction, "makes the trip really worthwhile!"

"I told you!" Sextant said smugly. "There may not be as much as we hoped, but there's more here than we ever laid eyes on before. How do you want us to get them out?"

"We'll make it in relays," Curtel decided. "One man every ten yards or so, with a lookout on the gate and the last man to stow each load in the *gazogène*."

"No more than half a dozen at a time," Sanglier said. "Those guns are heavy and we can't risk the clatter if one slips out and falls."

The theft and the following transfer of weapons were ridiculously easy. Apart from one alert—they had shifted about half the stuff when a whistle from the lookout warned them that a patrol was passing—the operation went off without a hitch. Fifteen minutes after they had entered the cellar, Curtel ordered all the men but Sextant to disperse. With Sanglier and the Pole, he walked to the *gazogène* panel truck that had been parked outside the empty house next door. He sat behind the wheel. The others pushed the vehicle to the end of the street, and from there he was able to coast down a grade without starting the motor, to a safe house where he was to spend the night.

It was the following day when the exploit came nearest to disaster. Gaston Ricatto, alias Raymond, Curtel's Number Two in the 40th Company, arrived on foot just before 11 A.M. With the help of Antibes MUR effectives who had offered Curtel asylum for the night, they chopped wood and stoked up the motor of the *gazogène*. The automatic pistols were to be dismantled and taken back to the arms cache in the avenue Fiésole by female members of the Company. But the submachine guns were far too cumbersome to be concealed in shoulder bags or slipped part by part into women's purses, and the grenades were too heavy. They would have to be transported, therefore, in the panel truck.

Raymond and Curtel loaded the back of the vehicle with sacks of leaf mold and plants in pots. The illegal hoard of arms was hidden beneath a carelessly bundled tarpaulin behind the seats, and the rear doors were left swinging open, in the hope that anyone looking in and seeing the nodding green heads of tomato plants and beans would assume that the driver had nothing to conceal.

They set off shortly before noon so that the greater part of the journey would be during the lunch hour, when police and military posts were at their lowest strength. Raymond drove through the pine woods toward the picturesque harbor of Golfe Juan. They were about to breast a rise in the neighborhood known as Les Eucalyptus when the trouble began. Halfway up the grade, the motor of the *gazogène* coughed, spluttered, and then stalled.

Raymond swore, wrestling with knobs and levers, but the motor remained silent. The truck began to roll backward down the slope. "*Merde!*" said Raymond. He steered the rear wheels into the curb and pulled up on the hand brake. Curtel swung out of the cab and ran around to the front of the vehicle. He cranked the recalcitrant engine furiously, but it refused to fire. Raymond was tapping on the windshield. Curtel looked up, following the direction of his pointing finger.

Helmeted German soldiers stood beneath the trees at the top of the hill, and standing talking to them, with their backs to the stranded truck, were two gendarmes from the local barracks. Suddenly Curtel's hands felt cold. If they should take it into their heads to order a spot check, to make a search . . . ! He turned the crank more violently still.

The motor preserved its obstinate silence. "If we could just get the damned thing to the crest . . ." Raymond clambered from the truck. "With a good run down, I could pick up speed and she'd probably catch when I let in the clutch." The two men walked around to the back, put their shoulders to the panels, and shoved with all their strength.

The grade was too steep and their combined efforts were not enough to move the truck. The Germans were staring now, and the gendarmes had swung around to look. "Jesus!" Raymond groaned. "If only those bastards . . ."

Curtel took a decision. "Leave it to me," he said briskly. He strode up to the group of uniformed men. "Forgive me for troubling you," he said, more to the soldiers than to the gendarmes. "It's the third time that bitch of a motor has let me down today—and I have kids at home waiting for their lunch. You know how it is. I wonder, could I possibly ask you . . . ?"

A burly corporal separated himself from the squad and walked back to the truck with Curtel. "What have you got there?" he said in his halting French. "Artichokes?"

"Actually they're hand grenades," Curtel said. "This is the mobile headquarters for the whole of the French Resistance in this area!"

The Wehrmacht man roared with laughter. "A Frenchman with a sense of humor!" he shouted. "Come on, boys! Let's give the little man a hand!"

The gendarmes stood aside as the grinning Nazis crowded around and manhandled the truck to the top of the slope. Raymond climbed back into the driver's seat and reached for the gearshift. "Before you go," the corporal said, "we'd better have a look at your papers. This is supposed to be a checkpoint, for God's sake. Fleichmann—see if there's anything among those pots in back."

One of the soldiers sprang to attention and then marched around to the rear of the truck. Curtel felt the sweat start on his forehead as he reached inside his jacket—and then suddenly, from somewhere nearby, the screech of an air-raid siren split the air. At the same time, the hollow, flat concussions of antiaircraft gunfire sounded from the Cap d'Antibes.

The corporal stared up into the sky. "The hell with it," he said to Curtel. "You'd better get that thing under cover or your kids may miss their lunch!"

Curtel pulled himself up over the tailgate. "Thanks," he said as the German gave the truck a shove. And then he added truthfully, "You'll never know how grateful we are!"

Raymond slid the gearshift into second and stepped on the clutch pedal. The hidden weapons clattered beneath their tarpaulin as the *gazogène* gathered momentum on the downgrade. He let out the clutch and the motor caught with a jolt. Twenty minutes later, they were listening to the distant thump of bombs from behind the tall gates of the Villa Fiésole. They heard that night that the Americans had made an unsuccessful attempt to destroy the railroad viaduct at Anthéor.

By 2:30, when they drove the empty truck away from the villa, Jean-Gabriel Domergue's gardener, unknown to his boss, had enriched the kitchen garden with several dozens of extra vegetables and a quantity of leaf mold. In the bluff behind, beneath the screen of eucalyptus and mimosa and African palms, the clandestine contents of the grotto had once more been increased.

A month later, on April 9, 1944, Curtel's company was well enough armed, and confident enough, to delay the munitions trains hastening to Italy by more than eighteen hours, when the tracks at La Bocca were sabotaged for the second time.

Flashback V

Autumn – Winter, 1943

I

ALONG THE northern coasts of the Mediterranean, the heat in the summer of 1943 was tropical. From Marseille to Menton, Polish workers in the Todt Organization toiled, stripped to the waist, sweating over the bulldozers and cement mixers concentrated on the littoral to build the redoubts of the "southern wall" designed to obstruct any Allied invasion from the sea. In Cannes, palms along the Croisette hung limp and brown in the windless air. Lizards panted in dry basins where once fountains had played, and the weeds that choked neglected flower beds drooped and died.

The morning of Tuesday, September 21, was hotter than most. There was a luminous haze uniting the sea and the sky; the atmosphere was breathless and humid. On the first floor of No. 5 *bis,* avenue du Grand-Pin, Ange-Marie Miniconi leaned his head close to the Arcor loudspeaker and listened to a news bulletin read by a man who spoke with a strong English accent. Prime Minister Churchill and President Roosevelt had announced that recognition of de Gaulle's Committee of National Liberation as de facto government of France was strictly temporary. Hitler had abandoned Sardinia, but German troops had consolidated their hold on Rome. A heavy force of RAF bombers had raided—

Miniconi switched off the radio and rose to his feet. He was a little late; he should have left for a meeting with Léon Noël. That would have been unforgivable in an outdoor rendezvous, but this time they were to talk in Noël's bicycle store. There were a hundred escaped Italian prisoners to look after. At the moment, these fugitives were hidden all over Cannes in garages, railroad warehouses, cellars, and apartments belonging to the men of Miniconi's 40th Company. But it was essential that they be directed as soon as possible to local Maquis formations: their chances of remaining undetected for long in town were slim. Apart from which, it was asking too much from the people sheltering them, who already risked deportation for belonging to the FTPF. The penalty for hiding refugees was death.

The Italians were therefore to be dispersed in small groups to different areas. Lieutenant Silvani of the AS, and a man named Boutières, who was an official of the Department of Rivers and Forests at Draguignan, had agreed to convoy some to Maquis units in the Massif de Ste. Baume, north of Aix-en-Provence, and others to a clandestine formation at Isola, in the high Alps. More still were to be sent to guerrilla companies based on the Esterel, La Duchesse, and the Massif des Maures, beyond Fréjus, and it was to finalize arrangements for this that the meeting was to be held. Curtel had already been to La Bocca to contact the escape network organized by Javel and Arnaud Le Manchot, the two railwaymen from the FER *réseau* who also belonged to Miniconi's group. Now the leader was to tie it all up with the Tonner brothers' activists via Léon Noël.

He made the routine checks before leaving the apartment. Radio knob tuned to a Vichy station. No paperwork visible. Weapons hidden in a rolled-up carpet in the cellar. The "escape line" in position behind the venetian blind in the bedroom. (This was simply a length of rope attached to a hook on the wall, which could be fed out through the window and used to swing, Tarzan-style, over a fence and into the back yard of a carpenter's shop in the next street. The apartment was well positioned for a man who might at any moment have to run for his life. It could be approached from the street in front or from a passageway leading around the end of the building. There was a door at the foot of the stairway and another at the top, both of which could be locked and both of which had bells discreet enough for code rings. There were, in addition, back stairs leading to the cellars—and from there a man could squeeze through low, frosted-glass windows onto the pathway in back of the house.)

Miniconi locked both doors and took his bicycle from the hallway. In order to supplement their meager salaries, they were obliged to look after other people's children during the school vacations, and Claire was in the park with Guy, Félix-Henri and several other small boys and girls. He wheeled the machine into the street and mounted.

The heat struck him like a blow as he pedaled out from the shade of the pine tree beside the house. It trembled above the patched macadam and softened the tar that sucked at his tires as he rode downtown. Most of the short journey to the rue du Titien was on a grade and he was able to coast the greater part of the distance, but his open-necked white shirt was plastered to his back by the time he glided to a halt at the intersection with the boulevard de l'Italie.

A small crowd had gathered on the shadowed sidewalk at the angle made by the two streets. Farther along the rue du Titien, there was another group opposite Léon Noël's store. A black Citroën with a driver at the wheel was parked nearby.

Miniconi frowned. It was a street of small businesses—a laundry, a watchmaker's, a cheap hotel, a hardware store, one or two neighborhood food shops. There was normally nothing to make even one person stop and stare. He looked at his watch. It was one minute short of eleven o'clock. He wheeled his bicycle along the sidewalk until he was opposite Noël's premises. There were no shiny new scarlet-and-cream drop-handlebar racing models displayed in the window of No. 23 rue du Titien now. Among the wrenches and inner tubes and saddles and pedal-rubbers a single used machine hung by its front wheel from a hook in the ceiling. A hand-lettered card announced in red capitals: BARGAIN.

The display window was backed by a wooden screen hung with puncture-repair kits, bells, mirrors, and showcards of accessories. The top half of the door was covered in pasteboard slips advertising bicycles for sale or wanted. It was impossible to see into the shop.

"What's going on?" Miniconi asked one of the idlers. The man shrugged his shoulders and moved away.

"Monsieur Miniconi! How unexpected to see *you* here!" exclaimed a thin, dry voice at his elbow.

Miniconi swung around. There stood a tall, elderly man wearing a gray alpaca suit and a panama hat. A gold-rimmed pince-nez sat slightly askew beneath the brim of the hat. "Monsieur Mosti! I could say the same. What's going on? Why is there a crowd outside this store?" The old man was a neighbor from the avenue du Grand-Pin.

Mosti shuffled closer. He stooped down and said in a low voice, "It's the police. They must have done something wrong. The police are in there."

"Police?" Miniconi looked at the black Citröen. It had ordinary civilian license plates.

"In plain clothes. They went in five or ten minutes ago."

Miniconi suppressed an exclamation. His date with Léon Noël had been for ten-fifty. A railroad engineer named Louis Lefers and an eighteen-year-old student called Louis Périssol, both members of the MUR, were due to have been there too, to discuss the transfer of the Italians to La Bocca. If he hadn't waited to listen to that radio broadcast . . .

He stared again at the Citroën. If they had been in there nearly ten minutes, they must be making a search. But if it had been a Vichy affair, they would have sent a meat wagon with uniformed men. Or members of the Militia in their battle dress and berets. Plainclothesmen operating in a Q-car spelled only one thing to him: Gestapo.

He leaned his bicycle against a wall, threaded his way through the small crowd, and crossed the street. He pushed down the handle, shoved open the door, and walked into the shop. Above his head, a bell clanged.

There were three hard-faced men in the place. One was standing by the counter, the other two by a closed door which led to Léon Noël's repair and stores department in the back. And also, Miniconi recalled with a sick feeling in the pit of his stomach, to his armory.

Of Noël and his two companions there was no sign. They must be holed up in that back room, Miniconi realized—and there was, he knew, no other entry or exit, not even a window. "Who the hell are you?" the man by the counter said. "What are you doing here?"

"Miniconi, Ange-Marie. Schoolteacher." You didn't act smart or try to answer back when the Gestapo might be concerned. And they probably were: the voice was guttural and heavily accented. Besides, the timing was a little too much of a coincidence; it smelled as though the meeting had been blown, or as if Léon Noël himself had been denounced.

"Your papers."

The other two men had come away from the door. They stood very close to him, very tall and very muscular. Despite the heat, they all wore dark suits. The onion odor of sweat swamped the thin stink of machine oil and gasoline in the shop. Miniconi reached for his hip pocket.

"*Halt!* Put your hands up! Up high. Quick!" A large Walther automatic pistol had appeared in the first man's hand. Miniconi obeyed. His palms were level with the shoulders of the men surrounding him. One came around behind him and ran practiced hands over his body, up the insides of his legs; the other stood to one side and twitched the billfold and papers from his pocket. The man with the gun had black-rimmed fingernails. Behind him, an inverted bicycle balanced on its handlebars and saddle, its wheels in the air. A length of oily chain looped down from the metal guard like the underskirt of a tipsy woman.

"What are you doing here? What do you want? Why did you come?"

"I wanted to get . . . I ordered . . . I have to buy a tire. For my bicycle." It was a routine he had worked out with Léon Noël long ago, a stratagem to meet just such an emergency, to give him a reason to be there. Whenever he came, he brought with him an order form, countersigned by the Mairie, giving him the right to purchase an object in wartime short supply, namely one bicycle tire, size so-and-so. "The authorization is with my papers," he said.

The men spread out the papers on the scarred wood of the counter—ration tickets, ID papers, an official attestation from his school, the order form, bills of various denominations. Then the contents of his pockets—lightweight coins, centimes with a hole in the center, keys. One of the men who had been by the inner door read through all the papers carefully. He turned back a couple of pages on Miniconi's passport, took out a small black notebook, and copied something down with a stub of pencil. The skin of his face was pockmarked and his eyes were like chips of flint.

He grunted something in German to the man with the gun, and

dropped the document back on the desk. "Stow this shit away and get out of here," he said.

"Thank you. But my bicycle tire . . . ? I need . . ." Miniconi raised his voice slightly, hoping the men holed up in back would recognize it and know that a friend was at least nearby.

"Shuddup!" the man with the gun shouted. "Get out of here, fast. Keep going. And don't come back if you know what's good for you."

Miniconi scooped up his belongings and got out of there. All three men were holding guns now. As the door slammed behind him, he heard one of them call out, "If you don't come out of there before I count to ten . . ."

He collected his bicycle, turned into the boulevard de l'Italie and rode as fast as he could to the railroad bridge. It was ten after eleven. By the Emerini antique furniture store he dismounted and ran through to the office. Curtel was sitting at his desk, going through some accounts. "Quick!" Miniconi panted. "Come and help . . . Léon Noël's place . . . three Gestapo with guns. Got to do what we can . . ."

Curtel unclipped a Webley automatic from the underside of his desk-top and thrust it into the waistband of his pants. Despite the heat, he was wearing a lightweight wool cardigan over his shirt, and this hid the bulge of the weapon. He collected his own bicycle from the rear of the store, and the two men pedaled furiously up the rue Fellégara, to enter the rue du Titien a little way beyond the Noël premises. As they dismounted and leaned their machines against a lamppost, a fusillade of shots rang out from the interior of the bicycle shop.

The crowd on the opposite sidewalk melted away, to regroup at the boulevard de l'Italie intersection. Miniconi and Curtel dodged into an open doorway. The door of the shop opened and a man came out with his hands in the air. Miniconi thought it was Louis Lefers, but he couldn't be certain. Behind him walked the Gestapo agent with the black fingernails, his pistol trained on the Resistance fighter's back. "My God," Curtel breathed, "I'm afraid we're too late, Jean-Marie."

"It isn't over yet," Miniconi said. "There are more of them in there." As he spoke, the man with the pockmarked face backed out onto the sidewalk and there was another eruption of gunshots, shockingly loud in the narrow street. From the reports, it sounded as though guns of several different calibers were being fired. Glass shattered in the display window, the secondhand bicycle dropped from its hook, and the man with the pockmarked face spun around and then collapsed in the gutter. They could see thin rivulets of blood running out from under him to color the broken glass. The first Gestapo man pushed his prisoner into the back seat of the Citroën and spoke urgently into a portable radio transmitter beside the driver. Miniconi and Curtel sprinted to the intersection and tried to rally the crowd. If they could persuade just a dozen men to rush the shop—the Gestapo were armed, but there were only two of them now, and one had a prisoner to look after. One, two, three, perhaps even four could get shot down or wounded, but after that the odds would tell: the Germans would be swamped and Léon Noël and his companions rescued.

They could have saved their breath. The men in the crowd lowered their heads, turned their backs, looked the other way, or simply hurried off. "What kind of people are you?" Miniconi shouted. "Those are Frenchmen in there! Caught like rats in a trap! Are you going to let the Boche drag them out and send them to death camps? Without raising a hand to save them?"

"For God's sake," Curtel cried, "isn't there one man among you yellow bastards? You! You! You! Come with us and set those people free!"

It was useless. Appealing to them individually was like putting a finger on a blob of quicksilver. The components of the crowd separated, eddied away, and then coalesced again somewhere else. "Forget it," Miniconi said tightly. "We're just wasting time and there's none to spare. Look—take the bike and go to La Bocca. Fetch the Tonners and anyone else you can drum up. And ride like the hammers of hell." He glanced quickly up and down the rue du Titien. "I'll go back to that doorway and keep watch here."

They ran to the bicycles. Curtel rode frenziedly away toward the boulevard Carnot and the road to La Bocca. It was still only 11:17.

Even in the shadowed doorway the air was almost too close to breathe. Miniconi passed a shirtsleeved forearm across his forehead. The upper half of his body was drenched in perspiration. Out in the street, the sun beat down on the Citroën and its three occupants. The German lying in the gutter hadn't moved. There had been no further sign of life from inside the bicycle shop.

At 11:21, the puffing of a locomotive sounded from beneath the railway bridge in the boulevard de l'Italie. Somewhere off to the east, the drone of an aircraft was audible. Then, with spine-chilling abruptness, sirens all over town wailed the alert. In the rue du Titien, the sound was deafening: there was an installation on the roof of the post office sorting center in the rue de Mimont, only a block away.

Miniconi cursed. The alert had nothing to do with the airplane. It must have been sounded in response to the SOS from the Gestapo man in the Citroën. During an alert, all traffic had to stop, the streets were cleared, and nobody was allowed outside. The Germans would use it to hasten reinforcements to the rue du Titien. At the same time, Curtel would be blocked before he even reached the outskirts of Cannes: it was more than two miles to La Bocca, and he had been gone less than five minutes.

There would be no reinforcements for the Resistance men in the store.

From the doorway, Miniconi watched helplessly as the drama approached its climax. A "salad basket"—an open patrol wagon with reinforced wire grills along the sides—pulled up with a squeal of brakes at the intersection. Uniformed French police jumped down and began hustling the crowd away. One officer strode up toward Léon Noël's shop with his revolver in his hand. Miniconi ran out from the doorway and stopped him. "Put that away!" he cried angrily. "There are no criminals concerned here. These are Frenchmen trying to defend themselves—and their country—against attack. You should be ashamed of yourself!" The policeman flushed, hesitated, and then shoved the weapon back into the stiff leather holster attached to his belt. Before he could reply, an armored truck full of helmeted German soldiers roared down from the far end of the rue du Titien. It was followed by a second detachment of French police in another *saladier*.

As Miniconi regained his doorway, the two vehicles pulled up outside the shop and uniformed men jumped to the roadway. The third Gestapo man hurried out and began shouting orders. A German officer ran up to the *brigadier* in charge of the police squad. "Just keep the street clear and don't interfere," he snapped. "So far as the rest is concerned, this is a German affair."

There were six or seven Wehrmacht men in the patrol. Two of

them stayed on the sidewalk to guard the store entrance. The rest went inside with the officer. Miniconi heard voices shouting, and then again the reverberation of heavy caliber revolver shots. The reports were obliterated by the ripping detonations of Schmeisser machine pistols. After that there was silence.

At 11:30 a Renault ambulance requisitioned by the occupiers turned into the rue du Titien and rocketed up to No. 23. A uniformed SS man who had been riding on the running board jumped down and hurried to the Gestapo agent lying in the gutter. Interns in white coveralls opened the rear doors of the ambulance and helped load him inside. The SS man climbed in beside him, the doors slammed shut, and the ambulance drove away. (Miniconi learned later that the wounded German was dead on arrival at the hospital.)

A few minutes later, young Louis Périssol was hustled out of the shop by a group of soldiers and pushed roughly into the black Citroën. So far as Miniconi could see, he was not wounded. The Third Gestapo man got into the car and was driven away toward the Hotel Montfleury with his companion and the two prisoners. It was not until almost noon that the ambulance returned. Léon Noël, pale as death, was carried out on a stretcher and taken to the German hospital installed in the Hotel Grande-Bretagne. By that time an SS search squad had arrived and was busy taking apart the interior of the store. Miniconi glanced at the curious faces pressed to first-floor windows all along both sides of the rue du Titien, and then went home. There was nothing he could do here. As it was, he had been foolhardy. The man who had gone to the shop and been questioned by the Gestapo was Ange-Marie Miniconi, schoolmaster; the patriot who had harangued the crowd and rebuked the French policeman could have been Commandant Jean-Marie of the Resistance. And it was vital that the two should never be connected.

At three o'clock that afternoon, he met Fauré, the head of his special police section, in the basement of La Régence. The *brigadier* had news of Léon Noël and his companions. Lefers and Périssol had been jailed at the Gestapo headquarters;* Léon Noël himself had received emergency treatment at the German hospital and then been taken to the Hotel Montfleury, where he was subjected to an

---

* To the surprise and pleasure of the resistants, Lefers was released several days later. Périssol was deported to Germany and died in a concentration camp.

initial "interrogation" of one hour. Having lost consciousness, he was then transferred under guard to the Saint-Dizier hospital in the Le Suquet quarter above the port.

"We must get him out," Miniconi said. "From the point of view of a rescue attempt, he couldn't be in a better place." Le Suquet was the neighborhood including the Mont Chevalier, his own school, the mail drop maintained by Monsieur and Madame Placide, and the homes of several FTPF members in its narrow twisting streets. Périssol himself lived in the rue de la Tour, which circled the fortifications at the top of the high ground overlooking the harbor.

Miniconi contacted a retired baker named Musso, who lived near the hospital—and whom he knew to be a member of Léon Noël's MUR group. Later in the afternoon, Musso went to visit a sick relative and contrived to "lose his way" until he found himself in the corridor leading to the ward in which Léon Noël was guarded. The door was open and no Germans were in sight. Musso tiptoed forward—but the injured man caught sight of him, shook his head, and made discreet signs pleading with Musso to go away, indicating that there was danger around the corner.

A rescue was nevertheless planned. But Curtel, interrogating an intern on the best way to retreat from the hospital, was told that Léon Noël was "absolutely untransportable." He had four machine-pistol slugs in one thigh and another in the shoulder, and the latter had punctured the top of one lung. Reluctantly, Miniconi was forced to abandon the idea.

Despite his critical state, Léon Noël was nevertheless taken back to the Hotel Montfleury during the night and dragged into the Gestapo's interrogation room. The inquisitors were determined to wring from the wounded man the names of all his contacts and the methods of communication they used. Léon Noël died under torture before dawn, without having spoken.

A number of arrests did however follow the drama of the Rue du Titien—probably, Fauré told Miniconi, as the result of the same denunciation. The SS searched many houses in Le Suquet and a dozen suspects were jailed. Perhaps in formal justification of their unilateral action, the Gestapo informed the French police that "an important stock of arms of foreign manufacture" had been discovered in the bicycle shop. For the Resistance, the most serious blow was the arrest of Captain Derché, the commander of AS.24. (Imprisoned first in Nice and then in Marseille, Derché was later deported to Mathausen concentration camp in Austria, where he died on August 18, 1944.)

Léon Noël's body was taken to the morgue at the Caucade cemetery in Nice, where his mother was obliged to identify the remains.* She was accompanied by Fernand Frossart, an old friend of the family who happened also—under his code name Le Teck—to lead the 3rd Detachment of Miniconi's 40th FTPF. And who happened to be the local organizer for the banned *Front National*.

Frossart and his wife hid Madame Noël and Odette Babée, the dead man's bride of only two months, when Fauré tipped them off some days later that the Gestapo were looking for them too. The two women stayed in the Frossart apartment, above a curio shop called *Le Vieux Paris* in the rue d'Antibes, until the heat was off. Then Miniconi arranged for them to be furnished with new identities and transported to a safer place in another *département*.

Some days after they had left, he was sitting in Curtel's office going over the tragic events which had led to the escape. The antique dealer was idly writing and rewriting Léon Noël's name on the back of an envelope. "That's curious," he said suddenly. "I never realized it before, but Léon's name is a palindrome."

"How's that?"

"A palindrome. It reads the same way whether you take it from left to right or from right to left. Like Yvon Novy, the Victorian critic."

Miniconi looked over his shoulder. "So it does," he said. "Mind you remember to burn that envelope. We can't afford to have any written connection with the rue du Titien, however slight."

"It's too neat to be a coincidence," Curtel said. "I guess Léon Noël must have been as much a fake name as the one we just gave his mother. Do you think he adopted it to avoid complications when he first came here? In case they found out he'd escaped from a POW camp, I mean?"

Miniconi sighed. "Once on the run . . ." he said. "I suppose he might have done at that."

---

* Léon Noël was buried in the Caucade cemetery. After the Liberation, the body was exhumed, transported to Cannes, and interred with full military honors—following an official procession and a memorial Mass—on November 14, 1944.

II

THE AUTUMN and winter of 1943–44 were the toughest the French had yet had to endure. Somehow the fact that the Allies had at last gained military supremacy seemed to make civilian privations even harder to bear. If victory finally appeared as something more tangible than a mirage, why was this not reflected in life on the home front? The picture was certainly somber enough. Nutrition experts had stated that the official rations were sufficient to sustain life and maintain reasonable health only if the recipient stayed in bed all the time. Everyone, therefore, was obliged to patronize the high-priced black market. But now, owing to the rapacity of the occupiers, even these quasi-legal supplies were drying up. Nazi "inspectors" were everywhere, and the moment a desirable item appeared it was requisitioned for consumption in the Fatherland. On the Croisette in Cannes the Carlton Hotel—last refuge of rich fugitives and the remnants of the international set—was reduced to offering as its luxury-priced "black market dish" a portion of plain white beans.

In some schools more than 70 percent of the children were tubercular. Epidemics of boils and carbuncles due to impurities in the "national" flour issued to bakers were common. Fresh vegetables had virtually disappeared from the market, and so had household articles such as polish, string, cooking utensils, and most kinds of hardware. Wine was rationed. Cigarettes were rationed (women were officially allowed none at all). Such clothes and shoes as there were, were reserved for pregnant mothers and children. The total shortage of any kind of cloth resulted in a bizarre outbreak of thieving among hotel guests: sheets, towels, pillowcases, drapes, even rugs were looted by women desperate for a new dress or a homemade winter coat. Finally managements were obliged to make an inspection of rooms before departing guests were given back their grips.

Nor could the prevailing gloom be lightened by artificial gaiety. Cosmetics had vanished and only the coarsest of kitchen soaps could be bought. Public dancing and music were forbidden because the aging Pétain held that France's defeat had been due to moral laxity —and as some kind of crazy penance, the Marshal had decreed the previous year that there must be three nonalcoholic days each week, when it was illegal to serve liquor in cafés and bars. (It was, as one writer put it, a "curious coincidence" that this law should have been promulgated at the very moment that snowbound German troops immobilized in Russia manifested their greatest need for alcohol.*)

Intolerable though they were, commodity shortages were not the only crosses French civilians had to bear. There had been a 10 P.M. curfew when the Italians occupied the coast, but nobody took it very seriously—no more than they took the blackout regulations seriously. Who would want to drop bombs on Cannes anyway? Although their officers strutted around jauntily enough, Mussolini's troops were scared of being attacked by patriots, so if they went out after dark at all, they tended to stay in groups, keeping to the center of the wider streets. The habit, with its accompanying lack of spot checks, suited the inhabitants very well: leaving the boulevards to the occupiers, they returned home, by sidewalk and by alley, as discreetly—and as late—as necessary.

The situation changed abruptly as soon as the Italians were replaced. Curfew breakers risked a fusillade of shots, or at best, a period in jail. ID checks by street patrols were frequent and rigorous. As far as the blackout was concerned, the Germans had been instructed to open fire without warning any time they saw a light showing after dark—and to keep on shooting until the source of the offending gleam was destroyed.

It was now doubly dangerous to harbor refugees—and, ironically, the Master Race were severest on those sheltering deserters from the army of their former ally. It was perhaps fortunate, therefore, that the very last Italian soldier to leave Cannes fell by chance into Miniconi's hands.

One day early in November, soon after the hundred deserters had been safely handed over to the Maquis, the Resistance chief boarded the train for Nice, on his way to spend a few hours with his parents. As usual, the train was crowded; as usual, there was standing room only—if you could fight your way in at all. Miniconi was aware of the atmosphere as soon as he jammed himself into the compartment. A sudden silence, followed by an obscure rearrangement of bodies, and then everyone talking at once, too quickly and too loud. He realized later that it was his clothes that had caused the

* Eda Lord, *op. cit.*

trouble: he was wearing a trench coat and a fedora with the brim pulled down—and this was, as it happened, the costume often favored by plainclothes Gestapo men and Vichy security police. If this coincidence had alarmed the other passengers, it followed that they must have something to hide. It was not until the train stopped at the third station that he found out what it was.

Nobody in the compartment moved at Golfe-Juan or Juan-les-Pins, but at Antibes a woman got out. Her departure left a momentary gap in the phalanx of bodies. Before it closed, Miniconi saw a tall, dark, bearded man sitting hunched up on the seat. The sleeves of his jacket were four inches too short for him, and the pants ended above his ankles. His feet were encased in what were obviously Italian army boots. And, as if this weren't a big enough giveaway, he was carrying his belongings in an Italian government issue army kit bag.

Miniconi elbowed his way next to the man, explained in Italian that he was a member neither of the Milice (the French Gestapo) nor the Gestapo, and added, "I imagine you're heading for home? Well, you haven't a chance. There's a special cordon around Nice and the frontier's impassable. You're walking straight into the lion's mouth." He offered to show the deserter a better way, and the man eagerly accepted, but the immediate problem was to get him past the *Feldgendarmerie* stationed at the barrier when they arrived in Nice. With the help of the other passengers, they succeeded. Miniconi himself carried the kit bag. And the Italian, walking in a kind of Groucho Marx crouch so that he appeared no taller than the women surrounding him, was swept past the barrier with the crowd as the train disgorged its human cargo.

Miniconi took him to his parents' house in the St. Sylvestre quarter, where they persuaded him to shave off his beard and managed to find him clothes that very nearly fit. In the evening, they returned to Cannes—and once again there was the problem of the train. Most of the coaches were reserved for German troops, and if Wehrmacht men wished to board one of the few "civilian" compartments and it was already full, then the French had to get out to make room for them. The occupiers, moreover, were in the habit of making sudden swoops and spot checks on passengers between stations.

Miniconi decided to adopt the *Purloined Letter* technique of "hiding" something by putting it in the most conspicuous place possible.

He deliberately boarded a coach that was already crowded with Germans. "The French will stay away," he explained to the deserter, "and as for the Nazis—well, nobody's going to look for holdup men in the policemen's favorite bar!" The stratagem paid off and the short journey passed without incident.

On the way to the avenue du Grand-Pin, Miniconi saw for the first time new posters warning the population that the penalty for harboring Italian deserters was death.

When they reached the front door, the Italian at first refused to enter. "You have already done far too much," he protested. "I cannot possibly permit you and your family to risk your lives for me."

Miniconi insisted, and finally the two men went inside. Claire was equally insistent that the unexpected guest must stay, and in fact he was hidden there for almost a week. His name, he told them, was Romolo Tebaldi. He spoke no French at all. He was by profession a fisherman, and he came from Falconara Marittima, near Ancona, on the Adriatic coast. "The best thing I can do for you," Miniconi said, "is to put you in touch with an escape line run by friends of mine in La Bocca. They can arrange for you to be taken up into the hills, where there are already countrymen of yours waiting to be repatriated. But it may take a few days."

Tebaldi, who naturally knew nothing of Miniconi's position in the Resistance, protested again that he had no right to put his hosts at risk. "The Germans may have been better soldiers," Miniconi said years later, "but don't tell me that the Italians are lacking in courage. Tebaldi was one of the bravest men I ever met . . . with a natural courtesy and a sensitivity to match. Food was very scarce at that time, but naturally we shared what we had, and as the apartment was not watched, he was able to eat in the dining room with us." He shook his head. "I can't tell you what lengths that man went to in his attempts to convince us that he wasn't hungry, that he was never hungry. I shall never forget him."

On November 10, Miniconi received a message telling him that arrangements for Tebaldi's transfer to the Esterel Maquis were complete. They were to walk down to La Bocca in the afternoon. Arnaud le Manchot, the one-armed railwayman who acted as liaison between Miniconi's group and the FER network based in the freight yards, would then take charge of the fugitive. "You walk in front," Miniconi said, tucking his gun into the waistband of his pants, "and

I'll be close behind you. If anyone stops you—and it could happen, the patrols are always asking for papers—if anyone stops you, make them understand that you're dumb. Make signs showing them that you can't speak."

"No," Tebaldi said. "No, no, and again no. I have said it before: you have already done too much. Besides, you have a wife and children, and I am single. I will ask you just to let me have the weapon. Then I will go alone and I can look after myself."

"There's no question of it," Miniconi replied. "You'd never make it, speaking no French. Just do what I say. If you're stopped, make believe you're dumb; show them the false identity papers I've given you; count up to three . . . and then drop to the ground, because I'll have started firing."

"Yes, but . . . ?"

"And in that case—I hate to say this, but I do have certain other . . . responsibilities—in that case, we must split up immediately and you *will* be on your own."

As it turned out, they were not stopped. Near the tiny station at La Bocca, one-armed Arnaud appeared from behind a fence at the end of a vacant lot, the briefest of introductions were made, and then Miniconi turned around and headed for home. Tebaldi was to stay the night at Arnaud's home in the St. Joseph neighborhood on the high ground in back of the town. The following night, he would be escorted across the St. Cassien plain and up into the Esterel.

The following night, November 11, strong forces of American bombers from bases on Corsica attacked *Les Aciéries du Nord*. Owing to a navigation mistake made by the planes laying marker flares, the succeeding wave of incendiaries fell more than a mile and a half to the north of the target area, and the greater part of the bombs fell on the St. Joseph quarter. The ADN factory was undamaged. More than 350 people in St. Joseph were killed, among them Arnaud le Manchot. Miniconi never heard another word of Romolo Tebaldi.*

Out of the bad, the good will sometimes emerge, but the sole benefit derived from this tragedy—and from the arrests that fol-

---

* The probability, of course, is that he perished in the raid, although there is no record of a victim with the name on his false papers. Having his true name and address, Miniconi has tried by letter, by press advertising, and even by ham radio appeals, to contact him or obtain news of him, ever since the war. So far, with no success. But as I write, in 1979, he is still trying.

lowed upon the Léon Noël drama, which preceded it—was a closer relationship between Miniconi's FTPF and the patriots in the MUR, especially those who worked with the FER network in La Bocca.

A favorite meeting place for the leaders of these different groups was the Taverne Royale, a big brasserie directly opposite the central station in Cannes. The Royale was also popular with German soldiers off duty, and many useful pieces of information came to Miniconi through snatches of conversation overheard in its bar. Most of them were passed on by the owner, an extraordinary woman named Toinette Marcoux. Toinette was fun-loving and boisterous, a six-foot brunette whose body was encased in a steel corset because of a back injury suffered when she was a child. Both she and her husband, Marcel, were valued members of Miniconi's 40th Company. It was through them that he first met Colonel Jean Dussert, the railroad Chief Inspector who was in fact head of the local FER *réseau.*

Tall, lean, limping Dussert, still the typical soldier, with his officer's mustache, had already supplied information on the munitions train derailed in the first FTPF attack at La Bocca on November 2. Now, in a series of apparently casual meetings at the Taverne Royale, he was able to funnel through to Miniconi the details which permitted them to plan the assaults at Anthéor, Mandelieu, and La Source early in 1944.

Scene Six

By THE beginning of April, 1944, Miniconi's 40th FTPF Company had been in existence for six months; the 1st Company of Destruction, based in the railroad complex at La Bocca, had been completed for more than three months; and the third company, drawn from resistants in the outlying villages of Auribeau, Pégomas, and La Roquette, was nearing half strength. Between them, these units of the Groupe Jean-Marie—sometimes on their own, sometimes in liaison with the MUR—had been responsible for five attacks on the railroad: two at La Bocca, one at La Source, and one each at Mandelieu and Anthéor. In addition, they had raided a German small-arms depot at Antibes, saved most of the gasoline stocks that had been hidden from the Italians, and stolen the weapons from under the noses of a Nazi detail near Pégomas.

And, astonishingly, all these operations had been carried out without a shot being fired, without a question asked, without any reprisals being exacted. Better still, apart from the AS.24 losses following the death of Léon Noël, there appeared to have been no denunciations and no arrests.

It was hardly surprising, therefore, as the long-promised Allied invasion drew nearer, that members of the group should feel the scales of war tipping slightly toward them; that they should suffer perhaps a little from overconfidence.

Certainly they underestimated the odds against them when, at the beginning of May, they were asked by the Free French headquarters in Algiers to sabotage the workshops at *Les Aciéries du Nord*.

The request originated with the planners on General Koenig's staff and was transmitted by radio to the secret station operated by Captain Ardouin at the Villa Petit-Clos. It was passed on to Miniconi by Commandant Duvallon, the ex-soldier who acted as liaison between the Groupe Jean-Marie and the Free French clandestine information service in Cannes. Miniconi assigned the 2nd Detachment of the 40th Company, the unit commanded by Sam Kadyss, to carry out the operation. The instruction: to blow up the pylon supporting the electric cables bringing high-tension current to the factory; to destroy the transformer from which power at a lower potential was fed to the workshops; to wreck as many machines on the factory floor as they could. The aim of the operation was simply to put the place out of action for as long as possible, since this would hinder the rail traffic that carried vital supplies to the Todt Organization units fortifying the coast against the expected landings. It was clearly preferable, the voice from Algiers had said, that the job should be done "from inside"; another air raid that caused heavy civilian casualties among the closely packed population of La Bocca would scarcely increase the popularity of the invading forces when they arrived.

Miniconi sent a message to Mertens at Beausoleil. Two days later he took the train to Nice, walked down to the place Masséna, and bought a paper from a newsboy at the entrance to the arcades behind the casino. Leaning against one of the arches to scan the front page (Pétain was at Rouen and the Americans were mounting a final assault on Cassino), he slipped his haversack from his shoulder and laid it on the ground between his feet. A few minutes later, a man heading for the Menton bus queue stopped by the arch to light a cigarette. In order to free his hands to shield the match flame from the wind, he stooped down and parked a haversack by his feet. When he reached down for the second time, it was Miniconi's haversack that he picked up and took away. Miniconi folded his paper, slung the substituted bag to his shoulder, and sauntered back toward the station. The weight on his shoulder was now considerably heavier: in addition to the books, papers, and provisions visible when the flap was lifted, there were six pounds of plastic explosive concealed in the false bottom of the haversack.

Kadyss divided it among the leaders of the three triangles selected for the exploit—one for the pylon, one for the transformer, one for the machines on the factory floor. He himself would accompany the three men detailed to the transformer, as that was the most important—and the most delicate—task.

Apart from the administration and office blocks, there were three main buildings and a railroad spur accommodated within the 2,600-yard wall surrounding the ADN. The wall was topped with broken glass and barbed wire, and there were German sentries stationed by the tall corrugated-iron gates that sealed off the spur and at all subsidiary entries. A guardhouse protected by a sandbagged machine-gun emplacement flanked the main entrance. Since it was obviously going to be virtually impossible for ten men to gain entry secretly, Kadyss had picked his triangles from among resistants employed in the workshops. That way the sabotage could be effected by elements already inside the compound: they would simply conceal themselves sometime before the whistle blew, and stay behind when the other workers went home.

"But surely we'll be fingered as soon as the sabotage is discovered," Cigale, the leader of one of the triangles, protested. "All the security people will have to do is check the time cards. Those who didn't clock out will be guilty."

"No sweat," said Big Sam. "Providing we all agree to do a day's work for no pay. We go onto the shop floor with the others," he explained, "but we mingle with the crowd when we turn up *and we don't clock in*. So it won't show in the timekeeper's office that we never left: as far as the management is concerned, we never showed that day at all. It's just part of the absenteeism the Marshal is always complaining about!"

They were running no graveyard shift at *Les Aciéries* that month, so Kadyss persuaded an AS.24 contact who worked in the secretariat to put him and his nine men on the swing shift. The operation was planned for the night of May 15. It was a warm night with mackerel streaks of altocumulus blotting out some of the stars. A lozenge of moon was about to plunge behind the Esterel as the Resistance men emerged from the washroom soon after midnight and stole toward their targets.

Kadyss crouched behind a freight car just outside the main assembly shop. The transformer was housed in a metal cabin with louvered doors on which there was a red enamel plaque bearing a skull and crossbones and the warning DANGER DE MORT! The warning was timely, Kadyss reflected grimly as he surveyed the terrain. The cabin was on the far side of an open space 50 yards across. The doors were padlocked, and the hasp of that lock had to be broken and the doors jimmied open if the plastic explosive he carried was to cause more than superficial damage to the transformer. Two boxcars and a line of flatbed trucks hid the area from the guardhouse at the entrance, but somewhere beyond the dull gleam of rails, jackboots stamped as a military detail patrolled the yard. He waited until the sound of footsteps had receded, and then waved his three men forward. Together they sped silently across the open space and ducked down on the far side of the transformer. Kadyss wondered how the other two triangles were making out. He cocked his head and listened.

He could hear the sound of waves crashing on the shingle beach (there had been a mistral blowing the previous day and the sea was still rough). In the distance, a locomotive hauling a line of freight cars panted up the grade between Théoule and Anthéor. There was a murmur of German voices from the guardhouse, and close at hand the humming from inside the transformer, which laced the air with the aseptic tang of ozone. He had half risen to his feet, prepared to sidle around to the doors, when again he became aware of the *tramp-tramp-tramp* of marching feet.

Kadyss motioned his three men back to the rear of the cabin and flattened himself to the ground. This time the noise was coming from behind them. It was impossible for the first detail to have reached that position in so short a time, so he concluded there must be two patrols on the move.

"*Merde!*" Kadyss swore softly. He held his breath and strained his eyes in an attempt to pierce the darkness at one side of the repair sheds. Masked overhead lamps cast a glow on the ground between the transformer and the boxcars. Soon he saw the second patrol emerge from the obscurity: a *Feldwebel* and six men. They marched across the illuminated area and disappeared in the direction of the guardhouse. Then, before the saboteurs had time to react, there was the sound of heavy steel doors moving on rollers and a third group of soldiers came out of the assembly shop. The original detail had clearly made a tour of the perimeter—but by the time they returned to the entrance gates, the other two had marched out once more.

Kadyss swore again. With three squads of men on constant patrol, it would surely be impossible to break open the transformer cabin and lay the charges during the short periods when the open space was unguarded. Since one of the squads also patrolled inside the workshops, the same problem would deter the three men who were to wreck machines on the factory floor. Cigale and one member of his triangle, who were responsible for sabotaging the pylon, shouldn't find their task too difficult: the crisscross steel structure stood in deep shadow beside the administration block. Kadyss hoped that the third man would be equally favored by chance. It had been his job to prepare their escape route.

"What are we going to do?" the man behind Kadyss whispered.

The Detachment leader replied, "Get the hell out of here. We have to rethink the whole operation. We miscalculated the number of Boches guarding the place. It'd be suicide to try anything the way things are now."

"What about the others?"

"Same story with the guys inside the shop. Cigale might make out —but we have to wait and see. Right now, we're gonna head for the exit!"

Kadyss waited until the two shorter-range details had crossed the open space on their third sortie. The perimeter patrol, he calculated, should be somewhere near the farthest point of their tour. Followed by his men, he sprinted back to the cover of the boxcars. After that, it was a matter of dodging between tracks, ducking underneath more cars, stopping to listen for the tramp of patrols, and then dashing to the next safe corner until they reached the place labeled "Getaway" on the map Kadyss had drawn the night before.

It was a corner of the complex where a siding ran close to the outer wall. Cigale's man—Kadyss knew him only by the number 3178—had done his work well. There were boxcars parked along the siding, and he had laid an aluminum ladder—taken from the workshop during the dinner break—from the roof of one of the cars to the top of the wall. The barbed wire had been cut and neatly turned back, and there was a folded tarpaulin blanketing the broken glass. The man whose number was 3178 lay flat on the boxcar roof. "What happened?" he muttered as Kadyss and his team clambered up the iron steps at the back of the car.

Big Sam told him, and concluded, "I'm calling everyone off, as of now. We have to come back with a much stronger force if we're going to make out here." There was a police whistle hanging from a lanyard around his neck. He put the whistle to his lips, preparing to blow the prearranged signal for a general retreat—three long blasts, repeated. He was still drawing breath when a shout came from the far side of the yard, followed by a clatter of footsteps and then the ripping detonations of machine pistols.

"Shit!" Kadyss cursed for the third time. "What the devil . . . ?"

There were more shouts, from the gatehouse. The serrated roofs of the factory were suddenly silhouetted against the night sky as a searchlight at the main entrance was switched on. The machine pistols fired again. Kadyss could see the flashes reflected from the steel sides of a baggage car. The shots mingled this time with the deeper reverberations of heavy-caliber revolvers. Cigale and his companion must have been surprised by one of the patrols.

The machine-shop men were already standing below the boxcar. Kadyss helped them up onto the roof. "It was hopeless," the leader began. "We didn't have a chance to—"

"I know. Save your breath and split. The wire's already cut."

"But—?"

"Look, the more we spread our getaway, the better. You three take a powder now. My triangle can follow. Me and 3178 can cover Cigale and his mate . . . if they make it."

The man stared at Kadyss through the gloom, then shrugged and led his companions toward the ladder. There was another volley of shots. The first man was about to jump down from the wall into the street when the darkness was split by a vivid orange flash. For an instant they saw the tracks and the cars and the factory buildings etched against the night, and then the thunderclap of an explosion cracked in their ears. It was followed by a patter of stones and bricks showering to the ground, and a heavy metallic crash that seemed to prolong itself into the ensuing silence. Kadyss realized that the searchlight and all the overhead lamps had gone out. Cigale had managed to bring the pylon down.

Now there was confusion in the darkness below—shouted commands, the flicker of gunfire on the far side of the compound, the sound of running feet. Kadyss drew the Mauser from the waistband of his pants and lay flat on the boxcar roof. Beside him, 3178 thumbed back the hammer of an old American .38 Police Special. The footsteps pelted closer and somewhere not too far behind, others clattered in pursuit across the cobbled yard. Kadyss waited until the two fugitives were directly beneath him and then fired blind into the night. A moment later, the roar of the .38 joined the whip cracks of the German gun. From below, flame stabbed the blackness as the patrol returned their fire. Splinters of wood flew from the side of the boxcar, and a slug glanced off an iron bracket and screeched over their heads. But Cigale and his fellow saboteur were on the roof of the car and heading for the ladder. Seconds later, their magazines empty, the other two joined them on the sidewalk outside.

Two days later, Sam Kadyss met Stefan Vahanian, whose code name was Pierre, in a waterfront bar. Vahanian was in a small way an industrialist: he owned a boat yard and ran a ship repair business. He was also chief of the MUR in Cannes—and since the arrest of Captain Derché, the effective leader of AS.24. "He's a good man," Miniconi told Kadyss. "He doesn't share your views—or mine—politically, but he figures it's more important to win the war against Hitler than squabble about the way the country should be run. You can trust him."

Since the Germans had invaded the southern zone, Vahanian had spent a lot of time making sure that certain boats they might requisition were unseaworthy, and in this way he had become something of an expert on the subtler kinds of sabotage. He listened to the story of the raid that had gone wrong and then said, "It's a pity you didn't contact us first. Infiltration with a small number of men isn't going to work with a place as well-guarded as that. You were lucky—and courageous—to blow up the pylon. But it only put the ADN out of action for half a day. If you're going to do real damage, something that will stop production for a good time, you need a different approach."

Kadyss stared out the window. It was raining and the water in the harbor looked like a sheet of hammered pewter. "What do you suggest?" he asked.

"Something much nearer to a frontal assault. I don't mean an all-out attack but, shall we say, a penetration in depth, with a sizable body of men keeping all the defenders pinned down while a couple of specialist squads lay the charges."

"You mean like stage a diversion? Only the diversion's bigger than the actual operation? Sounds great. But I don't quite see . . ."

"I'm suggesting we join forces again, the way we did when we got the gasoline. A few more of your people, plus an action group from AS.24 —men who work at La Bocca and are familiar with the ADN layout. You know the Tonner brothers, of course?"

"You forget that I was a member of AS.24 myself," Kadyss said.

Vahanian smiled. "There's not much danger I'd do that! I'll contact Francis Tonner and get him to organize a squad. You can fix up the details with my Number Two, Tony Isaïa. All right?"

Sam Kadyss held out his hand. "It's a deal," he said.

To avoid any risk of attracting suspicion to the workers by using the same men as before, Miniconi decided that the main FTPF unit this time should be Javel's detachment from the 1st Company of Destruction. They would have the task of destroying machines on the shop floor and putting the pylon out of action again. Kadyss, with a different section from his detachment, would handle the transformer, while the AS.24 group would allow themselves to be discovered and draw the enemy's fire.

The operations plan was simple but daring. Members of the FER network would arrange a minor derailment somewhere between La Bocca and La Napoule—nothing that would seriously hold up traffic, but enough to warrant a wrecking car with a crane. When whatever it was had been lifted back onto the track, the car would return to the ADN yards—but this time Kadyss, Javel, and their men would be concealed in the caboose behind the crane. Once this Trojan horse was safely within the walls, the AS.24 action group would make what appeared to be a spirited attempt to shoot their way in. And the charges could be laid while the Germans were occupied beating them off.

In brief, the plan for the second assault relied on force as much as guile. The date chosen was June 5; the time, soon after midnight, when the swing shift had finished work and the guard had just been changed. The night was very dark: the quarter moon had already disappeared behind the Esterel, and now clouds had blown up from the west and it was raining again. Crouched inside the caboose as it rattled back to base, Kadyss hoped that the absence of light would favor the attackers, every one of whom knew the layout of the yards as intimately as he knew the arrangement of furniture in his own home. Around him, two of his own triangles, and Javel with eight men from the 1st Company sat steeling themselves for action. Kadyss had brought the Sten gun from the avenue du Grand-Pin, but the others were armed only with pistols: there were too many parcels of plastic, and tools, and lengths of Primacord, for them to manage anything more cumbersome. In any case, the weapons were intended for defense only. The AS.24 squad, with their heavier armament, were handling the attack.

There was a squeal of brakes and the puffing of the fussy little tank loco that hauled the crane ceased. The car lurched to a halt. They must have arrived at the gates barring the way into the factory.

Kadyss and Javel rose to their feet and stood one on either side of the sliding door, their guns at the ready. Kadyss could feel the beads of sweat cold on his forehead. He was aware suddenly of the rain drumming on the steel roof of the caboose. One of Vahanian's men had kept watch and told them that the Nazi guards never asked to look inside the van when it returned from a wrecking trip, but there was always a first time . . .

They could hear voices outside. A silence in which the nasal breathing of the brakeman, whom they had bound and gagged to save him from suspicion, seemed suddenly unnaturally loud. Javel bit his lip. Then there was a screech of metal as the gates were dragged open. The locomotive panted and they jerked forward. The wooden horse had passed through the arch into Troy.

The wrecker was shunted into one of the open sheds not far from the railroad entrance. For some time after the tank engine had gone away they waited in silence. It had been impossible to fix on a zero-hour with the AS.24 unit because they would not have complete control of the locomotive or the actions of the wrecking crew. They had to rely on the *Armée Sécrète* lookout seeing the crane car brought in, and then passing the signal on to Tony Isaïa. Their own signal to get going would be the noise of Isaïa's attack.

It started with an explosion that shook the caboose on its chassis, followed at once by a burst of machine-gun fire. Kadyss slid back the door of the caboose and dropped to the ground. Javel and the others followed him. In the darkness of the huge shed, lines of boxcars, baggage cars, Pullmans, and transporters stood waiting on the tracks for the attention of ADN's engineers. The damp air smelled of machine oil and soot. In single file, they moved between two lines of freight cars toward the exit.

The paler rectangle framed by the roof and the closed sides of the shed brightened fitfully as the sound of sporadic gunfire came to their ears. Kadyss listened to the now-familiar noise of jackboots pounding across the cobbles, the guttural shouts of Nazi commands. Isaïa and his men had been instructed to breach the wall at the far end of the compound with plastic and then to shoot their way through. It was hoped that the entire guardroom would be mobilized to fight off what appeared to be a break-in—but what was in reality the bolt-hole for the sabotage squads' exit. At the shed entrance, Kadyss looked out at the dimly lit yard. Squalls of rain gusted across the open space, silvering the tracks and shivering the streamers of lamplight reflected in the wet stone. The firing was coming from behind the main assembly shops to their left. Nearer at hand, beyond the corner of a small brick building, a helmeted German carrying a machine pistol stood silhouetted against the illumination from an open doorway. He was shouting something in the direction of the main gates. The man standing next to Kadyss raised a pistol and drew a bead on the Nazi. Kadyss roughly shoved the weapon down. "Don't be a fool!" he hissed. "You want every damned kraut in the garrison on your neck?" And then, to one of the men who was fluent in German: "What's the guy saying, anyway?"

"He says to leave the machine-gun crew and two extra men on the gates, and everyone else run double-quick to the breach in the wall."

"Great!" Kadyss whispered. "That's just the way we want it. Rougeole, Belette—you come with me to the transformer. The rest of you go with Javel to the machine shop and do as much damage as you can."

The German had run off toward the sound of fighting. A moment later, half a dozen more streamed out from behind the brick building and followed him. The shooting, which had temporarily died down, now broke out again with redoubled force. Kadyss hesitated long enough to make sure that there were no more reinforcements on the way from the main gates, and then dashed across the yard in the opposite direction, followed by his two men. Javel and the others melted away into the darkness.

Ducking beneath the lines of freight cars strung out along the tracks, Kadyss ran past a series of loading bays and out into the open, toward the transformer cabin. The rain stung his face and bounced up from the shining cobbles. He splashed through puddles, swerved around switch levers, and skidded to a halt, panting, a few yards from the cabin. He waited until the sound of the shots would be covered by a volley from the rear of the compound, then fired a short burst from his Sten at the junction of the padlocked doors.

Sparks flew from the steel as the slugs slammed home. Rougeole and Belette hurried forward with their canvas carryalls. They took out two jimmies and began to pry the doors away from the shattered lock. The doors swung open. They crouched down, readying plastic explosive and fuses for positioning where they would do the most damage. Above them, Kadyss stood guard with the Sten, his eyes, squinted against the rain, ceaselessly scanning the pools of darkness between the hooded lamps.

Rougeole was shining a masked pocket torch into the interior of the transformer cabin. "Still a five-minute fuse?" he asked.

Kadyss nodded. And then, realizing that they couldn't see him, he said, "Yes," in a low voice.

"And you still want us to do the pylon again afterward?"

"Why not?"

"We won't have too much *plastique* left if we're to do this one properly. And if the transformer's kaput, they won't be able to use the juice anyway."

"Algiers wants the pylon down, too. It stands on four legs. If you can blow one and damage another, the remaining two will buckle and bring down the whole lot. Couldn't you save enough for that?"

"Just about," Belette said, his hands busy in the semidarkness inside the cabin. Seconds later, Rougeole switched off the torch and rose to his feet. "All right," he said. "Let's go."

Javel and the twelve men drawn from the 1st and 40th FTPF companies were dispersed through the machine shop and the largest repair shed. Each man knew exactly where to go and what to do; only the extent of his actions was left to be determined by the time available, and this in turn depended on the success of the pylon and transformer sabotages that Kadyss was handling. They moved swiftly, passing from lathes to drills to punches to tapping machines.

As the sounds of battle ebbed and flowed outside the shops, bolts were loosened, iron filings and steel scrap dropped in between gear trains, bags of sand emptied into the moving parts of electric motors, and the belting of pulleys savaged. Here and there beneath the cowling of larger machines, small explosive charges were laid, and every sump and reservoir in the place was drained of oil. Cars and coaches in the repair sheds were similarly damaged: hoses and underbracings sawed through, coupling pins removed, the lines connecting air brakes pierced, and again quantities of sand fed into journals and axle boxes.

By the time the first explosion rocked the sheds, several dozens of electrical machines had been doctored and their motors put out of action—or would be as soon as someone attempted to start them.

Before the echoes of the detonation had died away, Javel and his men were heading for the exits. Their orders had been specific. Whatever they were doing, they must leave it immediately when the transformer charge went off. The reasons were practical: as soon as the guards realized that there were saboteurs within the factory, men would be withdrawn from the area around the breached wall and ordered to hunt them down. The first big bang was therefore to be their signal to get out—fast.

All the lights had gone out. In twos and threes, they fled through the darkness toward the assembly point they had been given—a corner close to the perimeter wall, where a coal bunker and a line of parked trucks should shelter them from the crossfire exchanged between AS.24 and the defenders.

The breach was only fifty yards away. They could see the shattered brickwork in the flashes of automatic fire as Tony Isaïa's assault team forced their way farther into the yard. The attackers were crouched down now behind stacks of lumber which had been unloaded there for just that purpose by truck drivers belonging to the FER network. Most of the Germans had taken refuge behind a small wooden building that looked like a yardmaster's office, though occasional volleys still blazed from beneath a line of boxcars away to the left.

The night was split by a livid green flash followed by a cracking explosion that echoed around the yard as Sam Kadyss arrived at the bunker. That would be the double charge placed at the foot of the pylon by Rougeole and Belette. Kadyss listened for the sound of steel girders tumbling, but sirens were screeching now, and the rattle of small arms fire was punctuated by the thump of grenades. The intermittent illumination showed him a German soldier lying with outflung arms on the wet cobbles and another dragging himself painfully back toward the yardmaster's office. Kadyss looked quickly around him. If the saboteurs were all there, it was time to quit: a siren alert meant that the streets would be cleared and reinforcements on the way. As he hesitated, a series of smaller explosions signaled that the charges in the machine shop were beginning to detonate. In the blackness, someone shouted a command and a group of men ran out from behind the wooden building and doubled back toward the sheds. It was all going according to the blueprint, Kadyss thought. Now was the time to act.

He still had the police whistle on a lanyard around his neck. He put the whistle to his lips and blew three shrill blasts.

Outside the wall, fifty yards up the narrow service road that ran along the back of the ADN lot, Francis Tonner pressed the starter button of a closed Unic truck. The motor, already warm, fired at once. The truck they had chosen was gasoline powered, for relatively silent operation, speed, and reliability. A *gazogène* would have been hopeless as a getaway vehicle. It hadn't been too much of a problem, "borrowing" the truck. The fuel was more difficult, but there were always fishermen prepared to sell some of their tiny ration on the black market, and all they needed was enough to get to the factory and then race the couple of miles through La Bocca to the Tonner farm. Francis eased the shift into first and drove slowly past the breach blown in the wall.

He stopped a couple of yards beyond the gap. Javel's men were already clambering through, covered by a withering fire from the AS.24 fighters, which was forcing the Germans to keep their heads down. The truck rocked on its springs as the saboteurs piled in over the lowered tailgate. Moments later, the first members of the AS.24 squad pitched in their weapons and climbed up after them. The last to leave was Sam Kadyss. They saw him standing on top of the bunker, silhouetted by the flames belching from the muzzle of his own Sten. Then, when there was nobody left to cover, he too dived through the gap and was dragged aboard as Tonner sped away.

Miraculously, apart from two flesh wounds and a few scratches from grenade splinters, the resistants had suffered no casualties.

Inside the factory, friends on the day shift told them later, the transformer was wrecked, the pylon had been brought down again, and more than fifty electric motors were ruined. Both assembly and repair shops were completely out of action for fifteen days.

Francis Tonner had turned onto National Route 7 and then swung off again along a byroad leading across the plain of St. Cassien, before the bewildered Nazis guarding the ADN had realized what had happened. By the time reinforcements had arrived with detachments of *Feldgendarmerie* to set up roadblocks, the attackers had all dispersed and the Unic truck had been abandoned on the road to Mandelieu.

That was in the early hours of the morning of June 6. As the guerrillas were making their strategic retreat, forward units of the Allied invasion force 750 miles to the north were advancing steadily toward the Normandy beaches.

Act II
In Attack

Being powerful is like being a lady—if you have to say you are, you ain't.
— TEAMSTERS UNION BOSS, IN ANCHORAGE, ALASKA

Scene One

THE ALLIED landings in the South of France were originally conceived as the second part of a master strategy designed to crush Hitler's forces in France between two opposing advances: they were to play Anvil to the Normandy invasion's Hammer. Two factors contributed to the postponement of this plan. The manpower for any Côte d'Azur attack would have to be drawn from Allied forces in Italy, and Churchill was violently opposed to this; he wanted to strike on up through Lombardy and Trieste and get to the Balkans before the Russians did—and every man available would be needed if this aim was to be achieved. In the second place, there simply weren't enough invasion craft available to mount two assaults at the same time. The code name for Normandy was changed from Hammer to Overlord; Anvil was shelved until later in the year and renamed Dragoon.

Allied Intelligence headquarters in London were unforgivably lax in informing Resistance networks of the delay, and in many parts of France, patriots took the Normandy invasion as a signal for local uprisings, with tragic results. While Operation Anvil was still a possibility, however, there were many calls on networks in the South for specific actions to weaken the German defenses. During the evening of June 8, two days after the successful sabotage at *Les Aciéries du Nord,* Miniconi received a message asking him to meet Duvallon at the Taverne Royale. It was an "alcoholic" day, and the German soldiers crowding the bar were singing over their beer. Above the rows of bottles and glasses, a radio blared out the Lale Andersen version of "Lili Marleen." The two Resistance men took their glasses of wine over to a corner where the noise was loudest, and the Commandant told Miniconi that he had come straight from the Villa Petit-Clos. "Ardouin," he said, "has just received a priority signal from General Koenig in Algiers. They want the railroad cut between Théoule and La Bocca the day after tomorrow."

A few minutes later, Colonel Dussert joined them. The aim of the June 10 operation, he told them, was to halt unusually heavy troop and munitions traffic. In view of the increased patrol activity since the Allies had landed in the North, they agreed, the smaller the sabotage squad, the better its chances of success. The bridges, Dussert said, were too well guarded, even the smallest ones carrying the railroad over streams or irrigation ditches. But there was a sector not far from the mouth of the Siagne where a few well-placed charges of *plastique* could not only destroy the rails but also provoke a rockfall that would effectively block both tracks.

The task, they decided, would best be handled by a small crack team, a nucleus of experienced fighters who knew the terrain intimately. The detail finally chosen comprised five men only: Sam Kadyss, Francis Tonner, Captain Beauregard of AS.24, who had led Tony Isaïa's men in the ADN raid, and two guerrillas from Sam's detachment, whose code names were Papillon and Confiture.

The night of June 10 was moonless and warm. There had been a minor air raid on the freight depot and marshaling yards at Nice–St. Roch earlier in the day, but the noise of distant bombs and the German DCA* barrage wasn't loud enough to drown the din of the cement mixers and compressors engaged in turning the seafront into a fortress wall. Now, during the short summer darkness, there was only the splashing of small waves among the anti-invasion blocks that studded the foreshore.

Between Cannes and La Napoule, the flat coastline bends south in an unbroken shallow curve—a strip of land on which only a

* *Défense Contre Avions*—i.e., antiaircraft batteries.

sidewalk and two walls separate the railroad, the highway, and a narrow, sandy beach. One third of the way around this bay is the suburb of La Bocca, which is itself separated from the Cannes conurbation by a 540-foot, pine-topped eminence known as La Croix des Gardes. Between this hill and the sea, the coastal strip is at its thinnest, and here, on the one rocky outcrop punctuating the monotonous shore, the Germans had built a blockhouse commanding the road for a mile in each direction. Kadyss and his companions therefore had to keep to the landward side of the railroad track until they were well clear of this dangerous area.

They made their way individually to a rendezvous not far from the ADN entrance, where a side road plunged beneath the tracks to link the coastal highway with a shopping street running parallel to it. There were sentries patrolling either side of the bridge, but three trains were due within the next twenty minutes, and the five men dashed underneath as they passed, trusting that the noise would cover the sound of their footsteps. Then it was only a matter of crouching down behind the wall until they were far enough away to cross the road and drop down to the beach. From there on, they moved silently through the sand between the reinforced concrete pyramids and posts.

Silently but not invisibly. They had almost reached the point where they would have to recross the highway in order to get to the section of track chosen for the assault when they heard the sound of booted feet on the pavement above. Twenty yards ahead, a culvert beneath the road fanned a thin stream of moisture across the sand. "Quick!" Beauregard urged in a low voice. "In there and lie low until whoever it is has passed."

He was too late. As they ran forward, they heard a shout, followed by a harsh challenge in German. Not far away, salvage teams were working under floodlights to repair the damage at *Les Aciéries du Nord*. In the reflected light, they could see that a uniformed and helmeted sergeant was leaning over the rail, peering aggressively down at them.

Kadyss was once more carrying Miniconi's Sten gun—affectionately known as Caroline—in pieces beneath his windbreaker. Beauregard, Tonner, and Confiture had Mauser automatics hidden among the packets of *plastique* in their haversacks. Papillon held a looted Schmeisser machine pistol under a voluminous jacket. They must at all costs avoid an identity check and search. "Act a little drunk," Beauregard muttered. "Tell him we've been painting the town red."

The acting wasn't too difficult, especially floundering about in soft sand. The explanation was something else. Through exaggerated mime and gesture and the few words of German they knew, they tried to convey the idea that they were returning from a party. The sergeant was not convinced. In the gloom, they saw him reach suddenly for the revolver holstered at his waist.

Before any of them realized what he was going to do, Papillon whipped up the Schmeisser and fired a short burst point-blank at the German's chest. In the night, the roar of the shots was deafening. The sergeant folded forward over the rail and thumped to the sand. "You cretin!" Francis Tonner swore. "What in hell did you do that for?"

"It was him or us," Papillon said calmly. "What are you going to do: allow one kraut to march five of us off to jail at the point of a revolver?" He leaned down and twitched the dead man's gun from its holster.

"Come on—no arguments," Beauregard said sharply. "What's done is done; now we have to get the hell out and make the railroad before they send a squad to investigate those shots."

Once again he was too late. As they scrambled up and over the rail, light blazed out of the darkness to the southwest and the long finger of a searchlight beam stretched down the highway. They were nearer than they had realized to the Nazi blockhouse guarding the bridge over the Siagne.

"*Run!*" Kadyss yelled. "Over to the other side and across the tracks!"

Down the road, someone shouted. The searchlight beam swung and then steadied. As they sprinted across the macadam and flung themselves down a shallow bank on the far side, the unmistakable hammering of a heavy machine gun sounded. Slugs whistled above their heads and parted the grasses silvered by the searchlight at the top of the bank. Kadyss was assembling the Sten. "Shall I shoot out the goddamn lens?" he panted.

"Don't waste your ammunition. It's way out of range," said Beauregard. He looked over his shoulder. They were at the eastern end of the abandoned golf course, where the highway curved away from the railroad. A hundred yards of undulating, unkempt grass separated them from the tracks. "You were right the first time," he said. "We'll be better off on the far side. That machine gun is fixed in position: they can only follow us with carbines and subs, and at least we can fight on equal terms with those."

Big Sam nodded. "All right, let's go!" he said.

Black shadows swelled and diminished among hillocks beneath the parasol pines as the searchlight swept the disused golf course. The monotonous stammer of the machine gun started up again as they rose to their feet and raced inland, dodging from bunker to bunker, zigzagging across what had once been a fairway. Down toward the river, they heard the tramp of feet and the jingle of equipment: a patrol was being ordered out to hunt for them.

The railroad ran along the top of a shallow embankment here. They would be out of machine-gun range but silhouetted by the searchlight when they crossed it. There was no longer any question of sabotaging the tracks: it was a matter of saving their skins—if they could. "Papillon and I will stop them for a couple of minutes," Kadyss said. "The rest of you get down the other bank, and we'll meet up this side of the farm."

Darker patches of shadow moved now beneath the trees fifty, seventy, ninety yards away. Kadyss and Papillon crouched between bushes below the top of the embankment as Beauregard and the others scrambled up the slope and then wormed their way facedown over the tracks and ties. As soon as the German patrol started firing, they opened up with short bursts from the Sten and the Schmeisser, aiming for the flashes of gunfire between them and the sea. The movement ceased. For a few seconds the old golf course lay silent under the diffused beam of the searchlight. Then the crackle of carbines and submachine guns broke out again from the bunkers where the patrol had found cover.

The two resistants held their fire until the shadowy figures started a second advance. A longer burst at that critical moment, Kadyss figured, would send the Germans diving to the ground, and this would give him and his companion time to hurl themselves over the lip of the embankment while the enemy were still off balance. That was the way it worked out. Flame burst from the muzzles of their guns. The brass casings of ejected shells glinted momentarily as they spun into the light. A frenzied scramble in the sudden ringing si-

lence—the harsh scrape of granite chips against hands and knees
—smooth chill of steel rails—and then the plunge down the far
slope while the patrol's next volley sent bullets whistling over their
heads.

Among the small fields and allotments and occasional greenhouses studding the flat land beyond the railroad, it was not difficult
for guerrillas who knew the terrain to leave the pursuers far behind.
Past windbreaks of bamboo, through the soft earth plowed up beside dry-stone walls, they made their way to a trail leading toward
the Tonner farm. Half an hour later, they joined Beauregard, Confiture, and Francis Tonner on the Pégomas road.

They were four hundred yards short of the farm, creeping in
single file along the grass verge, when they heard movement ahead:
a faint creaking of leather, the smallest metallic jingle. Someone
shifting his position from one foot to the other? Lowering themselves noiselessly to the ground, they began crawling through the
undergrowth.

"*Wer da?*" a deep voice shouted suddenly, alarmingly close. "Who
goes there?"

In the obscurity, Kadyss saw the figures of several German soldiers outlined against the stars. Unwittingly, they had run into some
kind of roadblock. It wasn't the kind of situation you could bluff
your way through. "*Run!*" he shouted for the second time that night
—and almost as a reflex action he sat back on his heels, raised
Caroline to the firing position, and squeezed the trigger.

The gun roared and bucked in his hands. Two Germans fell,
mortally wounded. Then he was on his feet and diving for a low
wall on the far side of the verge. Tonner and the others had already
vaulted over. By the time the soldiers had recovered from the initial
shock, the saboteurs were in a thicket of young oaks, blundering
away from the road as branches whipped their faces. Behind them,
they heard shouts and the sharp crack of rifle fire. Tonner swung
around, dropped on to one knee, and emptied the magazine of his
Mauser in the direction of the road. Behind him, Kadyss aimed the
Sten again, but the mechanism jammed. For an instant, the copse
was illuminated in livid relief as a grenade exploded with a shattering concussion off to their right. They heard shrapnel slicing
through the leaves overhead.

Under their feet, the ground rose as they ran farther into the wood. A second grenade went off; the firing stopped and they could hear men crashing through the undergrowth. Now they were climbing a steep hillside beneath the trees. There was a final, ragged volley from below, then the crack of dry twigs and the swish of saplings, fading as they outdistanced their pursuers.

They came out onto a stretch of open heath, crossed a dirt road, scaled walls, and squirmed under wire fences, sobbing for breath each time they stopped to listen. Only when the progress of the patrol was inaudible did Kadyss and Beauregard call a halt. They were on high ground above the town, beneath parasol pines marking the boundary of the domaine of La Croix des Gardes. Miraculously, none of them had been touched. The worst injuries they had received were scratches from brambles and thorns. "We'll stay here until dawn," Beauregard decided. "We dare not chance our luck a third time in one night! Half the German army must be after us already. We can filter down toward La Bocca and join the day shift as they walk to work. That way we should be able to get back to the farm undetected."

"What about the *plastique*—and the weapons?" Confiture asked.

"We bury them right here under the trees. And come back for them in a couple of nights' time, when the panic is over." Beauregard was absently scraping up the earth with one hand. "That's curious," he said. "It smells kind of bitter, scorched . . . burned almost."

"Don't you remember?" Francis Tonner queried. He gestured toward a further group of pines. Against the paling sky, bare stumps and denuded branches stood stark as the skeletal trees on a battlefield. "This was where the Liberator came down last month . . ."

Flashback VI

May, 1944

GERMAN ANTIAIRCRAFT batteries on the Cap d'Antibes received the red alert at 13 hours 43 on May 25, 1944. Two minutes later, the air-raid sirens were wailing all along the coast from Nice to Fréjus. At 13 hours 50, the drone of approaching aircraft could be heard over the sea. Seconds later, they were visible—a formation of B-24 Liberators flying in from the south at an altitude of 10,000 feet. The batteries opened fire.

It was a sunny day with a cool breeze blowing. Soon the soiled puffs of white marking the shellbursts were being teased out between the tiny silver shapes high in the blue sky. The formation crossed the coast and wheeled through twenty degrees to head inland in a north-northwesterly direction. They must be on their way to attack German troop concentrations at Draguignan, Miniconi thought, glancing out of his living room window. Or perhaps they would wheel again and make a run on Toulon from behind the Massif des Maures. In any case, the All Clear should sound shortly and he could continue marking his essays on the history of the Second Empire.

The drone of aircraft engines faded. And then suddenly the noise increased to a harsh, shuddering roar that jarred the ear and set the inkwells chattering in the desks. Miniconi ran to the window, craning his neck to stare up into the sky. Now there was a long streak of black smudged across the blue. He went out into the garden. It was 13 hours 55.

One of the four-motor bombers had been hit. Both the port engines were on fire and, judging from the angle at which the plume of oily smoke was slanting across the sky, it was losing height rapidly.

The plane passed over the town at about 6,000 feet, limping after the main force in the direction of Draguignan. It turned to the west, and then south as though returning to the ocean. The rackety vibrations of the stricken motors diminished. Clearly, the pilot was looking for a suitable place to crash-land the Liberator.

Miniconi was back in the apartment, speaking urgently into the phone. ". . . as quickly as you can . . . I don't think he's going to make the sea. Watch closely and send as many as you can drum up. See if you can alert a couple of men to keep track of any parachutists: we must try to get to them first and then spirit them away to the Esterel." He hung up the receiver, ran out into the yard, and wheeled his bicycle into the street. The pilot had apparently given up the idea of the sea. Circling as he lost height, he was flying over the town again on another diagonal.

The third time the bomber passed over Cannes it was at less than 1,000 feet, moving perceptibly more slowly, with long streamers of flame now veining the smoke pouring from the dead motors on the port wing. It was lurching toward Mandelieu and the southwest. Of course!, Miniconi thought as he cycled furiously in the same direction—the aviators were trying for the St. Cassien plain; they were determined at all costs not to abandon their ship while it could fall in a densely populated area and sow death and destruction among the French. From a Resistance point of view, the location was perfect: it wouldn't be too far from the Tonner farm, which was the headquarters of the groups based on La Bocca; it was the nearest area to the Esterel, which would make it easier to get the crew away; and it was the farthest from the German barracks on the heights above the town.

That is, if they made the plain. Miniconi glanced over his shoulder as he rode. The Liberator was perilously low, and the laboring motors sounded as though they were about to die. He tried to cram on more speed: there were still two miles to cover before he reached the plain.

At the controls of the bomber, Captain Robert Wornbaker of the United States 464th Bombardment Group, 15th AF, wrestled with the stick and reached for the wheels that operated the trim tabs in an attempt to compensate for the total loss of power on the port side. The ship was wallowing like a whaler in rough seas, shuddering from stem to stern as the remaining engines tried to tear themselves free of their mountings. The near-miss which had crippled them had riddled both wings, destroyed the radio, and shattered several panels in the greenhouse as well as killing the port motors. "Tell the bombardier, the belly gunner, and Tail-end Charlie to quit," Wornbaker shouted into his headset. "They got a better chance out there than they have in this flying boxcar."

Sergeant Lawrence E. Reinecke swung around in the navigator's seat. The two men had flown together since the group was activated in August, 1943. "Okay, Skipper," he yelled above the appalling clamor. "You gonna try for a Chinese three-pointer then?"

Wornbaker nodded. "Can't risk her tumbling into the town. You better bale out, too, son."

"Not on your life, Bob. You and me, we never played the gimper game and I don't figure on starting now. I'll stay with the ship as long as you." Reinecke flipped over the intercom switch to relay the Captain's orders, and then stared helplessly at the dials in front of him. The airspeed indicator was showing something only a fraction over stalling speed, the altimeter needle was sinking remorselessly, and the oil-pressure gauges were a joke in bad taste.

Pedaling up the grade at the beginning of the avenue de Grasse, Curtel saw the three white parachute corollas blossom behind the ailing bomber. At once, a thin crackle of rifle fire and the stutter of machine guns superimposed themselves on the noise of the airplane motors. German soldiers outposted on the heights around the town were shooting at the crewmen as they floated to earth. "Bastards!" Curtel cried aloud. "You callous, murdering sons of bitches!"

Helpless as targets at a fairground stall, the parachutists jerked at their shrouds, swinging from side to side in the hope of avoiding the hail of lead spraying skyward. André Féraud, adjutant of the gendarmerie brigade at Rocheville, stood outside the station house focusing his binoculars. "With this wind, they'll come down between here and Le Cannet, well to the north of the town center," he said to the gendarme Biales. "Call Crétin and Pollien. We'll see if we can intercept them before the huns get there—if they're not full of holes before they land."

A mile and a half away, Miniconi's view of the American plane was cut off by a tall apartment house. The trail of black smoke hung in the sky like a pall.

"Wouldn't you know," Wornbaker said to Reinecke. "We fly seventeen missions strafing long-range targets in Italy, Germany, Greece, Czechoslovakia, you-tell-me. We hit an oil refinery in *Vienna* yet! Without a scratch among us and not a hole blown in the old lady. And then we have to catch a packet on a goddamn milk run they shoulda given to rookies just out of air echelon training in Tunisia!"

"Yeah," Reinecke replied. "Thank God we're just carryin' Smokey Joes instead of the hard stuff. You want me to lower the undercart, Bob?"

"Sure." Wornbaker peered through the starred windshield. "If we can just make that stretch of flat ground near the river . . ."

The port and starboard olios thumped down, almost inaudible over the terrible vibration that seemed to be shaking the ship apart. Wornbaker's knuckles showed white as he clung to the control column. They were less than 500 feet above the palms and the red pantiled roofs racing up to meet them.

"We're losing revs!" Reinecke shouted. The throttles were already fully open. "For Chrissake, Bob! Those pines are pretty damned close!"

Wornbaker leaned back in the pilot's seat, dragging on the stick with all his strength. "Lift up your *nose,* you motherfucker!" he cried.

The needle on the airspeed indicator sank into the red quadrant.

Although it was more than half a mile away, the explosion nearly shook Miniconi from his bicycle. His ears were still ringing from the thunderous detonation when the huge column of smoke boiled darkly into the air. Between Cannes and La Bocca, the Liberator had flown into the high ground at the top of La Croix des Gardes.

He made his way there up the Chemin du Périer—and stopped at the crest, aghast at the scene of desolation that met his eyes. An area almost a hundred yards in diameter had been decimated by the impact. Within this scorched zone, trees had been stripped of their foliage and most of the pines snapped off halfway up their trunks. Twenty feet off the ground, the Liberator's tail assembly was impaled on one of these skeletal spars. A wing and one of the motors had plowed a long trench in the earth beside the road. The rest of the plane was a mangled ruin of twisted metal still smoking among the blazing undergrowth.

Miniconi dismounted and wheeled his machine up to the small crowd of spectators staring helplessly at the holocaust. Curtel and Sam Kadyss were already there, and so was Edmond Pierazzi, one of the auxiliaries Miniconi had recruited from among the local police. "Poor bastards," the policeman said. "There's nothing we can do here." He shook his head and gestured toward the wreckage. The headless body of one of the aviators, still strapped into a seat, lay clear of the flames. The other had been literally torn in two, the torso lodged in the fork of a blasted pine with the entrails hanging down like some obscene fruit.

"They sacrificed themselves to save the town," Miniconi said. "We must see to it later that their heroism doesn't go unrecognized.[14] Right now, we'd better do what we can to help the ones who escaped."

The three parachutists all landed safely between Rocheville and Le Cannet—one in the grounds of the Villa Féa, another on the Franc property, and the third behind the Cottage Sévigné on the Clamens estate. Mercifully, none had been wounded by the rifle and machine-gun fire directed at them as they descended.

Féraud and his three gendarmes split up and hastened toward the landing places. So did Paul Honorat, an *agent* from the police station at Le Cannet. So did a number of resistants belonging to Miniconi's 40th Company. It was lunchtime and most of them were at home. They came by bicycle and on foot. Some, who had already stoked up their *gazogène* motors in preparation for the return to work, came in automobiles. But the Germans were not going to lose their prey as easily as that. From barracks in Le Cannet and Super-Cannes, from the Gestapo headquarters at the Hotel Gallia and from blockhouses in Rocheville and St. Antoine, they roared across town in half-tracks and personnel carriers, throwing a cordon around the sector that was already in place before the patriots arrived. Féraud, Honorat, and the others could only watch impotently while they quartered the area and finally made the inevitable arrests.

"But at least," Big Sam said to Francis Tonner as they hid beneath the charred pines a month later, "we were able to save the Americans' lives."

"How do you mean—save their lives?"

"God knows what they'd have done if we hadn't been around," said Kadyss. "But with all of us standing there looking on, they didn't dare shoot them in public once they were on the ground . . ."

Scene Two

HÉLÈNE VAGLIANO was arrested on Saturday, July 29, 1944. A black Citroën drew alongside as she cycled down the rue d'Antibes on her way to the Mutual Aid Center, forcing her to brake abruptly and pull in to the curb. Two members of Darnand's infamous Militia and two Gestapo men in plain clothes leaped from the car and pulled the girl from her machine. Without a question being asked, without even a demand for her ID papers, she was bundled into the Citroën, her blue-and-white-striped dress torn, her blond hair mussed, and driven away to the Gestapo headquarters at the Hotel Montfleury.

Later in the day, her father and mother were arrested at their house and questioned throughout the afternoon by the same four men. Before dusk, they too were driven to the Montfleury, in an open Mercedes.

Miniconi discovered that the kidnapping of the girl was due—like so many arrests—to a denunciation: a young woman who worked with Hélène Vagliano in the Tartane *réseau* had been unable to withstand the persuasions of the Nazi torturers and had told them everything she knew. The parents were imprisoned as a precautionary measure—and in case they could in some way be used as a lever when the girl herself was interrogated.

For some time before this blow fell, the Côte d'Azur had been the scene of furious activity on the part of both occupiers and resistants. Field Marshal Erwin Rommel had visited the area early in May and pronounced himself dissatisfied with the anti-invasion measures taken by General Friedrich Wiese, the man in charge of the German 19th Army, which defended the coast from the Spanish to the Italian border. As soon as he had gone, Blaskowitz, overall chief of all Hitler's armies in the South, summoned Wiese to a conference at which Wehrmacht sappers and the Todt Organization were instructed to accelerate the building of the *Sudwall* and strengthen its redoubts. Villas, hotels, and restaurants overlooking the shore were bricked up, concreted, and turned into strongpoints. Every beach, creek, and inlet was surrounded by a network of trenches, antitank ditches, machine-gun nests, and emplacements for flamethrowers. The number of blockhouses was increased. Between Nice and Marseille alone more than 600 casemates or isolated batteries were constructed, their armament ranging from 75s and 88s to long-range guns of 340mm. caliber. Along the wilder, uninhabited stretches of coast, mines were sown between rocks and among the scented herbs covering steep banks that plunged into the sea. But any strand that looked remotely suitable for landing craft was protected by three separate lines of defense: first a bed of Rommel's famous "asparagus" (underwater posts supporting 75mm. shells that exploded on contact); secondly, rows of concrete antitank tripods attached to Teller mines; and finally a complex of barbed wire and cheval-de-frise spikes linking huge blocks of stone and scattered with Italian antipersonnel mines.

Nor were these preparations confined to the littoral. Wiese never believed that he would be able to contain a full-scale Allied landing with the limited forces at his disposal. Of the eleven divisions originally comprising the 19th Army, three had already been plundered to bolster Von Rundstedt's crumbling defenses in Normandy. And of the 250,000 men remaining, many were battle-weary veterans of the eastern front, troops who had been wounded and then redirected to active units, or non-Germans press-ganged into service with Hitler's armies. It was unlikely therefore that such a nondescript force would be able to throw back into the sea the half-million trained invaders that Nazi intelligence agents reported avail-able to the Allies. In addition, Wiese's air cover had been reduced to a mere 185 planes, against 5,000 British and American aircraft said to be based on Italy and Corsica. Clearly, then, he had to plan for a defense in depth, and work was started up to twenty miles inland, strewing stretches of level country with antitank obstacles, more strongpoints, minefields, wires designed to cripple glider landings, and sharpened stakes, invisible from the air, which would impale descending paratroops.

All this activity was watched, noted, mapped, collated, and then radioed to Allied intelligence by the estimated 24,000 men and women of the Resistance in the area. The 650-odd members of Miniconi's Groupe Jean-Marie were as busy as any. In addition to relaying information on troop movements, fortifications, munitions, and supplies, there were increasing numbers of Polish and Arme-nian deserters from the Todt Organization and the 148th Infantry Division* to be sheltered and then convoyed to the Maquis units in the Esterel and the Alps. There was, too, an important propaganda operation to be carried out.

On May 26, the day after the Liberator crashed at La Croix des Gardes, a combined force of British and American bombers at-tacked marshaling yards and the St. Roch freight depot in Nice. The raid started at 10:20 in the morning, when the city's work force had long since left home. Official casualty figures were: 283 civilians killed, 499 wounded, and 500 houses destroyed. The day before the sabotage at *Les Aciéries du Nord,* USAF fighter-bombers attacked and partially destroyed the viaduct at Anthéor. Three days later, 27 bombers attacked and destroyed the bridge over the Var River, effectively cutting off St. Laurent, Cagnes-sur-Mer, Antibes, and Cannes from incoming food supplies. In the same week, St. Laurent itself suffered heavy civilian casualties when American medium bombers tried to sink German patrol boats anchored in the estuary. There were rumors, too, of a devastating raid on Marseille—and it was said that, as a punitive measure, the Germans had refused to allow the city authorities to clear the streets or remove bodies from the rubble for burial.

One of the most important tasks facing the Groupe Jean-Marie

---

* The German 242nd Infantry Division defended the coast from Marseille to the Esterel; the 148th was responsible for the sector from there to the Italian border.

and all other Resistance formations was the dissipation of anti-Allied feeling engendered by these raids. It was essential to get across to uncommitted members of the population that the real responsibility for these tragedies lay with the occupiers—and that before they could be defeated it would be necessary to subject the region to heavier raids and even greater trials.

Nevertheless, despite the anger and outrage of those personally affected by the bombing, the general attitude was one of acceptance, almost of relief. Imperceptibly, ever since the news of the Normandy landings, the pendulum had commenced to swing: the tide of battle had turned; victory was now a possibility rather than a dream; fortitude and hope gradually replaced apathy and despair. People rejoiced that at last something positive was being done, and the stories of huge Allied losses carried by the Vichy press were simply not believed: they were liberating the North; who could doubt that soon they would appear in the South as well?

This new mood of faith and expectation translated itself into action in a variety of ways. All over France, the different elements of the Resistance began, so to speak, flexing their muscles. Railroad and factory sabotages multiplied. Electric lines were cut. French Fascists and prominent collaborators were assassinated, German patrols and installations attacked.

There were, of course, terrible reprisals (and it must be remembered that at this time the mere chalking of a V-sign on a wall, or listening to a forbidden broadcast from the BBC, could in certain circumstances merit the death sentence). On June 8, no less than 99 hostages were hanged at Tulle, in the Corrèze, after an SS officer had been shot.[15] Two days later, the same SS division perpetrated the Oradour-sur-Glane atrocity. On the Côte d'Azur, FTPF guerrillas "executed" collaborators, stepped up their attacks on the Marseille–Genoa railroad, dynamited electricity pylons, organized strikes, and bombed a refectory for members of Darnand's hated Militia in the rue Pertinax, Nice. Hostages lost their lives at Gattières, Vence, Utelle, Nice, and in the Verdon region, where five highschool boys were among eleven patriots murdered. Soon afterward, nine more youths were arrested in Nice and a further thirty during a roundup in Vence, which had been a reception center for Jewish refugees before the Germans arrived. Three of the Niçois and twelve of the boys from Vence were deported to concentration camps, where more than half of them died.

At the beginning of July, Maurice Thorez and Jacques Duclos, the leaders of the outlawed Communist party, appealed to all left-wing resistants to prepare themselves for the liberation of their country. Many of the more impatient elements, instead of regarding this as an invitation to cooperate with the Allies, took it as a call to immediate action. Four of the *départements* in the southeast were in open revolt, with armed bands controlling whole towns and villages where the German garrisons were depleted. In the Indre, railroad lines were cut eight hundred times in the month of June; in Brittany, no trains were able to run at all, and the whole of the interior of the peninsula was in the hands of 20,000 *maquisards*.

It was at this time that *all* the Allied intelligence services were placed under the command of General Koenig in Algiers, and the various Resistance formations theoretically amalgamated into the FFI (French Forces of the Interior). In fact, many groups were unwilling to lose their autonomy, others suspected the political motivations of De Gaulle and the Allied High Command, former military *réseaux* refused to take orders from civilians, and right-wing patriots were unable to accept the good intentions of those on the left. The system nevertheless imposed some order on the chaotic Resistance scene and laid the basis for the kind of coordination that was to prove so helpful to Allied forces later. Because the Groupe Jean-Marie now comprised three whole companies, Miniconi— Commandant Jean-Marie, as he was called—was appointed Lieutenant-Colonel in the FFI. Soon afterward, when the FFI's Colonel Voisin was transferred to Nice, he became Chief of Staff for all units east of the Var River—in charge, that is, of an area between Nice and the Esterel, south of the Alpine foothills.

Acting on another tipoff from the Pole, Smilevitch, he authorized a raid on a house at La Roquette-sur-Siagne, between Pégomas and Auribeau, where a detachment of German infantry stored their arms. The operation, carried out on June 20 by members of the third, "exterior," company, gained for the group a quantity of pistols and carbines with a stock of ammunition. But Smilevitch must in some way have been careless, or left a clue pointing to his involvement in the raid. Five days later, his bullet-riddled body was discovered face-down in a ditch beside the road from Cannes to Mougins.

The mystery of exactly how he came to die was never solved. It was logical to assume that the Gestapo were responsible, but it was odd, if that were the case, that he had not been interrogated (the body bore no marks of torture). There was, too, the puzzle of his wife's arrest some weeks before. According to the Pole himself, she had been jailed by the Gestapo—who had then offered to release her against a considerable sum of money. Smilevitch didn't explain how he came by the ransom—which was a sum far in excess of anything he could have raised in his position as a clerk at the OPA —but Madame Smilevitch duly reappeared several days later. There was therefore the possibility that the money had been borrowed from black market contacts in the underworld, and that he had been "put on the spot" because he failed to repay it. What was more likely (Miniconi thought privately) was that Smilevitch had been some kind of double agent, and that his German masters had found out he was crossing them.

At the beginning of July, Vichy security services turned their attention toward Gabriel Davaille, leader of the 4th Detachment in Miniconi's 40th Company. In addition to hiding all the paperwork concerning the Groupe Jean-Marie in his wine shop, Davaille also acted as mail drop for Henri Pourtalet, a prominent Communist living underground in Cannes. There was therefore a quantity of incriminating material on the premises when a squad of militiamen armed with sub-machine guns raided the place early one morning.

Davaille himself had not yet arrived. The personnel were lined up facing a wall, and the French Fascists settled down to wait. After a few minutes, a woman clerk complained that fear had turned her bowels to water: could she go to the toilets on the first floor? The request was refused.

The woman pleaded once more to be allowed to leave the store, and again the militiamen refused. When, in tears, she asked for the third time, the man in charge of the squad relented. Having satisfied himself that there was no rear exit, he gave her permission to go.

Fortunately, nobody accompanied her. The Fascists had not yet searched the premises, and she had already contrived to secrete all the incriminating papers beneath her clothes. In the tiny toilet, she chewed up and swallowed the thicker documents and flushed the others away. Then she opened the small window and called out to passersby in the lane below, beseeching them to wait in the street for Davaille and warn him not to enter the store. Not one of the three men whose attention she drew was prepared to take the risk, and Davaille was arrested.

Gestapo and French security suspicions, however, centered on his relationship with Pourtalet, and since there was now no evidence to connect the two men, Davaille was released three days later, his association with Miniconi's group still a secret.

On July 14, Bastille Day, huge forces of police and Militia, backed by detachments of German infantry, invested the place Masséna in the center of Nice. A command post was set up in the municipal casino. The Maquis, it was said, planned to march on the town from the mountains. No Maquis arrived—but resistants raided the Pasteur hospital, at the other end of town, and freed one of the chiefs of the *Armée Sécrète,* who was lying there under Nazi surveillance. In Cannes, members of the combined Resistance movements marched down the avenue Félix-Faure with the intention of placing a wreath on the war memorial. Vichy police, supported by Militiamen in an armored car, ordered the marchers to disperse. The parade continued and the wreath was laid nevertheless.

The gesture, and the bravado of those who made it, somehow marked a turning point. Imperceptibly, the initiative had passed to the Resistance: now it was the occupiers' turn to look fearfully over their shoulders, wondering how long this state of affairs could last.

Behind Nice and Cannes, armed bands of FFI, wearing berets and tricolor brassards, could be seen on the country roads. Strikes of public employees increased as the food situation worsened. The main post office in Nice was attacked and burned; ration tickets were stolen and distributed in an attempt to cancel out the reductions imposed by Vichy. A German troop train was machine-gunned at Anthéor, waiting its turn to cross the single-track temporary span that sappers had thrown across the damaged viaduct. Then, on July 16, following a request from Koenig's headquarters, Miniconi's 1st Company exacerbated the railroad chaos by cutting the tracks at La Bocca yet again. On the 29th, the day Hélène Vagliano was arrested, the 37th Company of the FTPF, assisted by members of the MOI, came down from the hills and occupied the village of Peillon, in the valley below Miniconi's old home. The action was largely symbolic —they withdrew the next day, in order to spare the inhabitants a bombardment from the Nazi coastal batteries on Mont Agel—but it had a profound effect on local morale and went a long way toward counteracting the effect of increasingly heavy air raids along the coast. Nobody could doubt now that the Allies were on their way. The only questions were, When would they attack—and where?

Colonel Schneider, the officer commanding the 148th Infantry Division stationed in Cannes, Le Cannet, and La Bocca, clearly expected a seaborne assault along the sandy beach below La Croisette. An army of Todt workers toiled in the summer sun, installing rows of sharpened stakes eighteen inches below the calm surface of the water, with half-submerged mines attached to every post. At the same time, Wehrmacht engineers strengthened the fortifications built into hotels and villas along the promenade, and the number of waterfront blockhouses was increased. In addition to the mock-Tudor pavilion on the rocks at La Bocca and a number of emplacements camouflaged as bathing huts and beach cafés, there were now no fewer than five strongpoints opposite the islands on the Pointe de la Croisette, with others at the Corne d'Or swimming pool, the Palm Beach harbor, and the site now occupied by Port Canto.

The whole of the Croisette and all of the strip between the railroad and the ocean was evacuated, the inhabitants being housed in deserted villas among the steep zigzag roads of the Californie residential district to the east of the town. This in fact put them at greater risk than if they had been permitted to stay nearer the shore, because the biggest blockhouse of all was situated by the Col St. Antoine—a pass carrying departmental Route 803 across the wooded ridge above La Californie. And the big naval guns behind the Col St. Antoine casemates, dominating the whole of Cannes and the beaches as far as La Napoule, were now the target for frequent raids by British and American fighter-bombers. So far, the sunken, armored bunkers, 600 feet above sea level, had escaped damage, but civilian casualties on the surrounding slopes were high.

On July 31, Hélène Vagliano was transferred to the Gestapo headquarters in Grasse. A red-haired inquisitor burned her breasts, back, arms, neck, cheek, and chin with a hot smoothing iron in an attempt to make her reveal the names of fellow resistants in the Tartane *réseau* and details of how it worked. Her mother and father were lodged in adjacent cells, in the hope that the sound of her screams would persuade them to part with the same information. In fact, the parents knew nothing of her clandestine activities, and the girl herself withstood the torture and revealed nothing.

Three days later, the Vaglianos were taken to the military prison in Nice. That evening, the Allied air forces stepped up the weight and frequency of their raids to preinvasion level. Nice and Cannes were attacked on August 3, 4, 6, 7, and 8. On the 6th, 360 tons of bombs were dropped in an eight-hour assault on Toulon; the following day, a force of 300 bombers hit targets all the way from Monte Carlo to Montpellier; the 10th and 11th saw German radar installations pulverized; and on the two following days, succeeding waves of aircraft followed each other so quickly that the authorities stopped sounding the sirens—the Riviera was on continuous alert.

"In the blue August sky," an eyewitness recalled, "formation after formation of silver planes no longer contented themselves flying overhead with that majestic indifference which until now had only drawn the glances of the curious: now the whole coast was itself attacked, point by point. Little by little, the fires caused by the explosions coalesced and huge eruptions of black smoke rose menacingly behind the rocky scarps. . . . Thunderbolts and Liberators staged a veritable rodeo over Cap St. Pierre, near St. Tropez, and above the tiered vine terraces of Ste. Maxime Allied aircraft making the most fantastic maneuvers seemed to be playing cat-and-mouse with the coastal batteries, shooting up minefields and blockhouses, showering the corniches with explosions of water and flame, brewing up colors that even our skies had never known until that day."*

On August 14, along a front of 40 miles, 244 Mitchells and Marauders attacked German positions in the Esterel; four-engined bombers of the RAF blasted Nazi airfields and depots; American 12th Air Force Liberators blocked German reinforcements mustered near Genoa; and radar stations were once more strafed by Spitfires and Lightnings piloted by Free French flyers.

Two sets of figures suffice to underline the intensity of the bombardment: Between April 28 and August 10, 1944, Allied aircraft flew more than 10,000 sorties over the Côte d'Azur and dropped 12,500 tons of bombs; yet the five days after August 10 alone saw a further 5,000 tons dropped.

During the hideous clamor of these raids, when for almost a week most of the population remained hidden in cellars, without food, water, or light, Hélène Vagliano was taken each day from the German military prison in Nice to the Gestapo headquarters at the Villa

* Quoted by Jacques Robichon in *Le Débarquement de Provence,* Série: Ce Jour-Là, Robert Laffont, Paris, 1965. (Translation mine.)

Trianon. There, the same red-headed Gestapo agent daily interrogated her, still demanding a confession that she was a "spy," still demanding details of her "accomplices" and their work. It is hard to understand why the Nazi torturers persisted in their unsavory task: they must have known that an invasion was imminent and that they would have no opportunity to use the information, even if they got it. For two weeks nonetheless the girl was subjected to a series of atrocious treatments which included beating, more burning, and—according to one reliable witness—the actual boiling of her hands.

At the Hotel Montfleury in Cannes, equally bestial tortures were practiced on Conchita Biacca, Pierre Chalmette, Georges Krengel, and five other resistants working for the MUR, named Biny, Albertini, Séguran, Froidurat, and Martini.

Despite the inhuman severity of her injuries, Hélène Vagliano betrayed nothing and nobody. On August 14, however, in order to obtain the release of her father and mother, she signed a confession that she herself had acted as a courier and sent radio messages for a British network. With the confession, which she knew was tantamount to her own death warrant, she supplied a list of fictitious names and nonexistent addresses purporting to be her contacts all over France.

On the same day, among the hundreds of sorties flown by the RAF was a low-level attack on the viaduct at Anthéor. Previous raids by the Americans—including the one that cut the tracks—had been oriented laterally, the flyers making their approach at right angles to the bridge. The British fighter-bombers followed the curving line of the railroad, and this time direct hits on the structure were scored: two of the viaduct's nine great arches were destroyed; the last vestiges of rail traffic on the coast were halted. Monsieur and Madame Vagliano, exhausted, hungry, and fearful for the life of their daughter, were obliged to walk the sixteen miles from the military prison to their home in Cannes.

Fifty miles to the north, leaders of the ORA, the AS, and the FTPF met in secret at Beuil, a small town near the ski resort of Valberg, 4,500 feet above sea level. An FFI general staff was established, and all resistants in the region were warned to listen to their radios and stand by for action.

The call came that same night. Straining to distinguish the voice from London over the susurrus of Nazi jamming, Miniconi and

Claire leaned close to the Arcor radio and heard the general news bulletin, a report on the insurrection in Paris, and communiqués on Soviet successes and Allied advances in Normandy. Then came the so-called "personal messages"—those apparently nonsensical statements that were in fact full of coded meaning for those leading an underground existence. *Gaby is sleeping on the grass . . . Nancy has a stiff neck . . .*

Miniconi clasped his wife's hand. Throughout the South, the pulses of 24,000 resistants quickened. It had come at last: the signal for which they had waited so long. The Allies would be landing tomorrow!

Scene Three

COLONEL SCHNEIDER'S beach defenses in Cannes were not after all tested when the Allies invaded the South of France on August 15, 1944. General Patch's 7th American Army, and the French 1st Army led by General de Lattre de Tassigny, ten divisions in all, landed along a 35-mile stretch of coast east of Toulon, an area of sandy bays and rockbound creeks backed by the wooded hills of the Maures and the Esterel. An eleventh division, airborne, was dropped inland around the town of Le Muy. Miniconi's Groupe Jean-Marie therefore had nothing to do with the actual establishment of the beachhead: the nearest disembarkation point was several miles beyond La Napoule, and Maquis formations from the mountains were on hand to guide the invaders and liaise between airborne and seaborne forces. There were, however, a great many other problems to be tackled.

Foremost among these was the organization of the three companies so that they could most usefully be employed once the tide of battle did surge around the town. Allied to this were arrangements for the distribution of arms from the Villa Fiésole, and contingency plans for the occupation of key positions when the liberation of

Cannes became a possibility. Curiously, it was a relatively minor point that caused the most headaches. All FFI formations had been instructed, once the time came to move out into the open, to identify themselves with tricolor armbands overstamped with the Cross of Lorraine. This would enable Allied troops to distinguish them from collaborators or ordinary inhabitants, or, it was hoped, permit them to be recognized as military prisoners rather than spies or *franc-tireurs* if they fell into German hands. Claire Miniconi had agreed to provide these brassards for the 650 members of her husband's group; but when it came to making them, the difficulty of obtaining some 240 *yards* of blue-white-and-red material without raising the suspicions of shopkeepers in a time of catastrophic shortage taxed the ingenuity of the young Frenchwoman to the utmost. It was only after a modiste in the group had unearthed a stock of prewar dyes, and other women had sacrificed precious sheets and pillowcases, that the full number of armbands could be completed.

The most important of all the tasks facing Miniconi was perhaps the need to silence the batteries firing from the blockhouse at the Col St. Antoine. The casemates on the heights above La Californie had been attacked daily by twin-boom Lightnings of the Free French and the American air forces, but so far both the guns and their redoubts had escaped damage. Now they were being assaulted from the sea as well. Six battleships, four carriers, 21 cruisers, and more than 100 destroyers had escorted the 500 transports and 1200 smaller craft engaged in the landings. Once the troops were ashore, 27 of these warships had quit the main force and taken up station between the Iles de Lerins and La Napoule, and shells from their turrets had joined the bombs bursting among the pines around the blockhouse. Civilian casualties in the area were already heavy. If a continued massacre of the population was to be avoided, the strong-point had to be rendered inoperative so that the Allied raids would cease.

But so long as there were several thousand Wehrmacht men quartered in La Californie, it was clearly hopeless for the Resistance to attempt a direct frontal attack on the batteries and their 30-strong crew. Even if Miniconi were to throw in all the available men from his three companies, they wouldn't stand a chance against four or five battalions of motorized infantry. For the moment, the best he could do was wait and hope that his agents could give him a line on the intentions of the German military. His most fruitful source of intelligence here was Toinette Marcoux. He had already instructed her to be as pleasant as she could to the occupiers who patronized the Taverne Royale; now he asked her to be doubly sympathetic, in the hope that the officers would confide in her.

For the first few days after the invasion, however, the garrison in Cannes seemed to be as much in the dark as the inhabitants. Colonel Schneider was not the only German to have been misled about the exact location of the landings. The huge invasion fleet, assembled off Corsica from points of departure as far apart as Naples, Oran, Palermo, Taranto, and Malta, had of course been spotted and then tracked for three days by Luftwaffe reconnaissance planes. But its maneuvers on the 13th and 14th led the Nazi High Command to believe that they faced a two-pronged assault on Marseille and Genoa. The deception was fostered by false information leaked to German intelligence agents; by flocks of rubber mannequins parachuted from troop transports over the mouth of the Rhône; by the release of tens of thousands of metal-foil streamers which fooled what was left of the German radar into registering the approach of an air armada over Toulon; and, above all, by a deliberate pattern in the preinvasion bombing. When the fleet changed course under cover of darkness and the landing craft surged in toward the beaches at Cavalaire and St. Raphael and Dramont and Anthéor, the defenders were therefore taken almost entirely by surprise, and by the time the August heat haze lifted in the middle of the morning, many of the primary objectives had already been taken. Winston Churchill, watching the assault on Pampelonne Beach, near St. Tropez, from the bridge of the US destroyer *Kimberley,* reported that the warships were no longer firing when the sun broke through the mist because the shore defenses were offering no opposition.

Things were less quiet nearer Cannes, and the earth shook all day with the thunder of distant artillery as Germans and Americans battled for possession of the beaches at Agay and Dramont. One of the toughest fights of all was over the tiny inlet of Anthéor, where Oerlikons firing from each side of the breached viaduct kept the attackers at bay until late in the afternoon of the 15th.

But the most unfortunate and unluckiest unit in the invasion force was one of French naval commandos landed at two o'clock in the morning on the Pointe d'Esquillon, only four miles from La

Napoule—the nearest the assault came to Cannes itself. Each of the 67 men in the group carried a tommy gun and sixty pounds of Melinite explosive. Their mission was to scramble up the rocky scarp of the Esterel and to blow up, first, the coastal highway and then Route 7, five miles inland, so that the Germans would be unable to rush reinforcements to the beleaguered defenders farther west.

Last-minute information radioed to the Allied High Command by the local Resistance tagged the point as one of the few areas around the Esterel that was free of mines. But during the 24 hours between the sending of the signal and the commandos' arrival, German sappers had laid a minefield among the red sandstone outcrops of the headland. Eleven of the commandos were killed instantly and a further seventeen horribly wounded. Marooned in the darkness with death all around him, the sole surviving junior officer was forced to surrender in order that the lives of the remaining men could be spared and the injured removed to a hospital.

The officer and the senior NCO were taken by armored car to the German Divisional HQ in Grasse, where intelligence officers questioned them at length in an attempt to discover where the main weight of the invasion was to fall (they maintained that it was at Port Vendres, near the Spanish frontier). The rest of the commandos were to march to Grasse under armed escort—a sad and humiliating return to their native land.

It was suffocatingly hot. Above the forest of mimosas crowning the Montagne de Tanneron, humidity still hazed the blue of the sky. The thirty-odd prisoners of war were exhausted after the terrors of their sleepless night. They had covered just over half the nine miles separating them from their destination when the column overtook an elderly peasant woman carrying a basket on her head. It was not clear whether the woman was deaf—and therefore astonished suddenly to see a crowd of soldiers swing into view—or whether she simply tried too hastily to get out of their way. In any event, she appeared to lose her balance, and suddenly the basket was on the ground and there were apples and tomatoes rolling across the dusty roadway.

Ignoring angry shouts from the escort platoon, one of the commandos who broke step to help the woman retrieve her precious cargo was astounded to hear her whisper, "Watch out—the Boche are going to be fired on. The Resistance will set you free in the middle of the wood around the next corner . . ."

Before the Frenchman could pass the message on, the old woman, still grumbling and swearing, had climbed a stile and taken a footpath across the fields. A few hundred yards farther on, not far from the village of Auribeau, a fusillade of revolver shots erupted from a thicket at the side of the road. Two of the Wehrmacht men at the head of the column spun around and slumped to the ground. The others unslung carbines, drew pistols, and returned the fire. The commando who had helped the old woman collect her fruit jumped over a low stone wall, followed by several of his companions; the remainder of the prisoners flung themselves flat in a ditch.

For a few minutes, as the wood echoed with the sound of small-arms fire and the sunbeams penetrating the branches became veiled with blue smoke, the lane resembled the last reel of a Western. Among the trees, Francis and Fernand Tonner, with four other members of the AS.24 action group, called urgently to the prisoners as they shot up the escort. The two brothers were supported by Pierre Borghese, Lucien Albis, and Raymond Barbéris of La Roquette-sur-Siagne, and by Humbert Giordamengo of Mandelieu, who had seen the column pass and hurried to the Tonner farm to organize the ambush.

Borghese and Fernand Tonner were both wounded in the head during the skirmish, and two more men from the German platoon were injured. But before the Resistance fighters ran out of ammunition and were obliged to break off the encounter, ten of the commandos had been rescued, several carbines and pistols had been snatched from the fallen Nazis, and the wounded guerrillas were safely carried away.

The rescued men, one of whom had been slightly injured, were hidden at the Tonner farm. Two days later, a man from Pégomas who knew every track and bridle path in the Esterel as well as he knew his own back yard led them by a roundabout route to the American lines behind Fréjus.

But the ambush at Auribeau was not the only drama to be played outside the battle zone. At about the same time that Francis Tonner gave his group the order to fire, a similar command was being given in very different circumstances six miles to the southeast. Conchita Biacca, Pierre Chalmette, and the six other members of the MUR imprisoned by the Gestapo at the Hotel Montfleury were taken out into the yard at three o'clock in the afternoon and killed with a single volley from the execution squad.

In Nice, an unknown voice had cried outside the window of Hé-lène Vagliano's cell, "The Allies have landed at Fréjus! The Allies have landed at Fréjus!" The voice was abruptly stifled, but the message had penetrated the jail. There were shouts of acclaim from all around. Maimed and emaciated, Hélène clung to her cellmate, whose name was Lucie, and cried aloud, "They're here! I don't care what happens now: my work is finished; they're here at last!" Weeping, the two girls held hands and sung the "Marseillaise."

When, at three o'clock again, they came for her, Hélène removed an enameled clip from her dress and handed it, together with a pair of earrings, to her friend. "Keep these for me, Lucie," she said. "If I don't come back, give them to my mother . . . and tell her not to be sad: I did what I wanted to do."

There were twenty-one other prisoners in the jailhouse yard, among them two teenage girls, two schoolboys, a chaplain, and a young blond nurse in a state of great distress. All of them were herded into a black prison van. As they drove out through the gates, Hélène was doing her best to calm the nurse. "They landed at Fréjus this morning!" she kept repeating.

Instead of turning right, in the direction of the Villa Trianon, the van turned left and headed out of town. There were two French militiamen with the Gestapo agents in the black Citroën that followed it.

Half an hour later, they stopped by a vacant lot in l'Ariane, a suburb three miles to the northeast of the city. The wasteland was bounded on one side by a steep hill, on the other by a dried-up river between shingle banks. A peasant and his daughter, working in a nearby field, saw the arrival of the convoy and hurried back to their cabin, beyond a footbridge on the far side of the river. Through the slats of their closed shutters they saw three machine guns set up near the far end of their garden.

"All the prisoners were lined up," Hélène Vagliano's mother wrote later. "Soldiers from neighboring barracks advanced to receive their orders. Some of them crossed the bridge and took up position behind the machine guns. You, my darling, stood next to the priest, with the little nurse on your left and then another girl. They made you wait, motionless, while your tormentors exchanged pleasantries: the echo of their laughter was audible on the far side of the river. The farmer had closed all his shutters now, and his daughter was praying. There was a sudden crackle of machine-gun fire, then the dry snap of revolvers, the sound of cries brusquely strangled.

"Later, much later, the Vichy police came to remove the bodies. One of them fainted, for several of the victims, who had at the last minute attempted to escape, had been cruelly shot in the back.

"You, my little Hélène, had not moved. The farmer told me that you held your small head very high and looked away into the distance, toward the top of the hill where, above a miniature church all in white, the Cross shone in the sun.

"You fell like a wounded bird . . . your bruised face, defiled by the executioners, lost in your bloodied hair."*

Unless it was to silence possible witnesses to Gestapo atrocities, it is difficult, again, to understand the reasons for these senseless massacres. Neither Nice nor Cannes was directly threatened as yet, but the Allied bridgeheads were mushrooming inland and it was clearly only a matter of time before they were attacked. The Germans must have known that their days on the coast were numbered.† There was no point, therefore, in regarding the executions as deterrents. Yet in the enclaves so far untouched by the invasion, repression by the occupiers became more pitiless than ever.

For this reason, Miniconi frowned upon unplanned, unpremeditated actions like the ambush at Auribeau, and he gave strict orders that members of his own group must lie low—and above all carry no arms—until the signal was given for the Resistance as a whole to rise up and take action. There were always hotheads to be reckoned with, nevertheless, no matter how disciplined a unit might be. Two such men, Gabriel Berrone and Charles Costa, decided on August 18 to stage a private war against the Wehrmacht. Berrone was in fact the leader of Javel's Detachment in the 1st Company of Destruction at La Bocca; Costa was in command of the Company's 4th Detachment.

The ADN workshops were on strike. The freight yards had been

* In a privately printed booklet titled *Hôtes de la Gestapo (Guests of the Gestapo).* (Translation mine.)

† As early as May 27, the Militia headquarters in Nice circularized members in the Cannes region with a warning that aerial bombardments, or "coastal alerts," were to be expected. Militiamen must be prepared, with their families, for "a hurried departure at any time," the circular said.

wrecked by bombs. In the center of town there was now a total curfew: women only were permitted on the streets for two separate hours each day to shop for provisions—if they could find any. Above the deserted squares, shells whistled from the offshore warships and the batteries at the Col St. Antoine. It seemed a good time, Berrone and Costa thought, to increase the arsenal at the Villa Fiésole.

Prowling behind the railroad embankment near *Les Aciéries,* where the highway, the tracks, and a thin strip of sandy shore ran side by side, they surprised a soldier in field gray carrying four carbines and a canvas bag with grenades in it toward the blockhouse at the Pointe de La Bocca. It was an opportunity too good to be missed. The German was held up under the menace of their Mausers and relieved of his burden.

A double problem then arose: how were they going to dispose of the arms in broad daylight, and what could they do with the Wehrmacht man meanwhile?

Neither Costa nor Berrone had the courage to shoot the sweating and fearful German in cold blood. They decided to seek help from their superiors: both Raybaud and Tosello, their Company Commander and his Number Two, lived nearby. In the meantime, they stowed the weapons in a platelayers' hut by the railroad and—after some discussion—decided to bind and gag their prisoner and lock him in with them.

Lightning fighter-bombers were attacking the Col St. Antoine when they came out into the sunshine, and the afternoon was loud with the clamor of antiaircraft gunfire and bursting shells. Dodging from doorway to doorway, they made their way toward the St. Joseph residential quarter. But neither Raybaud nor Tosello was at home. The two guerrillas would have to deal with their problem on their own.

An hour later, they returned to the hut and unlocked the door. A small window at the back had been smashed and then ripped from its frame—and the German had gone.

Berrone and Costa turned to run. They were too late: the place was already surrounded by a Wehrmacht patrol. Identified by their former captive, the two resistants were marched outside, stood against the squared-off limestone blocks forming the wall at one side of the railroad, and immediately shot. Their bodies were left lying by the iron railings between the sidewalk and the beach.

Not far away, a third patriot, named Barbier, a railroad worker like Berrone and Costa and a member of the FER *réseau,* was arrested and shot in the rue des Mûriers.

The following day, August 19, a section of the third "exterior" company ignored Miniconi's instructions to lie low and his call for prudence. Led by Palanca and Thomas, the Company Commander and his aide, they attacked a German squad preparing defensive positions near La Roquette-sur-Siagne. The aim of the operation was apparently to annihilate the Germans and take their arms, but the plan went badly wrong. The Resistance fighters were outmaneuvered, beaten off, and dispersed. Palanca and Thomas were captured. Later in the day they were executed and their bodies left by the roadside between La Roquette and Auribeau.

It was in an attempt to find out exactly what had happened—and in particular to discover whether the two men had been interrogated before they were shot—that Curtel offered to investigate the next day. "All right," Miniconi said. "But take three good men with you . . . and for God's sake go unarmed!"

Curtel left before dawn on the 20th. He was accompanied by Teyssier, Ferraris, and Vietto, who had been a famous racing cyclist before the war. There was no zooming along the roads of the St. Cassien plain today, however. The four men arrived in the tiny *place* at Auribeau at 7 A.M. They had only just dismounted from their machines when three armed Gestapo men in plain clothes materialized from an alley and demanded their papers.

Judging by the questions they asked, the Germans too were investigating the dramatic events of the previous day. Since their papers showed that they lived in the center of Cannes, Curtel and his three companions were safe from suspicion. They said they had ridden out into the country in the hope of finding a farmer who would sell them black market vegetables. All went well until the Gestapo men started to search them. Curtel, Vietto, and Teyssier were clean, but Ferraris had disobeyed Miniconi's orders: there was a revolver concealed in the saddlebag of his bicycle.

He was immediately arrested. The others were told to be on their way.

Curtel arrived at Miniconi's apartment in the avenue du Grand-Pin at noon to report the arrest.

Miniconi was furious when he heard what had happened. "How many times do I have to tell these fools that I know what I'm doing?"

he raged. "Why can't they understand that I have good reasons whenever I give an order?" He sighed, shaking his head. "Now we shall have to mount a special operation to try and spring the bastard before they put him inside. Where did they take him, do you know?"

Curtel thought the arrested man had been taken into the Mairie at Auribeau. "But he could be anywhere by now," he said glumly. "We'll have to hope that Teyssier can get some inside information from Fauré and the other boys in the police group." But the two men had scarcely begun to consider the possibilities open to them before there was a code knock on the outer door. Frossart, the "man of teak," was filling the hallway. "Ferraris is hiding in my cellar," he announced.

"But . . . ? In the name of—! But what *happened?*" Miniconi sputtered.

Ferraris, it seemed, had played a true poker hand, and won. He had pretended complete ignorance of the gun in his saddlebag. He had never looked in the saddlebag in his life, he said. And when the Gestapo men had asked—in somewhat rougher terms—how come, he had said because the bicycle wasn't his.

"What do you mean, not yours? Whose is it?"

"I don't know."

"Don't give me that!" the senior Gestapo officer shouted. "How can you not know?" He seized the Resistance man by the lapels. "Answer me!"

"I stole the bike this morning," Ferraris said calmly. "I don't know whom it belonged to. I'm in the black market and you take what you can get."

The German stared at him. "Where did you steal it? Who was there?"

Ferraris played his trump card. "I stole it from a group of terrorists at La Bocca. They were so busy talking, nobody noticed me take it."

Suddenly the Gestapo agents were very interested. How many terrorists were there? How did he know they were terrorists? What were they talking about?

Ferraris said there were about a dozen. He knew they were terrorists because they had weapons. They had been saying something about a blockhouse on La Croisette . . . something about a quantity of *plastique* . . . he hadn't really paid attention because he was anxious to get the bike.

All at once, Ferraris found that the Gestapo were no longer concerned with him. After questioning him closely about the number and appearance of the "terrorists," and insisting that he specify exactly where he had seen them, they got into a car and drove rapidly away toward the coast. Ferraris jumped on his bicycle and pedaled hell-for-leather back to Cannes. "He dared not go home," Frossart said, "because the Boches had taken his name and address —and once they discovered there weren't any terrorists, and there wasn't a plot to bomb the blockhouses on the Croisette . . ." He paused and shrugged his shoulders significantly. "So he figured he'd better drop out of circulation. That's why he came to me. The thing is—what are we going to do with him?"

"I'll make arrangements to have him taken up to the Esterel Maquis tonight," Miniconi said. "He's best out of the way until it's all over."

"Ferraris is not the only one either," Frossart went on. "An old Party member phoned Davaille at his store this morning and tipped him off that the damned Militia are after him again—and this time they mean to put him away for sure. He skipped just in time too, and came over to me."

Like Frossart, Davaille was a Detachment leader in the 40th Company, commanded by Curtel—an invaluable man at a time of crisis like this. "Can you do anything for him?" Curtel asked. "I'd rather he didn't disappear into the Esterel right now. If there's anything . . . ?"

Frossart nodded. "I know folks with a big house in La Californie."

"Good," Miniconi said briskly. "I'll leave that to you then. Curtel and I have to go to an important meeting downtown."

The meeting was in fact historic. It took place in the basement of the Vauban Garage. The four men seated around a deal table on upturned packing cases were Miniconi, Curtel, Vahanian, the acting head of AS.24 and the MUR, and his assistant, Tony Isaïa. The purpose of the conference was to apportion zones of responsibility, so that there would be no overlapping and no querying of orders when the time came for the Resistance to act.

The instructions to be discussed were contained in a document headed *Plan of Occupation and Protection to Be Used in Case of Departure by Occupation Troops*, dated July 25, 1944. Originating from General Koenig's headquarters in Algiers, the plan had been relayed to Miniconi and other group leaders by the FFI General Staff at Beuil.

Now that the Allied beachheads were firmly established, it seemed that the time had come to put it into operation.

The aim of the plan in its broadest sense was to enable each Resistance unit "to take over effective control of its sector and to maintain order therein." To this end, all government posts and positions of authority were to be occupied by officials authorized by Koenig's headquarters, public services were to be restored, Allied forces in the neighborhood were to be aided by the FFI, and any attacks by Vichy forces repulsed. In particular, the document said, Resistance forces must:

> (a) OCCUPY vital public service installations such as waterworks, gas and electricity supplies, post offices, railroads, bridges, and police stations;
> (b) KEEP WATCH over, and if necessary protect by force, food stores, refrigeration plants, gasoline dumps, and banks;
> (c) SEARCH all premises previously occupied by Germans or collaborationist groups;
> (d) SEEK OUT and arrest (or kill in the case of resistance) all Germans still in the area, whether in uniform or plain clothes;
> (e) KEEP ORDER in the streets; arrest or shoot any trouble-makers, especially all looters caught in the act.

The three-page document also specified, among other points, that: revenge killings and reprisals were expressly forbidden (collaborators would stand trial later in properly constituted courts); Vichy authorities were to be given the chance to cooperate before any overt action was taken; violence was to be avoided unless absolutely necessary; captured Germans and Militia were to be interned in suitable camps and their leaders jailed. Resistance chiefs were nevertheless warned strongly to make certain that German troops in their sectors were in full retreat before any of these steps were taken, since any return of the occupation forces could "result in terrible reprisals on the civilian population." The signal for Resistance forces to go into action was to be a continuous, uninterrupted sounding of the air-raid sirens for fifteen minutes. Thus the capture of the posts from which the sirens were controlled would be a first priority for all groups.

A second document, dated the same day, requested group leaders to inform FFI headquarters as accurately as possible of the strength and disposition of forces under their command.

Miniconi undertook to pass on these instructions to networks operating in Antibes, Cagnes-sur-Mer, St. Laurent, and other towns in the area east of the Var River for which he was Chief of Staff. He and Vahanian then decided how their respective groups would organize the liberation of Cannes. Fortunately, the geographical division of the area was simple. Miniconi produced a map that was printed on the back of a restaurant menu and drew a thick red line down the length of the boulevard Carnot, which bisected the town center from north to south. It was agreed that neighborhoods to the west of this line, including Rocheville and La Croix des Gardes, would be the responsibility of the MUR and the FER *réseau,* while Miniconi's 40th FTPF handled the east. The 1st Company of Destruction was assigned St. Joseph and La Bocca; and the line of villages behind the ridge sheltering Cannes inland—Auribeau, Pégomas, La Roquette, and Mougins—would be left to the third company.

The four men emerged from the basement at five-minute intervals. Out in the bay, the French cruiser *Montcalm* had steamed up from St. Tropez and was now shelling with impeccable accuracy the German batteries below Grasse, in the Alpine foothills.

That night, Toinette Marcoux learned from Colonel Schneider that the Gestapo were preparing to evacuate the Hotel Montfleury. Elements of the 148th Division, she was told, were also about to be withdrawn from Cannes to strengthen the garrison in Nice. The information was passed on to Miniconi the following day, and he in turn reported it to the radio liaison at the Villa Petit-Clos.

The German infantry were not the only foreigners to be leaving Cannes. For many months Miniconi had been arranging the safe passage of a steady trickle of Poles, Armenians, and Hungarians who wished to desert from the Todt Organization or flee the ranks of the army they had been forced to join. He had found an invaluable helper in Mme. Kasimiera Wdziconski, an émigrée Polish interpreter who lived near his school at Le Suquet, and on one occasion they had between them engineered the escape to the Maquis of an entire Polish platoon, complete with their weapons, from a Nazi unit stationed at Le Trayas, near Anthéor. Another time, not long before the Allied landings, Curtel was driving a *gazogène* away from Mme.

Wdziconski's house when he was stopped by a Vichy police patrol. "What are you carrying in that truck?" the officer demanded when he had examined Curtel's papers.

Miniconi's Number Two glanced at the man from beneath lowered brows. With an invasion expected any day, there was an even chance that he would be sympathetic. "Merchandise," he said briefly.

There were in fact a dozen Poles beneath the canvas top of the truck, and a small store of carbines, grenades, and pistols. "Let's have a look," the officer said.

Curtel swallowed. He got down from the cab. "I told you," he repeated. "Just merchandise."

"Open it up."

Curtel twitched aside the curtain above the tailgate. "Have you seen enough?" he asked meaningly.

The policeman looked briefly at the twelve pairs of eyes glaring at him out of the gloom. Then he turned away. "You'd better get going: that's perishable stuff," he said.

Another Polish woman who had been of great help, hiding refugees and then handing them over to guides who would escort them to the Esterel, was Madame Soden, who lived at the Mas St. Antoine, just across the road from the German batteries below the Col. The Mas was an old farmhouse which, excepting blast damage to the windows, had remained miraculously untouched by the shelling. From its stone-walled courtyard on the morning of August 22, Madame Soden stole down toward the network of steep streets zigzagging through the Californie neighborhood. She had a message for Miniconi that was perhaps the most unexpected of any he received that dramatic summer.

Many of the big houses in the quarter were damaged. Branches torn from pines and eucalyptus and mimosa lay across the roadway, and there was a burned-out automobile perforated by shrapnel lying on its side in the avenue de Vallauris. But the shelling had stopped, cicadas were rasping in the hot sun, and somewhere beyond a cypress hedge Madame Soden could hear the laughter of children evacuated from the town below. She found the man she was looking for among a dozen families camping in the grounds of a derelict mansion. She gave him the message.

An Austrian by the name of Victor Turderer had come to the

farm that morning with two friends. He was the NCO in charge of the gun crews at the Col St. Antoine—and he and his friends wanted to desert. What should they do and where could they go?

Madame Soden sat down in the shade of a jacaranda tree to wait for the reply to her message. She gazed over shattered roofs of red tiles toward the sea. Out on the blue water, the anchored warships looked as inoffensive as toys in a shop window: even the salvos from the *Montcalm,* still firing at the German guns in Grasse, sounded scarcely louder than the bees humming around the neglected roses. "It's terrible, the shelling," said a woman in black nearby. "There were fifteen dead yesterday. Why don't they realize . . . ?"

It was an hour and a half before the courier returned, and by then the Lightnings had started their daily assault. This time the Col was spared and a gasoline dump at Antibes was the target. A huge tower of black smoke stood against the sky to the east. The three Austrians were not to desert, Commandant Jean-Marie said. It would be better if they took possession of the blockhouse and surrendered it to the Resistance. A detachment would be sent as soon as possible. Madame Soden got to her feet and began the long walk back to the Col.

Miniconi delegated the task to Frossart and Davaille, the two 40th Company Detachment leaders whose territory, under the plan agreed with Vahanian, was centered on La Californie. The "man of teak," furthermore, would already be in the area fixing up Davaille's new hideout.

Each of the Detachment commanders took with him a full section of thirteen men—the first time such a large group of Resistance fighters had dared to appear openly in Cannes during the daytime, and the first time any of them had worn the FFI "uniform" of beret and tricolor brassard.

German troops falling back on Nice seemed mainly to have been withdrawn from the heights above the old Gestapo headquarters at the Hotel Gallia, and the neighborhood was surprisingly free of field gray and gutturals. They had been warned nevertheless to be extra careful, and the routes to the Col chosen by Frossart and Davaille could have served as textbook examples of guerrilla tactics. From the bluff behind the Villa Fiésole, where pistols and grenades were issued to the men of each section and submachine guns to their leaders, they climbed diagonally upward through thickets and gardens and stretches of private park. As the fierce midday heat was dissipated by a thin veil of cirrus spreading over the sky from the west, they scaled walls, skirted the big Victorian houses, and moved silently through shrubberies, never staying in the open longer than was necessary to gain the next piece of cover or sprint across one of the roads looping up the ridge. Davaille and his men were to approach the blockhouse from Super-Cannes, slightly above and to the east of the Col; Frossart's section would advance from the other side, under cover of the woods fringing the Chemin des Collines, which ran along the crest.

Gabriel Davaille lay beneath a mastic tree near the water tower that crowned the highest point of the ridge. To his left, the Observatory stood at the top of a funicular railway, leading up from Montfleury, that hadn't been used since the beginning of the war. Focusing a pair of field glasses, he surveyed the terrain in front of him. Beyond a group of trees that half hid the roofs of Mme. Soden's farm, he could see the great blue sweep of the bay and then, over the dwarf street-map of the town, the sugarloaf humps of the Esterel. There was a low rumble of artillery from behind the wooded slopes, where several columns of smoke marked the sites of German rearguard actions against the Americans. At one side of the farm, just above the saddle, a tiny chapel was sheltered by an earthen bank. Nearby, the menacing snouts of the guns showed through the blockhouse casemates.

Davaille studied the clearing around the huge concrete bunkers. There was no sign of life between the shell holes or among the bomb-shattered trees. Overhead, a single reconnaissance plane circled the ridge and drowned the rattle of the cicadas. It would be nice, he thought, if they could get the operation over with before the spotter pilot called up the next wave of fighter-bombers. Rising cautiously to his feet, he signaled the men concealed in the bushes on either side to follow him down the hill.

The heavy oak door of the chapel was open. Inside, there was just enough space for two short benches, two rush-bottomed chairs, and a simple wooden altar beneath a statue of the saint. Four more figurines stood in niches carved from the stone wall, and a single candle burned on an iron stand by the door. Davaille stood beside a pillar surmounted by a small calvary on the far side of the dirt road. The date 1850 was carved into the stone. He crossed the road and climbed the bank beneath an immense black cypress that towered over the chapel. There was still no sound from the bunkers, and no movement on the martyred land surrounding them.

Davaille cupped his hands around his mouth and gave a code whistle. It was answered immediately from the far side of the clearing. Frossart and his section were in place. The owner of the wine store positioned his men beneath the lip of the bank, and then stepped out into the open himself. He unslung his Sten and fired a short burst into the air.

Before the echoes of the shots had died away, the cicadas had fallen silent; before Davaille could shout out his prepared invitation for the gun crews to surrender, a white cloth tied to the end of a carbine was poked out through one of the casemates.

Warily, Frossart, Davaille, and their guerrillas emerged from cover and encircled the blockhouse. Three men in Wehrmacht uniform walked out with their hands in the air.

Instead of risking a refusal, Turderer had preferred not to ask the thirty soldiers manning the battery if they wanted to surrender. He had pretended to receive a signal and ordered them to march back to Nice and report to the regimental headquarters there. Under his direction, the Resistance fighters now removed the breechblocks and put the big naval guns out of action. They took possession of a heavy machine gun and a number of carbines. And then, surrounding their willing prisoners, they marched jubilantly back to the Villa Fiésole.

Later the same afternoon, a young lieutenant who had adopted the code name Auribeau led an armed attack on the big blockhouse at the extremity of the Croisette point, and took it without loss to the Resistance. That night, Miniconi radioed news of his success to Allied headquarters—and since the guns were now no longer a menace to the invaders, both the systematic shelling and the fighter-bomber attacks on the Col St. Antoine were called off by the Franco-American High Command.

That night, for the first time in several weeks, the inhabitants of Cannes were able to relax a little. They might have no water, very little electricity, and hardly any food, but at least they could sleep in peace now that the danger from the air was past.

Neither they nor Miniconi knew it, but they were about to be threatened by a danger even more acute.

Scene Four

THE MORNING of August 23 was humid and close. From the bedroom window overlooking the avenue du Grand-Pin, Miniconi and his wife could see across the roofs of the town to the waterfront. An hour after dawn, the sun was hidden behind the mist uniting sea and sky, and none of the Allied craft lying offshore were visible beyond the gray silhouettes of the big hotels along the Croisette. Black smoke, occasionally crimsoned by bursts of flame, thickened the haze to the east. The gasoline dump beyond Antibes was still burning.

At 7:30 the stutter of automatic fire broke the heavy silence somewhere inland. Fifteen minutes later, a squadron of Lightnings streaked overhead and vanished from sight behind the mountains. Soon afterward they heard the distant thump of falling bombs and the racket of exploding antiaircraft shells. Then the noise of battle was varied with salvos of artillery in the direction of St. Raphael. In Cannes the streets were eerily quiet after the previous days' bombardments. Nobody seemed to be taking advantage of the two-hour no-curfew period: few of the stores were open and there was nothing to buy anyway. Miniconi studied the map of Vahanian troop dispositions he had drawn up. He could think of no way to improve them. Forcing his mind from the ache of hunger that gnawed at his belly, he realized that the sounds of conflict had ceased. In the apartment, the stillness was so intense that the discreet code knock, when it came, startled him as much as a grenade exploding.

Miniconi checked the back window, the knotted rope on which he could swing into the adjoining yard, the graveled pathway running along the side of the house. There was nobody to be seen, but the precautions were standard routine, like cockpit drill before flying an aircraft. There was always the possibility that someone had broken and given the codes away. He covered the map with a folded newspaper, motioned his wife into the bedroom, and eased open the apartment door.

Curtel was standing outside, his sallow face creased with anxiety. "What is it?" Miniconi asked, ushering him into the sitting room. "I thought we agreed that while this curfew—"

"I know, I know. But one of Rougeole's people working in the Mimont postal center intercepted this. Rougeole thought you ought to see it." Curtel produced a square brown envelope from an inner pocket and handed it over. The envelope, which was unstamped, was addressed in crude capital letters to THE OFFICER COMMANDING: GERMAN FORCES IN CANNES. The flap had been carefully steamed open. Inside were two sheets of cheap, ruled paper covered with an untidy script written in the same blue indelible pencil as the superscription on the envelope. Miniconi read:

> We feel we should inform you that we know you have orders to destroy certain buildings in the town as soon as Allied forces increase their pressure sufficiently to make you withdraw. A soldier who fights always has the right to the respect of his conqueror. This is a military code the Wehrmacht has always extended to its unfortunate adversaries, and there is no reason for things to change just because you are now on the side of the vanquished rather than the victor. But useless acts of destruction masquerading as military necessities have nothing to do with the duties of a soldier. We therefore leave it to you to decide whether anything could be gained by increasing the distress of a population which has always behaved correctly toward your troops, always carried out your wishes with good grace, and reacted neither with recrimination nor hostility to the scarcities which daily grow more acute.
>
> The planned destruction to which we refer is that of the Mairie, the

Hotel de Ville, the Palais de Justice, the Records Office, the Post Office,
the Place Massuque, the Carnot bridge, and the hotels of the Croisette—
establishments which are essentially French, essential to the life of the town,
and essentially civilian. We therefore appeal to your conscience as a soldier
to renounce any act of destruction which would, without any military
advantage, uselessly lay waste our town, and could in any case make no
difference to the result of the battle, not even for a few hours.

The letter ended with a meaningful reference to the difference
between the Wehrmacht and the Gestapo, which would "one day
have to answer for its crimes at the bar of justice," and suggested
that the distinction could best be maintained by the granting of its
plea. It was signed simply: A GROUP OF FRENCH PATRIOTS.

Miniconi compressed his lips as he read it. He turned the two
sheets over and glanced at the reverse sides. "Who gave this to
Rougeole?" he asked.

"Gaudriole. Three-one-eight-five in Belette's triangle. He
thought—"

"He was quite right!" Miniconi cut in angrily. "This is a crawling,
spineless effort. Whoever wrote it sounds as if he almost *approved* of
the damned occupation! He's making the whole town sound like a
bunch of collabos. Talking of Nazis and respect in the same breath
—I never heard anything like it!"

"Yes," Curtel said. "But do you think it's true? Do you believe they
have orders to blow up all those places? It would be a disaster."

"Certainly, I believe it. It would be just like the bastards. But we'll
check anyway."

Curtel frowned. "How could they have—? I mean, the people
who wrote this letter: how would they know?"

"The same way we know about the letter, I guess," Miniconi said
drily. "You don't imagine Gaudriole is the only man in Cannes capable of intercepting a message, do you?"

"What are you going to do?"

Miniconi folded the sheets of the letter, slid them back into the
envelope, and tossed it onto the table. "I think I'll deliver a similar
message—in person," he said. "Only I shall express it a little more
forcefully."

"You mean . . . ?"

"I mean this kind of rubbish is worse than useless." He gestured contemptuously at the envelope. "An anonymous begging letter! What the hell kind of good is that going to do with a man like Schneider? It's got no weight; it's got no leverage. It'll go straight into the trash can."

"What kind of leverage do *we* have?" Curtel asked.

"When you're dealing with the Boche," Miniconi said, "it's useless appealing to his finer feelings; it's not even a great deal of help pointing out the advantages to him of a certain line of behavior. You won't get an army man to show mercy by telling him you know he's not as bad as the Gestapo. If you want to negotiate, you have to do it from a position of strength: it has to be do-it-my-way-Fritz-or-else. You know that."

"Sure. But do we have enough muscle for a show of strength to be convincing? Even now?"

Miniconi's gold tooth glinted as he smiled. "It's up to us to make it convincing, isn't it?"

Outside the window, the sun's heat had dispersed the early morning haze. The shadows of lamp standards lay like iron bars across the empty sidewalk. Curtel unfastened the buttons of his jacket and sat down. "What do you have in mind?" he asked. "And what can I do to help?"

"I think we should take a leaf out of Ferraris's book, and play a poker hand," Miniconi said. "But first we must check if the information in this letter is accurate."

It was Toinette Marcoux who was able to answer that question. Claire Miniconi met the owner of the Taverne Royale during the second of the two hours set aside for marketing. An infantry lieutenant, Toinette said, had drunk a little too much the previous evening and confided the whole story to her. They did indeed have orders involving a massive destruction of property in Cannes—and any move to prevent it would have to be made fast, because the 148th Division would be moving out almost at once, effecting the demolitions before they left.

The Wehrmacht were not, however, quitting the area without a final show of resistance. Late that afternoon, batteries situated at Rocheville and La Croix des Gardes started to bombard selected targets in the Esterel massif, the whole of which was now in American hands. At the same time, small parties of infantry were dug in on the left bank of the Siagne River with orders to delay any Allied thrusts across the St. Cassien plain.

Patch's staff officers dealt with the situation in two ways. They called on the warships lying off Cannes to shell the German artillery positions, and they asked for a Resistance patrol to liaise with their advance scout columns, in the hope that these could in some way be led around behind the enemy lines.

Captain Ardouin received the message on the radio at the Villa Petit-Clos, and passed it on to Colonel Pétrequin, who in turn contacted Vahanian of the MUR. "It sounds like a job for the Tonners' action group," Vahanian said. He looked at his Number Two. "See if you can get in touch with them, Tony—but be very careful: the krauts may be deployed all around the farm by now."

"Don't worry," Tony Isaïa said. "There's more than one way to get into that property, and I've been there often enough, for God's sake! We'll contact Francis and Fernand all right."

Vahanian clapped him on the shoulder. "That's my boy! I'd go myself but I have a rendezvous with Commandant Jean-Marie: we have to finalize arrangements for putting the liberation plan into operation."

Untypically, Miniconi was late for the meeting. He had been a few blocks away from Vahanian's store when the ships fired their first salvo at the German artillery positions. Unhappily, the first salvo fell short. Miniconi heard the screech of the shell and flung himself to the sidewalk as the roadway erupted in a fountain of saffron smoke tinged with flame. Stones and fragments of rubble pounded his shoulders and the backs of his knees while the shattering effect of the concussion drained from his ears. He got shakily to his feet. The shell had exploded less than fifteen yards away from him, slicing off the corner of an empty house and leaving a crater in the road. He had been lucky, so far as the blast was concerned, to find himself in a "dead" area: apart from a grazed knuckle and a cut on his cheek caused by a splinter of stone, he was unharmed. A couple farther up the street had not been so fortunate. They lay like bundles of discarded clothes by a wall that was webbed with scarlet.

Choking on the stink of cordite, Miniconi hurried over to see if he could help. An old woman and a man of about forty—white bone fragments showing through the ruin of the woman's chest and the man bleeding from the ears. Haddad Simon, a doctor who was a member of the Groupe Jean-Marie, lived in the next street. He came at once, when Miniconi called, but by the time the two men returned, crunching over the broken glass that littered the cobbles, both the victims were dead.

Francis Tonner heard the shells burst as he crawled along behind a bamboo windbreak with his brother and two other men. Later, when they had reached the river and the naval gunners had corrected their aim, he saw the salvos blossom like dusty alien flowers among the pines on La Croix des Gardes. The Siagne was overhung with trees and flowed fast and shallow, no more than fifteen or twenty yards across. They forded it near the old golf course and headed back inland toward Mandelieu—Francis and Fernand, Henri Bergia, and Marius Mascarello, each with a machine pistol and three grenades.

The shelling had stopped when they saw the American patrol. It seemed so natural, so matter-of-fact when it happened that Francis Tonner almost took the whole thing for granted: there were three jeeps drawn up on the grass verge around a corner of the lane, and, a little way in front of them, a group of men in steel helmets, one of whom was speaking into a walkie-talkie. It was only later that he realized this was an historic moment: these men were the first non-Axis soldiers he had seen in over four years!

Henri Bergia at first took them for Germans and instinctively raised his machine pistol. Then he saw the white star painted on the hood of the dun-colored jeep, the unfamiliar rank and divisional markings on the helmets. Bergia knew one phrase in American, which he had picked up from prewar movies. He used it now. "Well, waddya know!" he said.

Fortunately, the young lieutenant in charge of the patrol spoke a little French. He and his men appeared equally unsurprised at the meeting. They had already been contacted by several *maquisard* groups in the Esterel, the lieutenant said. He called up his headquarters to report the liaison.

"Four guys. It seems they come from some outfit calls itself the MUR," he said in answer to a question. "Yeah, they're the ones who were supposed to contact us anyway."

"Listen, Fletcher," the distorted voice in the speaker ordered, "you forge ahead until you make the river. These guys can show you the best way. When you get there, turn north and reconnoiter the land on either side until you make a bridge over a narrow canal. It's near a place called the St. Cassien Hermitage. I want you to hold that bridge until Martino shows, okay?"

"Yessir, Captain," the lieutenant said. "I'll call you when we're there."

The sun had vanished behind the Esterel by the time they arrived at their goal. Beyond the parasol pines between them and the shore, they could see the last rays of golden light gilding the sea, but inland, dusk was gathering already among the olives and eucalyptus that studded the wide, flat valley. Beneath the bridge, the Béal canal flowed noiselessly and fast.

Lieutenant Fletcher leaned his elbows on the iron railings to steady the field glasses he held to his eyes. Somewhere on the far side of the water German troops lay hidden behind the corn patches and rows of vines, but the bamboos growing on the canal banks impeded his view. The dirt road ran straight for two hundred yards and then curved out of sight behind a cypress hedge around a farm. "It's good tank country," Fletcher said, "but I didn't see no Tigers when we came down from the hills."

Francis Tonner shook his head. "They are all on the far side of town," he said when the observation had been translated for him. "People say they will be retreating tomorrow or perhaps the day after. Here there are just isolated infantry detachments, and some artillery up there." He gestured toward the wooded outline of La Croix des Gardes.

The attack came without any warning. Flame belched from the bamboo thicket across the canal. Suddenly the evening was hideous with the racket of small-arms fire. There were twelve Americans in the patrol. Two of them fell with the first volley. The others leaped behind the jeeps, seized their weapons, and began blazing away at the thicket. Tonner and the lieutenant dropped flat and wormed their way back under cover, thankful that the Germans had not dared approach closer than fifty yards.

There seemed to be about twenty of them, dodging behind the bamboos, looking for an opportunity to cross the road and perhaps enfilade the patrol from the other side of the bridge. But they were armed only with machine pistols and carbines. Among the arsenal deployed by the Americans were two antitank rifles and a bazooka, and as the shells from these heavier weapons went ripping through the canes, the enemy fire diminished and finally ceased altogether.

Fletcher waited, listening to the sudden silence in the valley. Some distance away a night bird called. Beneath the bridge, water swilled. He rose to his feet, absently dusting off his knees, and a fragment of glass from one of the jeeps' windshields tinkled to the ground. "Well, I guess that's it—for now," Fletcher said. "But if we're supposed to hold this goddamn bridge, I can't see how the hell—"

He never finished the sentence. Thunderous detonations on every side blacked out the sky. For ten minutes they were engulfed in an inferno of noise and heat as a barrage from German mortars and 75s pinpointed the bridge with merciless accuracy.

When the smoke cleared, the place looked like the inside of an abattoir. One of the jeeps had been overturned and was now on fire. Two more Americans had died. Fletcher had been wounded in the shoulder and Marius Mascarello was unconscious and bleeding from multiple injuries. Fernand Tonner was unhurt, but of his brother Francis and Henri Bergia there was no trace. They had been blown to pieces by the first salvo.

The senior American NCO made the decision. "We're getting the hell out of here!" he said. They collected the wounded, loaded them into the remaining jeeps, and drove away. It was a quarter after eight.

An hour later, unaware of the tragedy, Miniconi and Curtel crossed the Carnot bridge spanning the railroad tracks just outside the station. Although it was some time since darkness had fallen, the asphalt that covered the sidewalk and patched sections of bomb-damaged *pavé* still breathed out the sullen, tarry heat of the day. The two men were dressed in the blue serge fatigues of *Défense Passive* workers; their papers, forged by Buffet at Le Cannet that afternoon, identified them as regular members of the Vichy-run-civil defense corps; and they wore hastily faked brassards similar to those issued to the port lookout detail. None of the Wehrmacht sentries posted outside public buildings in the boulevard Carnot had challenged them as they marched briskly in step toward the town center. Evidently they assumed that two Frenchmen so openly defying the curfew must have special permission to be out. Not for the first time, Miniconi's preference for the calculated risk had paid off.

On the far side of the bridge, at the foot of the iron stairway leading down to the station yard, they paused. Curtel produced the components of the Sten gun which he had somehow secreted in his oversize pockets and beneath his tunic. When he had assembled the weapon, Miniconi handed him the three magazines he had concealed in his own clothing. Then, treading silently now on the outside edges of their boots, they moved toward the canopy sheltering the entrance to the terminal.

The station was deserted. Stars shone through gaps in the arcaded roof, and the glass doors were shattered. It was nine days since a train had rolled along the tracks, though the building still emanated the distinctive station odor mingling soot, fish, and stale cigarette smoke. There were signs of life, however, on the far side of the *place*. From behind the blacked-out shutters of the Taverne Royale came the sound of drunken singing. Besieged and surrounded though they were, the rear guard of the 148th were determined to put a brave face on it so long as there was beer in Toinette's cellar.

Opposite the entrance to the bar, there was an alcove that had once housed three public telephone booths. The instruments were long gone and the doors had been ripped off, but the partitions were still in place and the recesses were in the deepest shadow. Miniconi took Curtel's elbow and steered him toward the center booth. "Give me ten minutes," he whispered. "If anything goes wrong, shoot at the doorway around waist height. I'll duck down and try to crawl out beneath your line of fire."

"You'll be lucky!" Curtel said mournfully. "You know this bastard always jams halfway through the first magazine!"

"Never mind that. Just try and look like two hundred men surrounding the square," Miniconi replied with a rare attempt at humor. He settled the beret more firmly on his head and walked quickly across the darkened *place* toward the brasserie. "Good luck, Jean-Marie!" Curtel called after him.

Miniconi skirted two *gazogène* cabs and a staff Mercedes parked by the curb, approaching the doorway from the direction of the port. Twitching aside the black drapes, he slipped inside.

Across in the station yard, the noise had been loud. Now it was deafening. Although a number of units had been withdrawn, there were still a thousand German troops quartered in Cannes, according to Miniconi's latest information. More than half of them, he thought to himself, seemed to have been crammed into Toinette's bar to-

night! The place was jammed from wall to wall with men in field
gray, singing, shouting, laughing, struggling to fight their way to the
zinc counter and bawl for a refill. A *Feldwebel* and half a dozen
troopers were banging their tankards in time to a marching song
around one table in the window. A larger group chanted the words
of "Lili Marleen" to three local whores sitting, flushed with drink,
on a disused shuffle-pool table. Beyond a crowd of perspiring sailors
from the *Kriegsmarine,* Toinette Marcoux carried a tall pile of plates
from the kitchen toward the bar. A few of the Germans near the
entrance had glanced at Miniconi as he came in, but none had approached him yet. There were two other DP men already in the
Taverne, but they were on the far side of the room and their backs
were turned.

Toinette saw him at once. She jerked her head imperceptibly at
the door beside the bar leading to the back room—and dropped the
plates.

At once confusion reigned. Over the smash of breaking crockery
and the big woman's simulated scream of dismay, men cheered and
laughed. The crowd heaved and swayed as the drinkers around her
bent down to help gather up the broken fragments. Those at the
back pressed forward to see what was going on. Under cover of the
diversion, Miniconi jerked open the door beside the bar and stepped
unnoticed into the passageway leading to the back room.

Colonel Schneider was sitting alone at the only table laid with
knives, forks, plates, and a white cloth—a short, gray man with
crew-cut hair and a tired face. There was a carafe of red wine in
front of him. His head was lowered over a soup plate piled with
unappetizing, grayish spaghetti: there was no cheese, no sauce, no
bread, and no salt on the table; it was five days since the last food
shipment had arrived in the town.

Miniconi swallowed. For over two years he had been subject to
police surveillance, required to report his movements outside
Cannes, probably on the Gestapo "suspected" list. Only extreme
care and concentration, right down to the minutest detail, had enabled him to keep his Resistance connections, and those of his companions, from being discovered. Now, in a desperate gamble to save
the town from destruction, he was deliberately renouncing the effect of all those months of security, deliberately jeopardizing his
own freedom. He took a deep breath and then, walking briskly

across the room, he pulled a chair out from an adjoining table and sat down opposite the German.

"Colonel Schneider?" he said. "I am Commandant Jean-Marie, the officer in charge of Resistance forces in this area."

Schneider didn't look up from his plate. He continued rhythmically forking the tasteless pasta into his mouth. Miniconi paused for a moment. His right hand eased off the safety catch of the revolver in his tunic pocket. "I have to tell you," he lied, thinking of Curtel alone with his unreliable Sten, "that my men have this place entirely surrounded. Furthermore, four Companies of the French Forces of the Interior, fully armed, have encircled the town and cut off your retreat. In the circumstances, I have a proposition to put to you."

Still the German made no reply. He didn't even raise his eyes to glance at the stranger who was interrupting his meal. The creased red flesh of his neck bulged momentarily over his tight uniform collar each time he swallowed. Miniconi cleared his throat. He wished that time—and the curfew—had allowed him to contact and assemble even one Company of the French Forces of the Interior; the knowledge that they were there could have made his bluff that much more convincing. "I understand," he resumed, as belligerently as he could, "that you have orders to destroy certain buildings and facilities here when you withdraw."

Schneider reached for the carafe, poured, lifted his glass, and gulped down wine. He said nothing.

"Now bridges, railroad marshaling yards, power stations, and port installations," said Miniconi, "are acceptable military targets. If you were to blow up such things, I should naturally regret it—but I wouldn't have a legitimate grievance under the rules of war: you'd simply be carrying out the normal duties of a retreating commander to hold up the enemy and protect his rear. But they tell me you have also been ordered to dynamite public buildings, civic utilities, monuments, even the hotels along the Croisette, and this I cannot tolerate."

Schneider's gray brows lifted fractionally, but he continued staring at his plate as he chewed.

"I cannot under any circumstances permit the destruction of the amenities on which the social life of this town will depend," Miniconi insisted. "It is barbarous, it is unnecessary, and it is useless. It cannot affect the outcome in the slightest degree." He watched the German as he ate. Dark pouches sagged in the flesh beneath Schneider's eyes. It was said that his wife came from Alsace. Perhaps that was why the writers of the anonymous letter had resorted to a Gallic appeal to the man's honor as a soldier. Miniconi sighed. "Such an action," he urged, "would brand the Wehrmacht as a whole—and your Division in particular—as spiteful, vengeful, uncivilized. Whereas in different circumstances . . ." He left the sentence unfinished and hitched his chair closer to the table.

"Here's what I suggest, Colonel. Give me your word as a soldier and an officer that you will restrict your demolitions to targets of purely military character . . . and I will promise you on my honor that you and your staff shall have safe conduct out of the town. Refuse my offer and we shall attack—in which case I cannot answer for the consequences. Any prisoners taken will be executed for a start, if those demolitions are carried out."

He pushed back his chair and stood up. "You have until dawn to decide. People will know where to find me if it is necessary. And if by any chance you were thinking of raising the alarm and having me arrested as I leave . . ." (Miniconi moved the hand holding the gun in his pocket) ". . . let me tell you that there is a revolver here loaded with six shells." He paused and then added significantly: "That means five for you . . . and the last one for me."

Schneider was still bent over his plate eating as the Resistance chief turned and strode from the room.

No gun roared in the silence behind him. No voice called angrily or urgently. No footsteps clattered across the tile floor. The German soldiers and sailors were still drunkenly singing in the outer bar. Miniconi shouldered his way to the door, lifted the blackout curtain, and walked out into the night.

Fingers gripped his shoulder to waken him at 3 A.M. "Two men in the alley beside the house," Curtel murmured. "Too dark to see, but they threw pebbles at the window in the hallway. I thought I'd better check with you before I took any action."

Miniconi was awake in an instant. He flung aside the covers, padded across the room, and kneeled down beside a loose board flanking the tallboy. "Where is Claire?" he whispered, lifting the board and feeling for the precious flashlight that he kept there with the spare Sten magazines.

"Keeping watch by the window. She didn't want to wake you, but I figured it might alert the neighbors if we challenged them on our own."

"You were quite right. Are the children still asleep?"

As Curtel nodded, Miniconi rose to his feet and carried the torch out into the hallway. His wife was peering down through the window, blocking off reflections with the palm of one hand. "There's still one man there," she said softly. "The other has walked around to the front."

"Wait here." Miniconi hurried back to the bedroom, unhitched the knotted rope where it hung from beneath the eaves, and lowered the free end gently to the stones paving the terrace. A man could be over the wall and into the builder's yard in seconds, swinging Tarzan-style from the tiny balcony, if the intruders proved to be hostile. Back in the hallway, Curtel was cradling the Sten in his arms. "The second one's back," he muttered. "If it was anyone we knew, surely they'd— Watch out, Jean-Marie: it could be some kind of trap."

Miniconi nodded. "Finger on the trigger," he breathed. In a single movement he jerked open the window and switched on the flashlight, lancing the powerful beam down at the two men on the pathway below. At the same time, Curtel sighted the muzzle of the gun over the sill.

Marcel Marcoux and Colonel Dussert stood rigid in the pool of light.

"My God, you came damned near to breathing your last!" Miniconi said when Claire had let them in. "Lucky for you I had that flashlight, or we could have shot at your silhouettes! But why in hell didn't you come up and give the code knock?"

"The outer door was locked," Marcoux explained. "We were afraid of waking the whole house if we knocked loudly enough for you to hear."

"That idiot janitor!" Miniconi scowled. "Anyway, now that you're here—what's new?"

Dussert smiled thinly beneath his drooping mustache. "A message," he said. "An urgent message from the Herr Colonel Schneider, Officer Commanding the forces of the Third Reich based in Cannes, no less!"

The Resistance chief's breath quickened. "And the message is?"

"It was given to Toinette, who passed it on to me. The Herr

Colonel desires to make a rendezvous with the Herr Commandant
—outside the station, as soon as possible."

Miniconi's thin face creased into a grin of pure joy. "You see?" he
exclaimed, gripping Curtel's arm. "You *see?*"

Forty minutes later, Dussert and the two FTPF fighters stood
beneath the station canopy while Marcoux returned to the darkened
brasserie to alert Schneider. He came out immediately, accompanied by Toinette. "We have to go to the far end of the rue
d'Antibes," he said without any preliminaries.

It was a curious group that traversed the *place* and turned left up
the town's main street that August night. Curtel, like Commandant
Jean-Marie, was short and wiry. Schneider, who was exactly the
same height, was beefy and solid. Behind them, a full head taller in
each case, walked Toinette and Colonel Dussert—although the lean,
stooping ex-soldier moved with a loping stride, while Toinette, because of the steel corset encircling her bosomy frame, was forced to
take short, quick, rigid steps. With the German strutting in the lead,
they marched the whole narrow length of the street between silent,
shuttered storefronts. Then, a little way up the grade toward the
avenue de Madrid, Schneider halted in front of a narrow five-story
building set back behind a terrace with a rusted iron pergola that
had once been covered by vines.

Miniconi stared up at the peeling stucco facade. The moon had
risen over the rooftops and in the wan light he could just make out
the words HÔTEL SPLENDIDE over the cracked portico. He knew the
place by reputation. It was the kind of *maison de passe* which had
hired out rooms by the hour to prostitutes patrolling the port and
the side streets off the Croisette. He knew also—it was his business
to know—that the Germans had recently requisitioned the hotel
cellars as some kind of stores depot for their sappers. Why would
Schneider be bringing them here now?

The Wehrmacht colonel was rapping loudly on the entrance
doors with his knuckles. "Open up! Open up! In the name of the
Führer!"

The knocking echoed in the empty street. Somewhere overhead,
a four-motored plane was flying out over the sea toward Corsica.
Schneider thumped the doors again. Inside, they heard a complaining voice approach, the shuffle of feet, the rattle of a chain. One of
the entrance doors opened a crack. "What is it? What is it? Do you
know what time it is?" a man's voice demanded querulously.

"Open up, you fool. It's Schneider. Let us in at once and fetch the key to the cellar."

The chain rattled again. The door opened wide, revealing an elderly white-haired man wearing pajamas and carpet slippers. They could see in the light of the oil lamp he was carrying that he had hastily pulled on a pair of pants over the pajama trousers: the fly gaped open and suspenders trailed to the floor behind him. "Of course, Colonel," he stammered. "At once. I'm sorry. I didn't realize . . ."

Schneider motioned the others inside and pointed to a flight of stairs leading down at the rear of the hallway. The old man took a key from a row of hooks behind a scarred olive-wood reception desk and padded down the stairs. He unlocked a heavy wooden door and pushed it open. Schneider led the way in, switching on a low-power electric bulb as he passed through the doorway.

After the stale, bug-ridden odor of the squalid entrance hall, the air of the cellar struck cool, moist, and sour with the smell of newly mixed cement. It was about fifteen feet square, empty except for a large box of black metal screwed to a concrete podium rising from the center of the floor. The box was like the nucleus of a spider's web: from holes bored in its sides, several dozens of different colored electrical leads rayed out across the floor and disappeared into conduits projecting from the walls. Schneider walked across, took a key from his pocket, and unlocked a padlock that secured the lid of the box. He opened the lid. "Here is the master control for detonating all charges for the demolitions," he announced. He took a pair of wire cutters from a shelf near the door and handed them to Miniconi. "You know what to do," he said.

Miniconi looked down into the detonator and saw wires, junction boxes, a plunger of the type they used in the limestone quarries above Peille. Holding his breath, he advanced the tool toward the nearest lead. He squeezed the handles together. The two ends of the severed cable sprang apart as the steel blades sliced through insulation and wire.

He reached for the next lead, moving slowly around the podium until every cable issuing from the black box was cut. When he had finished, he exhaled a long sigh of relief and turned to Schneider. "You have honored your side of the bargain," he said. "Now I will keep mine. If you will come with me, I shall at once arrange the safe conducts I promised you."

The German shook his head. "I am a soldier," he said stiffly. "I am obliged to you, Herr Commandant, but my place is with my men." Saluting, he turned on his heel and strode briskly up the stairs. They heard his footsteps cross the hallway and then the slam of the front door.

"What an extraordinary mentality," Dussert said. "Absolutely correct in some ways, completely perverted in others. If more of them were less obstinate . . . if only they would allow themselves to listen to reason . . ." He shrugged and left the remark unfinished.

Toinette Marcoux was leafing through an exercise book she had found on the shelf. "Look, Jean-Marie," she said. "Here is a diagram of the wiring plan you have just destroyed, with details of where each cable goes and how much explosive it sets off."

Miniconi and Dussert turned the pages of the book. Dussert, the railroad engineer, was the first to appreciate the significance of the diagram. He whistled. "Those Boche sappers certainly did their work thoroughly," he said. In addition to blowing up the bridges, monuments, and public buildings listed in the anonymous letter, the Germans had indeed planned the destruction of the Croisette: every hotel and villa between the casino and the Palm Beach promontory was mined.

(When Larteguy and Donazolo, the Groupe Jean-Marie's bomb-disposal experts, defused the complex some time later, they found that more than three tons of explosives had been used. The material, mostly Donarite, had been secreted in cellars and fed with long strings of Bickford cord and Primacord into the drains beneath the Croisette. Fifty canisters, each with its own detonator, had been destined for the Carlton Hotel alone, and there were almost as many buried beneath the other big, evacuated buildings. If the German High Command's orders had been carried out, and the plunger in the black box depressed, any Allied troops braving the half-submerged mines and underwater obstacles to land supplies around the shallow crescent of sand would have found the way inland blocked by a continuous wall of ruins sixty or seventy feet high.)

By the time Miniconi and his companions emerged from the Hôtel Splendide the sky was already paling to the east. And the night—still windless and humid—was no longer silent. From the direction of the port they could hear the whirr of caterpillar tracks and the grinding of gears; nearer, to left and right and on the fringe of the evacuated Croisette zone, there was the tramp of marching feet and the guttural shouts of military commands. The Resistance leader turned to Dussert. "They're pulling out!" he exclaimed exultantly. "Schneider would never have played ball unless he was on his way!"*

The man from the FER *réseau* nodded. "It's been in the cards for some time," he said. "They're virtually surrounded here, and there's no military objective worth defending. What's the next move for us, Commandant?"

"We sound the sirens and activate the plan we drew up with Vahanian into action!" Miniconi cried. "We've been lucky enough to save the town from destruction: now it's up to us to liberate it!"

---

* In fact, the German Commander's humane disregard of his High Command's orders cost him his life. Escaping to Nice with the remnant of his forces, he was court-martialed for dereliction of duty and executed there by firing squad four days later. Only minor demolitions around the Cannes port area had been carried out.

Scene Five

ALL SECTIONS of Miniconi's three Companies had been assigned their areas of operation and told what to do when the signal for action was given. In the 40th Company, which shared the town of Cannes with the MUR, Sanglier's 1st Detachment was responsible for the northern sector, including Le Cannet. The 2nd Detachment under Sam Kadyss was to be in charge of the center, between the railroad and the port. Frossart and Davaille would take La Californie and the east, and Curtel, the Company Commander, would hold a formation in reserve at the courthouse. It was here, too, that the Committee of Liberation and the joint headquarters of Miniconi and Vahanian would be established.

Miniconi had circulated an order two days previously, the text of which was short and to the point. It said:

> *If the call to action is sounded during the night, only Section Chiefs, of all ranks, are to proceed urgently to their Command Posts. Men are not to report until 0600 hours. Anyone on the street before this time will be arrested or, in case of resistance, shot.*

The decision had been made in order to avoid confusion in the dark, to minimize the risk of casualties, and to ensure that as few "freeloaders" as possible jumped aboard the Resistance bandwagon now that it was on the winning side. One disadvantage of the compartmentalized cell system was that almost anyone, once they knew about it, could claim to be a member of the group, since nobody in it would know personally more than a handful of the other members.* (There were of course numbers to be quoted and a password —it was *Tchad* on August 24—to be used, but who was going to waste time asking about those when the town was being liberated?)

To give his Company, Detachment, and Section leaders time to organize themselves at the various assembly points allotted to them, Miniconi ordered the siren to be sounded at 5 AM, not long after he left the Hôtel Splendide. But Louis Ceran, the postal clerk detailed to activate the system above the sorting center in the rue de Mimont, reported that by some twist of fate the departing Germans had cut the cable before they quit the building. It was in fact not until 5:30 that he was able to penetrate the post office in the rue Bivouac-Napoléon, a block away from the port, and set the alarm there wailing.

As the siren, whose warble had brought fear to so many, shrilled its fifteen-minute cry of triumph, men and women all over Cannes rose from their beds with pulses racing. Weapons were brought down from lofts, dug up in backyards, lifted out from under the floorboards where they had been hidden. In the avenue Fiésole, members of the 40th Company lined up outside the Domergue property to draw guns, ammunition and grenades from the arsenal in the grotto behind the villa. By 6:30 each unit was mustered at the relevant assembly point, ready to advance toward strategic positions through streets already filling with excited crowds sensing that here, at last, today, was the release for which they had hoped and prayed so long.

It was a perfect day, with no trace of the humidity which had hazed the air and hidden the sea during the past few mornings. At

* The efficacy of the system can be judged by the fact that, in 1979, some 35 years later, Miniconi was still trying to authenticate the real names of more than half the 650-odd resistants under his command whom he had known only by code names or numbers. Many of course claimed to have been members of the *Groupe* Jean-Marie—medals and sometimes government pensions could depend on it—but no claim was accepted as verified unless substantiated by at least two other resistants personally known to Miniconi.

seven o'clock, it was already hot, with the August sun, shining from a cloudless sky, scattering gold pieces among the shadows beneath the plane trees lining the Boulevard Carnot. Miniconi and Vahanian stood at the top of the steps leading to the courthouse. Bare-headed, newly shaven, Commandant Jean-Marie was wearing dark trousers and a freshly pressed white shirt with his tricolor FFI armband. Curtel, Raymond, and Isaïa stood beside him, receiving the reports as they came in.

Before eight, the port, the station, the town hall, the telephone exchange, gas and electricity supplies, and all the blockhouses were in Resistance hands. Through the genius of some Detachment leader who was also a hydraulics expert, there was even water running from the faucets!

Two-thirds of the German rearguard, including all the armor and all the artillery, had been withdrawn in the hours before daybreak. The 350 infantrymen left behind were mainly Poles, officered by Germans, and they showed no appreciable enthusiasm for the concept of fighting to the last man and the last round in defense of Hitler's New Europe. They surrendered meekly, allowing their quarters and emplacements to be occupied without a single shot being fired.

Jubilant guerrillas took possession of their arms and equipment and escorted them to a compound where they were placed under guard with the few notorious collaborators and members of the Militia who had not already fled the town.

Back in the Boulevard Carnot banners were waving. Tens of thousands of men, women, and children—laughing, cheering, weeping, embracing, singing the *Marseillaise*—jammed the broad, tree-lined avenue from side to side for as far as the eye could see. Before nine o'clock, Miniconi was able to announce to the delirious crowd that Cannes had fallen to his secret army.

An hour later, when celebrations were at their height, a breathless messenger arrived from Rocheville with the news that a force of German tanks was approaching the town from the direction of Grasse.

Panic.

"For Christ's sake, get these people off the street!" someone shouted. "If the Boche arrive in the middle of this lot, there'll be a massacre!"

Lieutenant-Colonel Pétrequin, military adviser to the *Groupe* Jean-Marie, turned to Miniconi. "Didn't you say that Kadyss had 'liberated' a truck from the German ordnance depot near the port?"

Miniconi nodded.

"And that his Detachment had the heavy machine guns you recuperated when the battery at the Col St. Antoine surrendered?"

"That's right."

"Send them up to Mougins," the soldier said. "If they can muster enough firepower, it could divert the Hun long enough for us to get this crowd dispersed."

It was not in fact too difficult to clear the street: once the word got around that the Germans were returning, the crowd melted away as if by magic—and the first to leave were those heroes and heroines proudly flaunting red, white, and blue brassards who had only discovered the will to resist since 5:30 that morning. The genuine resistants gathered around the courthouse steps, prepared to defend their newly-won territory if necessary, waiting for orders from Miniconi or Vahanian. Kadyss took a whole Section of his own Company, and four more triangles led by a man whose code name was Rodrigue, driving north up the boulevard as recklessly as a fire truck.

Below the village of Mougins, perched on a hilltop three miles inland, they stopped at a crossroads and Kadyss hastily deployed his troops among the pine trees, behind a high wall, and along the embankment beside a small canal. Within minutes, they heard the grinding of gears as the Nazi convoy climbed the grade leading up from Highway 567.

But the "force of German tanks" turned out to be three armored scout cars equipped with 8mm. Parabellum turret guns. As the first volley from the Resistance machine guns crackled out from either side of the intersection, followed by rifle fire along the canal, the leading car—clearly imagining that a sizable force blocked the road to Cannes—turned sharply left and took departmental Route 35 in the direction of Antibes. Close behind it, the other two scouts sped away, and in a few moments all three of them had vanished over the brow of the hill hiding St. Basile.

Miniconi heaved a sigh of relief when Kadyss reported, a half-hour later, that the danger was past. He turned to Vahanian. "All we have to do now," he said, "is redirect the local government machine, which has been going the wrong way for four years!"

A couple of miles to the west, Raybaud, Tosello, and Javel, whose men had just occupied the ADN factory and the gasworks at La Bocca, saw a jeep speeding along the coastal highway from La Napoule. The driver pulled up by the deserted blockhouse on the point. Two American officers climbed out and crossed the road toward the armed guerrillas standing in the sun.

General Leclerc's 2nd French Armored Division was within a mile of the Porte d'Italie in Paris. Von Cholditz wouldn't sign the German surrender of the capital for another 24 hours. It would be 48 hours before the Allies took Toulon and four days to the fall of Marseille. But thanks to Ange-Marie Miniconi and the men and women who had fought alongside him, Cannes was already liberated.

Epilogue

War has seldom brought anything for the people engaged in it . . . But the people are not usually asked.

— FIELD MARSHAL ERWIN ROMMEL

THE TIDE of battle now flowed northward. The Americans who had advanced on Cannes through the Esterel liberated Nice on August 30. But two days before that, Allied armor, supported by strong forces of FFI, had arrived on the outskirts of Lyon. Grenoble fell to elements of the US 6th Corps as early as August 23, when Colonel Schneider was still eating his spaghetti at the Taverne Royale. On September 12, a Free French patrol contacted southbound scouts from General Leclerc's French 2nd Armored Division near Châtillon-sur-Seine, and the Normandy-Provence link-up was complete. The invaders had advanced 500 miles in less than a month, and Operation Dragoon achieved its aim 77 days ahead of schedule.

In Cannes, the onerous task of replacing a Vichy-approved municipal administration was under way. In the early days there were many surprises. One of the most astonishing, for many people, was the revelation that a modest schoolteacher from Le Suquet was in fact the near-legendary Commandant Jean-Marie. A colleague who had repeatedly tried to persuade Miniconi to "join the Resistance" —and had as often been rebuffed or told "I don't want any part of it"—was so incensed at being successfully fooled that he wouldn't speak to Miniconi for weeks!

Subsequently Gabriel Davaille was appointed President of the Committee of Liberation. Miniconi became a member of the *Commission de Triage*—a tribunal set up to determine the innocence or guilt of collaborators. In addition to passing judgment on those who had openly fraternized with or worked for the enemy, the Commission had to examine the cases of people who had, according to captured files, denounced patriots or volunteered information damaging to them. Among the culprits who came before Miniconi were the schools inspector, Carpentier, accused of supplying information on teachers' political sympathies (he was released "to live with his conscience"); Mme. Lecourtois, who had perjured herself to gain possession of Miniconi's apartment (jailed for a short period); and the judge who had found for her without even allowing Miniconi to plead. The judge denied that the case had ever come up before him . . . until Miniconi revealed that he himself had been the victim of the decision. With the Resistance leader abstaining, the tribunal voted to send the judge to jail.

In November of 1944, as a lieutenant-colonel of the FFI, Miniconi was appointed by the Free French provisional authorities as Commandant of the 4th Company, *Forces Républicaines de Sécurité*—a kind of interim police force complementing the gendarmerie. The following year, when the war in Europe was over, he was moved to Nantes, south of Brittany, as head of the 158th Company, CRS.[16] He remained there until 1948, when, in one of its shabbier postwar maneuvers, the Gaullist administration purged itself of many of the radical elements which had helped win the war and put it in power. Eleven entire companies of the CRS were disbanded without warning during this operation. Miniconi's was one of them.

Back in Cannes, he refused all honors (and a number of sinecure jobs that were offered to him) and resumed his career as a teacher at a new school named after Hélène Vagliano, where he stayed until his retirement at the age of sixty, in 1971. "The country owes me nothing," he said once when refusing a citation for the Légion d'Honneur; "I gave it no more than the allegiance owed by any Frenchman."

The same fierce loyalty informed his many years as President of an organization devoted to the recognition—indeed the preferrment—of ex-Resistance fighters. Quite recently, the proprietress of a pastry shop in the ritzy rue d'Antibes withdrew permission for the placing of a wreath at the side of her premises—an annual ceremony marking the spot where Hélène Vagliano was arrested. "It was a long time ago," she said disdainfully. "Besides, it's bad for business: it embarrasses the customers." Miniconi was at the town hall within ten minutes. "If you don't have enough men detailed to ensure that the ceremony takes place as usual," he told the police chief, "I guarantee that *I'll* have 200 ex-resistants down there in half an hour—and that every window in the goddamn street will be broken!" The ceremony took place as usual.

It was largely due to Miniconi that there are today in Cannes an avenue Francis Tonner, a rue Léon Noël, a rue Louis Périssol, and a number of other streets and squares named in honor of heroines and heroes of the Resistance.

A proud grandfather with both his sons happily married, now in his eighth year of retirement, Ange-Marie Miniconi and his wife divide their time between a modern apartment overlooking the town that he saved and a small country property in the mountains that was inherited by Claire. In Cannes, Miniconi divides his time between the operation of an immensely powerful ham radio installation which has brought him friends all over the world, and the maintenance of his Resistance archives. Here, preserved with that meticulous attention to detail that always characterized his work, is the wartime history of Cannes in cellophane folders. From the schema of the 40th Company hidden by Davaille to the plain brown envelope containing the anonymous letter to Colonel Schneider; from FFI orders of the day to handwritten police reports on the Léon Noël tragedy; from a coded message scrawled on the back of a yellowing visiting card to a Militia circular, all the original documents are filed. Beneath the shelves of dossiers sit the first clandestine radios parachuted into France for Peter Churchill. In a drawer, carefully wrapped in tissue paper, are the blue enameled earrings and clip given to her friend Lucie by Hélène Vagliano before she was shot. And behind the Opel in Miniconi's garage, polished and oiled but otherwise untouched since July 29, 1944, is the Resistance heroine's bicycle.

With such a collection at his disposal, it is hardly surprising that people come to Miniconi from all over the South seeking elucidation of wartime mysteries or the verification of dates and times and places. Yet it is not just a magpie instinct or an obsessive predilection for the past that keeps the Resistance flame burning so brightly in his mind. Awarded the Croix de Guerre with Silver Star, the Médaille Militaire, two voluntary combatant's medals and a silver plaque from the municipality of Cannes, Miniconi treasures the past because of the spirit it bred and the unity it brought.[17]

"Nobody gave a damn for religious or philosophic conceptions then," he recalls. "A priest would go along with an atheist; someone descended from a royal house would be close to a militant Communist. You found tolerance all around you, because the Resistance was a kind of crucible fusing individual desires into the collective will that gave us the strength to survive until the liberation. But it shouldn't require the presence of danger to spark off such an amalgamation. Given understanding and tolerance, it's equally possible today—provided that personal interests are submerged for the general good, and that we realize a man isn't necessarily an enemy because he doesn't think or feel the same way we do. The divisions which are ruining us can and must disappear."

Bright eyes twinkle. The head tilts to one side with a characteristic, birdlike movement. "Just so long as folks really want them to," Miniconi says.

Notes

1. French deputies are elected on a system of proportional representation. While this gives a truer reflection of public opinion than a straight "first past the post" or two-party method of voting, it results inevitably in a proliferation of political parties, and this in turn often means that no party will have an overall majority in the assembly—and thus power to govern. It is therefore necessary to form coalitions, which inevitably disagree and founder on points of policy, causing the resignation of the government and frequently dissolution, with fresh elections.

2. In the unoccupied zone, apart from the Mediterranean ports there were only eight cities of any size: Clermont-Ferrand, Grenoble, Limoges, Lyon, Montpellier, Perpignan, St. Etienne and Toulouse. Of these, only the last-named, with a population of nearly half a million, plus Lyon and Marseille (each around a million), could be considered major industrial centers. Vichy, the "capital" of the zone, was a town of 30,000 inhabitants. Unoccupied France, in fact, was basically three barren mountain areas—the Alps, the Massif Central, and the Pyrenees foothills—plus the Rhône valley. The Germans occupied the entire Atlantic coastline, from Spain to the Low Countries, the whole of the industrial north, Paris, Burgundy, Champagne, and all of the east. The cost of this occupation, moreover, was borne by the French,

who discovered as time went on that practically everything they produced was channeled toward the Nazi war machine.

3. Under the armistice terms, the French fleet, disarmed, was to remain in Toulon, while naval units elsewhere were to allow themselves to be impounded in neutral ports or steam for French bases overseas and take no further part in the war. Hitler's sole concession was a promise not to sequester the fleet for German use. Churchill did not believe this promise was likely to be kept, nor did he believe French protestations that they would scuttle rather than allow their ships to fall into Nazi hands. The Italian army in North Africa was too near the units berthed at Oran. And the warships, if seized by the Axis, could neutralize the Allied blockade and turn the scales in the battle of the Atlantic. The Royal Navy was therefore ordered to present the French at Oran with an ultimatum: surrender to us or be sunk. The French navy naturally refused to comply with what it regarded as an act of piracy, and the British opened fire. In the ensuing twenty minutes, the warships were destroyed at their moorings and 1,200 French sailors lost their lives. The hatred engendered by this shortsighted act of aggression was largely responsible for French North Africa's refusal at first to cooperate when the Allies landed in Algeria and Morocco two years later.

4. The first victim of Nazi repression was a young Polish Jew who struck a German captain as the Wehrmacht marched into Bordeaux on June 27, 1940. He was immediately shot. The first lethal attacks on German soldiers were carried out by a lumberjack named Hérault (at Ste. Germaine-la-Poterie, in October), by the artisans Masson and Brusque (St. Valéry-sur-Somme, November), and by the wine merchant Mourgues (Bordeaux again, in December). These, all of them summarily executed, were the first martyrs of the Resistance.

5. The transistor was not invented until 1948, in the United States. Its precursor, the thermionic valve, either gas-filled or vacuumatic, was larger than a standard electric light bulb, and a good radio needed at least five. Miniconi confided the secret of his tinkering to another radio ham—and was astonished to see the system front-paged in an enthusiasts' magazine called *Le Haut-Parleur* (The Loudspeaker) under the heading "Astonishing New Discovery—A Breakthrough in Shortwave Reception!" When he attempted to commercialize the technique after the war, he was told it had "already been patented by someone else."

6. Henri Michel, in his *Histoire de la Résistance en France* (Presses Universitaires de France, Paris, 1972), points out that because the freedom movement in the south was directed mainly against Frenchmen, at

first it was "by definition revolutionary rather than nationalistic." It recruited many of its members "from among the opponents to [Pétain's] so-called National Revolution, less from among social or political conservatives. The classic Right . . . were, on the whole, on Vichy's side—even those of them who were avowedly anti-German." They included, Michel says, the high clergy, financial and industrial circles, career soldiers, and anti-Republicans.

7. In a secret-session speech to the British Parliament after the invasion of North Africa in 1942, Winston Churchill explained the apparently inexplicable loyalty to Vichy of so many French in these words:

> The Almighty in His wisdom did not see fit to create Frenchmen in the image of Englishmen. In a state like France which has experienced so many convulsions—Monarchy, Convention, Directory, Consulate, Empire, Monarchy, Empire, and finally Republic—there has grown up a principle founded on the *Droit Administratif* [the law of authority] which undoubtedly governs the action of many French officers and officials in times of revolution and change . . . For instance, any officer who obeys the command of his lawful superior is absolutely immune from subsequent punishment. Much therefore turns in the minds of French officers upon whether there is a direct, unbroken chain of lawful command, and this is held to be more important by many Frenchmen than moral, national or international considerations. From this point of view many Frenchmen who admire General de Gaulle and envy him his role nevertheless regard him as a man who has rebelled against the authority of the French state, which in their prostration they conceive to be vested in the person of the antique defeatist who to them is the illustrious and venerable Marshal Pétain.

8. The cost was in fact very high. The Germans decided to treat all persons under arrest, whatever the charges, as hostages. Later they picked hostages off the street, from cinema queues, from crowds at railroad stations, from among local dignitaries, completely at random. And each time there was an attack on Nazi personnel, those hostages died. Ten were shot on September 16, a further twelve four days later, and twenty-five at Chateaubriand the following month. Paradoxically, the severity of these measures, publicized with all the efficiency of the Nazi propaganda machine, served only to make martyrs of the dead and attract more people to the Resistance banner. (See also Prologue and Note 15.)

9. The word is used here and throughout in its commonly accepted sense. In fact the Gestapo (*Geheime Staatspolizei*) was the least impor-

tant of the security services of the Nazi party, working simply as the state secret police. It was the general security service, or SD (*Sicherheitdienst*), that was responsible for the savage repression in occupied countries. The ensemble, to which the Gestapo lent its name, was completed by the Sipo (*Sicherheitspolizei*) and a criminal division. Non-party security services included the *Abwehr* (Military Intelligence) and the *Feldgendarmerie* division of the military police. A great number of atrocities not directly concerned with security were carried out by formations of the SS (*Schutzstaffel*). Resistants in the south and east of France were hunted additionally by the Italian secret police (OVRA).

10. Some idea of outlaw life among the *maquis* may be gained from secret documents circulated among *eight hundred* separate groups in the spring and early summer of 1943.

Frenay, the acting head of the MUR, had charged an advocate named Michel Brault with the task of coordinating and rationalizing all these organizations in collaboration with the *Armée Sécrète*. Under his code name of Mezeray, Brault issued a Declaration of Principle for the *maquis* stressing the importance of having small formations because of their mobility and reduced risk of detection.

The document pointed out that it was almost impossible for men to live for months on end in the rough, far from human habitation, poorly equipped and subject to rain and cold. "The solution lies in lodging them in small parties, either in friendly houses, in stables, in mountain shelters, or in abandoned farms." There must be a lookout post several miles away from the main camp, and every member of a group must be familiar with all footpaths, mule tracks, shortcuts, and hiding places on the way to and from each possible target in his area.

Chiefs of units should cultivate friendly relations with local mayors, gendarmes, curés, and secretaries of Mairies where possible, especially if the latter could provide ration documents. But such contacts must never be told the password or the exact location of the *maquis*.

To "avoid the boredom which breeds apathy and carelessness," men were to help local peasants, *whether or not they helped in return*, with hedging, ditching, tree-felling, plowing, digging, or building repairs for half of each day. The other half of the day was to be devoted to group work of a military kind: arms drill and maintenance, survey of terrain suitable for parachuting supplies, map reading, and so on. To avoid antagonizing local populations, with the consequent risk of betrayal, theft was absolutely forbidden except in case of necessity, and then only from depots servicing the Vichy police, the Militia, or the occupying forces.

The documents assumed that men wishing to join a *maquis* were refugees from a slave-labor deportation order. Before they could be accepted, they must be warned "that the purpose of their existence is to fight; that they will live precariously, badly, often without enough to eat; that they will be totally separated from their families until the end of hostilities; that disobedience will be severely punished; that they will receive nothing in return; and that although we will try to help their families, no promise can be undertaken on this account." Contact with families, or specific help given, it was pointed out, could lead to jealousy and perhaps to denunciation by neighbors.

Once accepted, a *maquisard* must understand that the least thing coming to him had "been obtained and distributed only at the price of enormous difficulties and extreme danger for all those in higher positions or posts of liaison." A volunteer would be armed only when endurance, training, and discipline showed him "to be worthy of receiving one of our weapons, extremely rare and therefore very precious. He should then take the greatest care of it, service it with scrupulous cleanliness, keep it near to him or actually at hand unless it is necessary to hand it in to the camp armorer. Loss of weapons is punishable by death."

The same severe penalty was prescribed in the case of those who wanted to quit: "Nobody must be allowed to leave when his capture could put the lives of fifty or sixty comrades at risk." But the death sentence could never be pronounced by a group leader alone: it must always be the decision of a tribunal, preferably including the local mayor or some other official from the nearest village.

The *maquis* formations to whom these documents were addressed were not the only ones in existence. Others, almost equally numerous, adhered to the Communist party, the *Front National*, and other left-wing organizations. The one most closely associated with the FTPF was the *Main d'Oeuvre Immigrée* (MOI), or foreign labor force. The movement was mainly composed of refugees, Jews, and foreign workmen living in France, and it was to southern branches of the MOI that a great number of those escaping the Gestapo net in Nice and Cannes were directed.

11. Installed on the outskirts of Arles, Carte and his lieutenant agreed that their network should work only with Britain's SOE and repudiate the authority of de Gaulle's Free French. But they quarreled violently over how this should be done, and finally they were both summoned to London, Frager flying there with Peter Churchill in a Lysander. Since the breach could not be healed, Frager returned to Marseille to inaugurate a new *réseau* with full SOE support. Carte remained anti–

de Gaulle, but was considering amalgamating the rump of his network with Frenay's *Combat* when he heard that his wife and daughters had been arrested and deported. Shattered by the news, he emigrated to the United States and never returned to France. Frager was later denounced, arrested, and deported. He died in a concentration camp.

12. The worst of these were at Ascq, Oradour, and Tulle (see Prologue and Notes 8 and 15), but they were symptomatic and different only in sheer numbers from countless others (as witness the annihilation by the SS of the village of Lidice in Czechoslovakia).

13. Those who produced such documents, often the employees of town halls or mairies and therefore automatically suspect, were in great danger. If caught, they risked at best imprisonment or life in a Vichy internment camp, at worst torture and execution. Facing the same penalties, those who produced the clandestine news-sheets also worked under the most extreme difficulties. It was increasingly hard to locate supplies of paper and printing ink; frequently it was necessary to have official permission, and for this again forged documents were needed. Then most of the work, because of its nature, had to be confided to small, often outdated printshops, and carried out at night after the employees had gone home. Once the edition had been "put to bed," the type was rapidly distributed and any blocks melted down. But there remained the problem of getting the paper to its readers. By 1943, *Combat* was printed at the rate of 120,000 copies twice a month. *Libération,* in the northern zone, had risen to 100,000 a month. A year later, *Franc-Tireur* computed that the combined clandestine circulation was more than a million and a half copies a month. At such a figure, if the original printshop was sufficiently sophisticated, it was safer to transport a matrix or mold from region to region and run off separate editions. If not (in the words of one historian), "such a huge number could only be distributed by flocks of agents taking the train armed with suitcases carefully stowed on the rack of a neighboring compartment."

14. Miniconi in fact spent thirty years satisfying himself that the sacrifice of the two Americans did not go unrecognized. The first difficulty was to find out who they were. It took years to do this because the Germans had buried the bodies in a military cemetery, they had then been disinterred and taken to an American cemetery at Draguignan, and finally relatives had effected a second exhumation and had the remains transported back to the United States for reburial in their home towns. After innumerable checks, the Liberator was identified through a twisted and heat-warped fragment of duralumin bearing

the remains of a matrix number. The definitive proof that Reinecke and Wornbaker were the two aviators who had saved Cannes was not finalized until the late 1960s. But Miniconi was still not satisfied. He badgered the municipality until it was agreed that a monument to the two men should be erected. On June 1, 1976, a huge limestone plinth was unveiled at La Croix des Gardes, dedicated to their memory, and linked to the 40th Company, FTPF. A new traffic intersection at the place where the bomber crashed was baptized *La Place du Liberator*. At the inauguration ceremony, Miniconi was awarded the American Legion Valor Medal.

15. The massacre of hostages at Tulle was one of the most barbarous acts the Das Reich SS division perpetrated, exceeding in some ways even the Oradour horror. It was assumed as a matter of course that the officer must have been killed by "communists." Communists were therefore taken as hostages, the method of establishing who came into that category being quite simple: all workmen, the theory ran, were "communists," and so *ipso facto* anyone wearing the traditional French workman's blue coverall must be a party member. Ninety-nine men dressed this way were taken off the street. Many of them were not remotely left-wing; many radicals, on the other hand, escaped the net because they happened that day to be wearing a suit or a collar and tie. The records state that they were hanged. What is not usually mentioned is that few of them were executed by means of a rope noose around the neck: most had their hands bound behind their backs and were then drawn up to dangle from the balconies overhanging the river by means of a meat hook thrust in under the chin. Some of them took four days to die.

16. In France, as in the United States, police forces are local, answerable to the mayor of the town in which they operate, with no authority outside its boundaries and no central directive. The gendarmerie is national, with headquarters in Paris, and is attached to the army. It works in collaboration with police in the larger towns, replacing them in villages and country areas, much as the *carabinieri* do in Italy and the *guardia civil* in Spain. *Compagnies Républicaines de Sécurité* (CRS), resembling, like the gendarmerie, a federal body, are responsible for specific tasks including riot control, demonstrations, the handling of natural disasters, and certain highway duties.

17. The unity certainly extended to his own family. Miniconi was the eldest of five brothers—and all of them were members of the Resistance. The youngest, only 14 when the war started, acted as a courier. Next to him were two twins, who were members of a network based on Nice from 1940 to 1944. The second eldest was a policeman,

working with an information *réseau* in Marseille. When the Allied invasion was imminent, Miniconi was able to contact him and get him back to Nice before the landings started. The policeman then joined an urban guerilla unit with the twins and was active in the liberation of the city. In addition to all this, Miniconi's parents allowed their house in the St. Sylvestre neighborhood to the north of Nice to be used as a mail drop.